NELSON INTERMEDIATE ATLAS

CARTOGRAPHER ▪ Geoffrey J. Matthews

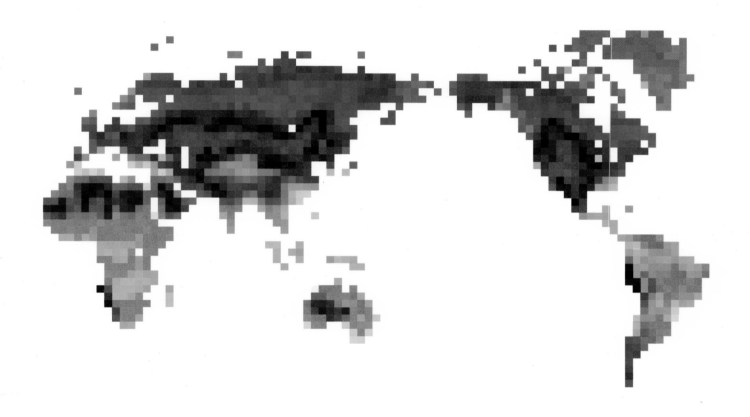

© 1989 by Nelson Canada, A Division of
International Thomson Limited

Nelson Canada
A Division of International Thomson Limited
1120 Birchmount Road
Scarborough, Ontario   M1K 5G4

Canadian Cataloguing in Publication Data

Matthews, Geoffrey J., 1932-
  Nelson intermediate atlas

For use in schools.
Includes index.
ISBN 0-17-602674-6

1. Atlases, Canadian.   I. Title.

G1021.M386 1988   912   C88-093929-X

CONTENTS

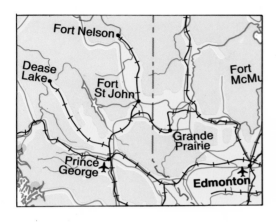

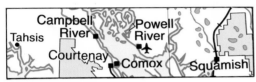

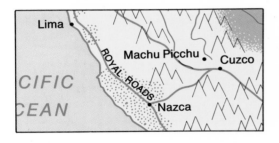

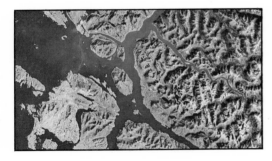

sound: a long narrow area of water be
and the mainland, or joining two larger

statistics: a collection of facts about p

An atlas is full of interesting and important information about places and people. Once you know what kind of information is in the atlas, it is important to have the skills needed to use that information. Your atlas will be much more useful to you if you read the information here and on the following pages.

Thematic Maps

A map that shows one thing, such as vegetation, transportation, or population, is called a thematic map. Information is usually shown as colours or shapes. When you read a thematic map, first look at the title, then the legend. This will help you understand the information on the map. Maps of the world can be drawn with either the Atlantic or the Pacific Ocean at the centre of the map. This atlas contains both, to let you see the world from two different points of view. You may notice that some of the continents have slightly different shapes on the two world views. This is because you have to "stretch" different parts of the map to flatten it when you change the location of the "split" on the round earth.

Regional Maps

A region is a large area which has some things the same. Regional maps show more details than maps of the whole world. The size of the map area is smaller, and the scale is larger than on maps of the whole world.

Historical Maps

Information about the past is shown on historical maps. This can include ancient cities that have been discovered, or the general areas once ruled by a certain group of people. A historical map is really a thematic map about the past. It can be interesting to compare a historical map with a current map of the same location, to see how the cities, roads, and boundaries have changed.

Landsat Photographs

Landsat satellites are in orbit around Earth. They have special instruments that can sense energy coming from the Earth. These satellites pick up energy signals from the areas they pass over, then they send the signals to stations on the ground. The signals are recorded on a tape by the ground stations. Later, a computer changes the information into a coloured photographic picture. Certain information, such as whether there are cities, farms, or forests, will show up as a specific colour.

Glossary

This list tells you the meanings of many words you will find when you work with the maps in this atlas. Once you know what a word means, you will be able to use the word again.

Index

How can you find a new place in the atlas? The easiest way is to look up the place name in the index. The index is at the back of the atlas. Look up your home town or a nearby large city. What information is shown? Is it enough to find out where the place is in the atlas? Try looking up some other places you have visited or heard about.

Before you read a map, you need to know about...

Looking Down from Above

Imagine you are looking down at a fairground from your seat at the top of a very tall ride. What can you see? Now imagine you are directly above the fairground in a cable car. Can you see anything else when you look down from directly above? Why is the striped tent hidden in the first picture? A map is a drawing of the land as seen from directly above. Many things can be seen when you look directly down on the land. Since it is smaller than the actual land, a map only shows the main important things, for example, roads but not sidewalks.

Grids

Straight lines have been drawn over this picture, dividing the fairground into squares. These lines cross each other to make up a grid. The grid has letters along the top, and numbers down the side. Each square is named by its letter and number, for example C3. By naming one grid square, or several grid squares, you can accurately describe the location of anything in the picture. Name the grid squares in which the following things can be found: striped tent, ferris wheel, roller coaster. In this atlas, the map grid is made from the latitude and longitude lines. The index lists grid squares to help you locate the places on each regional map.

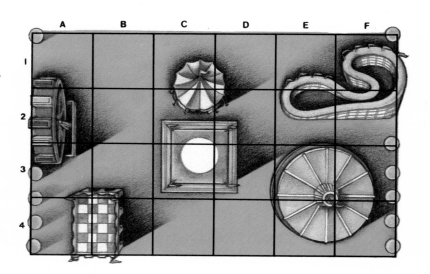

Symbols

Symbols are shapes or colours that stand for well-known things. The meanings of the symbols on each map are shown in a list. This kind of list is called a legend.

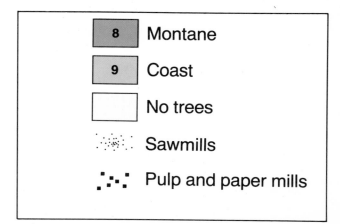

8	Montane
9	Coast
	No trees
:·:	Sawmills
:·:	Pulp and paper mills

4

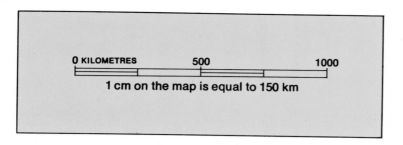

0 KILOMETRES   500   1000

1 cm on the map is equal to 150 km

Scale & Measurement

Scale is the relationship between the distance measured on a map and the real distance on the earth's surface. On a map, scale can be shown as a written statement or as a divided bar. You can measure on the map using a ruler or a piece of string, and then work out the real distance by referring to the scale on that map.

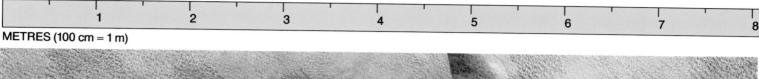

1   2   3   4   5   6   7   8

METRES (100 cm = 1 m)

Elevations

Since maps don't show side views of the land, heights and depths are shown by colours. Colours that stand for elevations will be explained in the map legend.

URAL MOUNTAINS
WEST SIBERIAN PLAIN
STEPPES
ALTAI MOUNTAINS
KOLYMA MOUNTAINS

Directions

On most maps, direction is shown by a compass needle pointing north, and by latitude and longitude lines. These lines each have numbers and compass directions, which are printed at the edges of the map. Latitude lines measure directions north and south of the Equator. Longitude lines measure directions east and west of the Prime Meridian.

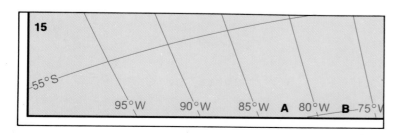

15

55°S

95°W   90°W   85°W   A 80°W   B 75°V

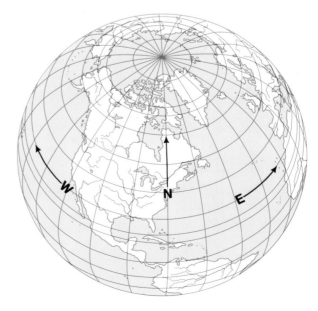

W   N   E

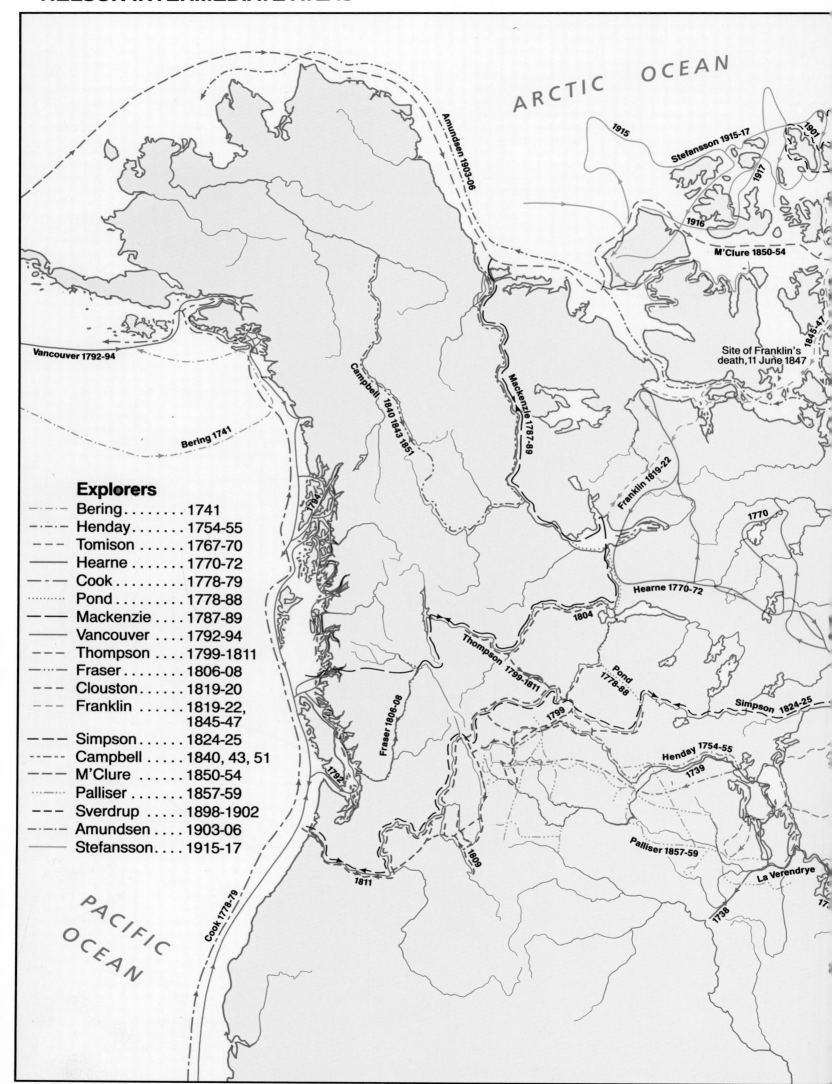

ARCTIC OCEAN

PACIFIC OCEAN

Amundsen 1903-06

1915

Stefansson 1915-17

1907

1917

1916

M'Clure 1850-54

1845-47

Site of Franklin's death, 11 June 1847

Vancouver 1792-94

Bering 1741

Campbell 1840 1843 1851

Mackenzie 1787-89

Franklin 1819-22

1770

1794

Hearne 1770-72

1804

Thompson 1799-1811

Pond 1778-88

Simpson 1824-25

Fraser 1806-08

1799

Henday 1754-55

1739

1792

1809

Palliser 1857-59

1811

La Verendrye

1738

Cook 1778-79

Explorers

Explorer	Years
Bering	1741
Henday	1754-55
Tomison	1767-70
Hearne	1770-72
Cook	1778-79
Pond	1778-88
Mackenzie	1787-89
Vancouver	1792-94
Thompson	1799-1811
Fraser	1806-08
Clouston	1819-20
Franklin	1819-22, 1845-47
Simpson	1824-25
Campbell	1840, 43, 51
M'Clure	1850-54
Palliser	1857-59
Sverdrup	1898-1902
Amundsen	1903-06
Stefansson	1915-17

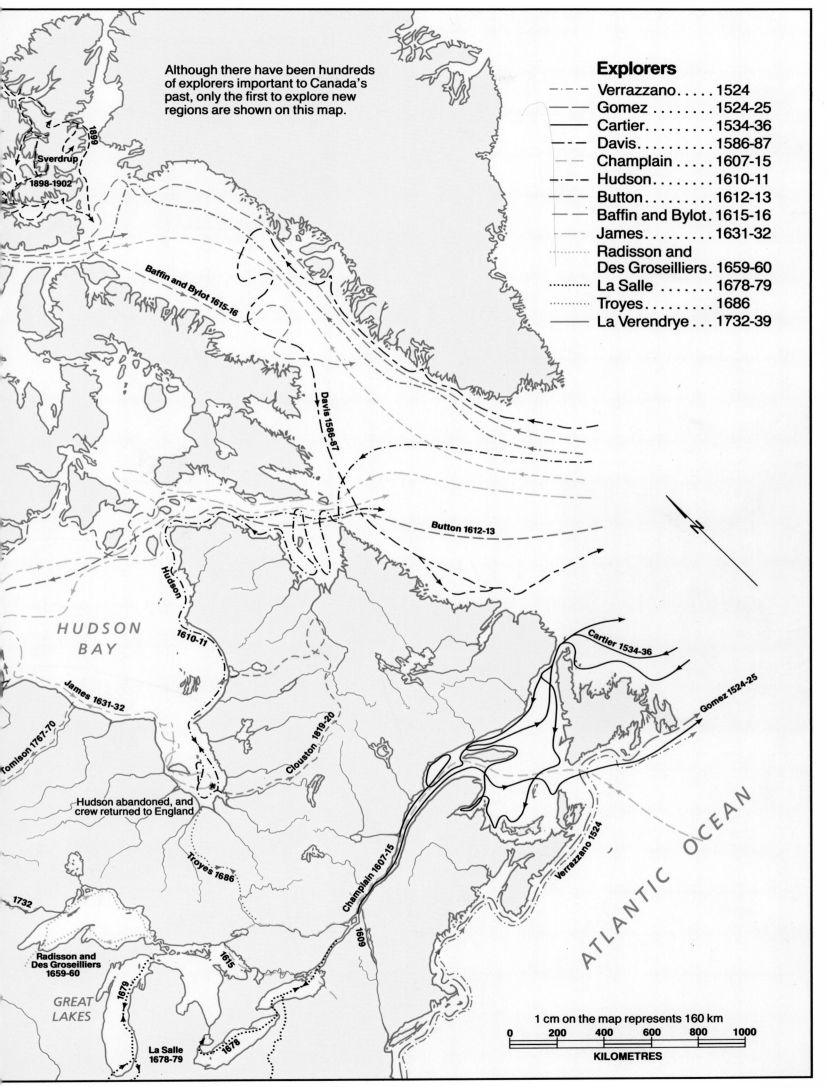

Although there have been hundreds of explorers important to Canada's past, only the first to explore new regions are shown on this map.

Explorers

—·—·—	Verrazzano	1524
— — —	Gomez	1524-25
———	Cartier	1534-36
—··—··—	Davis	1586-87
———	Champlain	1607-15
—···—···—	Hudson	1610-11
— — —	Button	1612-13
— — —	Baffin and Bylot	1615-16
— — —	James	1631-32
·········	Radisson and Des Groseilliers	1659-60
·········	La Salle	1678-79
·········	Troyes	1686
———	La Verendrye	1732-39

Sverdrup
1898-1902
1899

Baffin and Bylot 1615-16

Davis 1586-87

Button 1612-13

Hudson 1610-11

HUDSON BAY

James 1631-32

Tomlson 1767-70

Clouston 1819-20

Cartier 1534-36

Gomez 1524-25

Hudson abandoned, and crew returned to England

Troyes 1686

Champlain 1607-15

1609

Verrazzano 1524

ATLANTIC OCEAN

1732

Radisson and Des Groseilliers 1659-60

GREAT LAKES

1679

1615

1678

La Salle 1678-79

1 cm on the map represents 160 km

0   200   400   600   800   1000

KILOMETRES

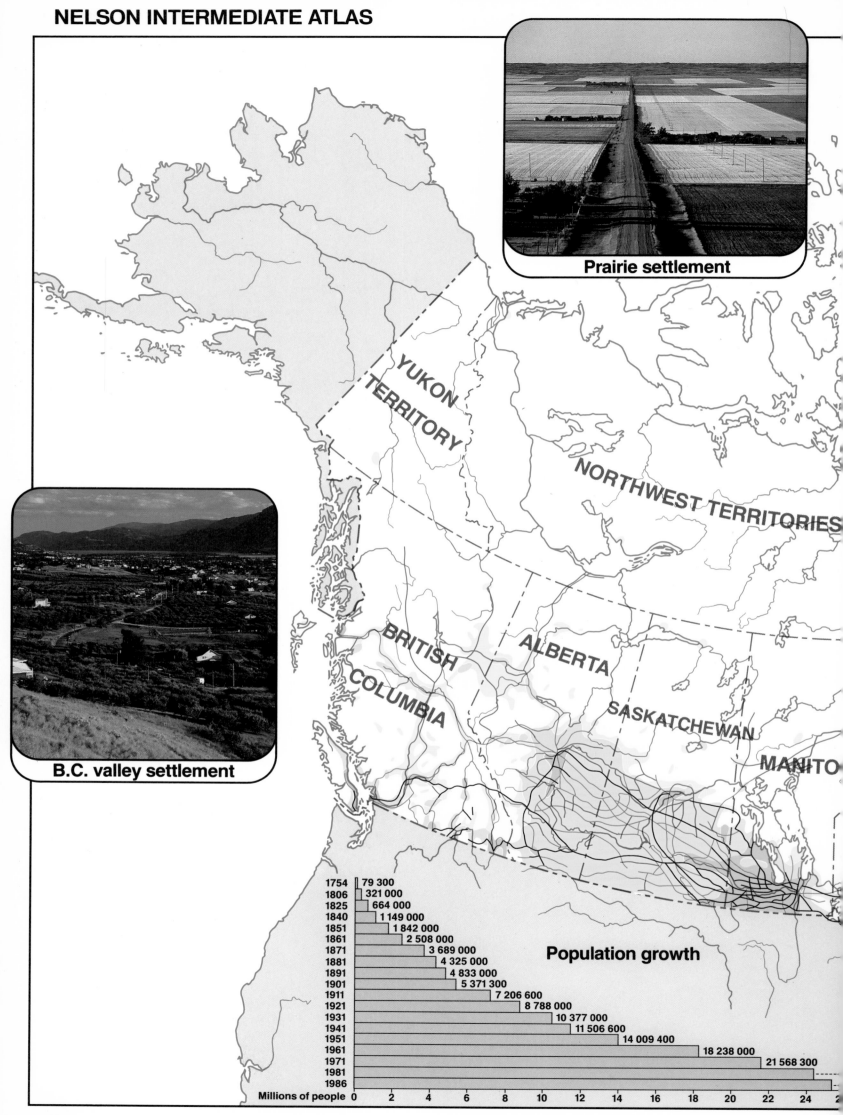

Prairie settlement

B.C. valley settlement

YUKON TERRITORY

NORTHWEST TERRITORIES

BRITISH COLUMBIA

ALBERTA

SASKATCHEWAN

MANITO

Population growth

Year	Population
1754	79 300
1806	321 000
1825	664 000
1840	1 149 000
1851	1 842 000
1861	2 508 000
1871	3 689 000
1881	4 325 000
1891	4 833 000
1901	5 371 300
1911	7 206 600
1921	8 788 000
1931	10 377 000
1941	11 506 600
1951	14 009 400
1961	18 238 000
1971	21 568 300
1981	
1986	

Millions of people   0   2   4   6   8   10   12   14   16   18   20   22   24

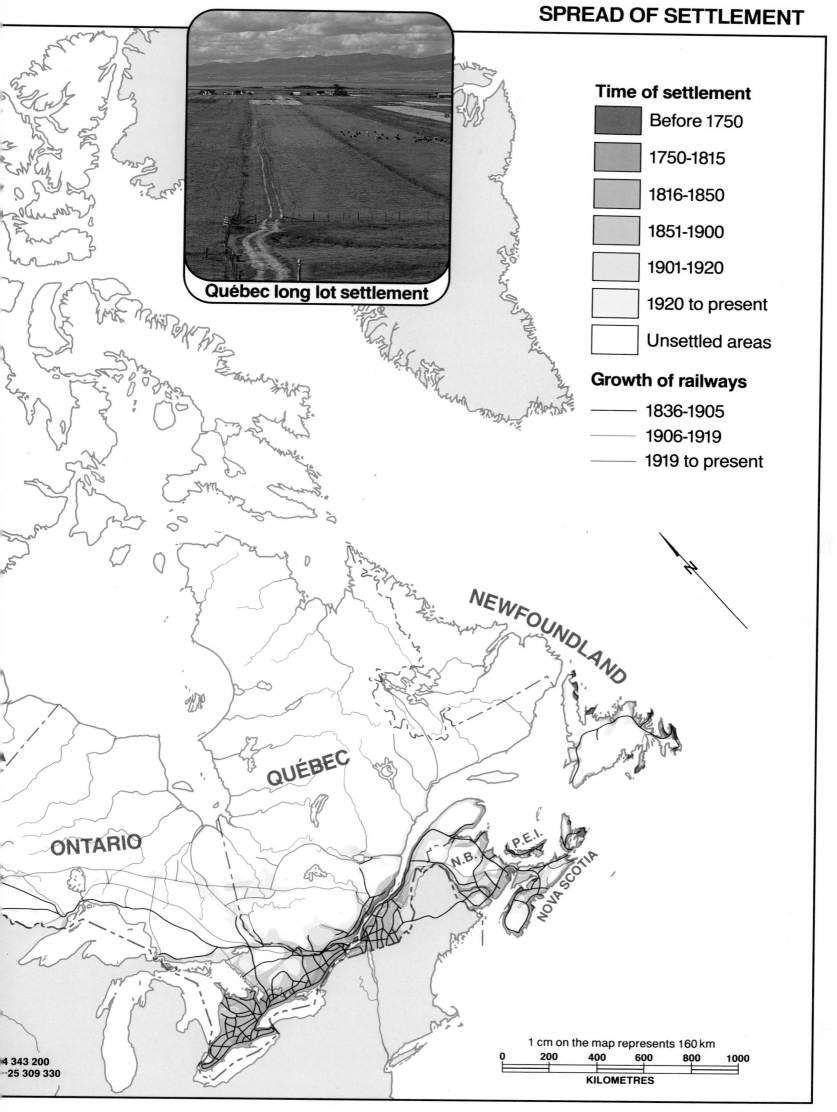

Québec long lot settlement

Time of settlement

Before 1750

1750-1815

1816-1850

1851-1900

1901-1920

1920 to present

Unsettled areas

Growth of railways

1836-1905

1906-1919

1919 to present

N

NEWFOUNDLAND

QUÉBEC

ONTARIO

N.B.

P.E.I.

NOVA SCOTIA

4 343 200
25 309 330

1 cm on the map represents 160 km

0   200   400   600   800   1000

KILOMETRES

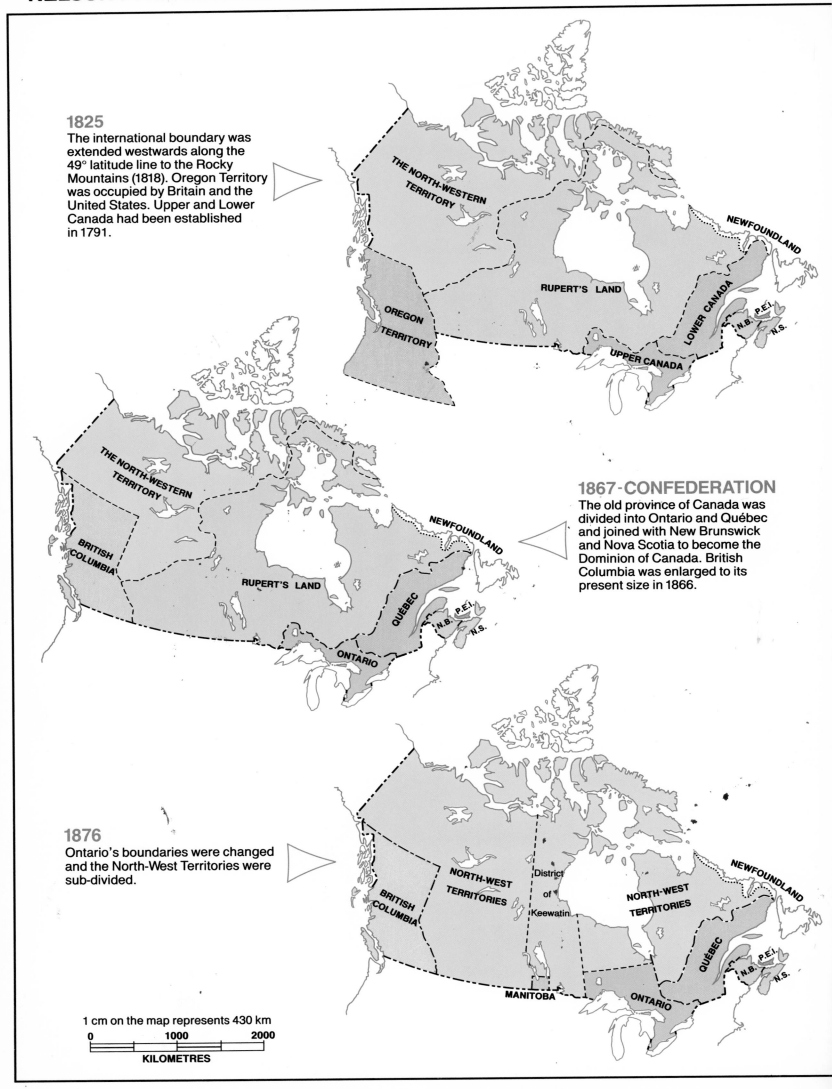

1825

The international boundary was extended westwards along the 49° latitude line to the Rocky Mountains (1818). Oregon Territory was occupied by Britain and the United States. Upper and Lower Canada had been established in 1791.

1867 - CONFEDERATION

The old province of Canada was divided into Ontario and Québec and joined with New Brunswick and Nova Scotia to become the Dominion of Canada. British Columbia was enlarged to its present size in 1866.

1876

Ontario's boundaries were changed and the North-West Territories were sub-divided.

1 cm on the map represents 430 km

0   1000   2000
KILOMETRES

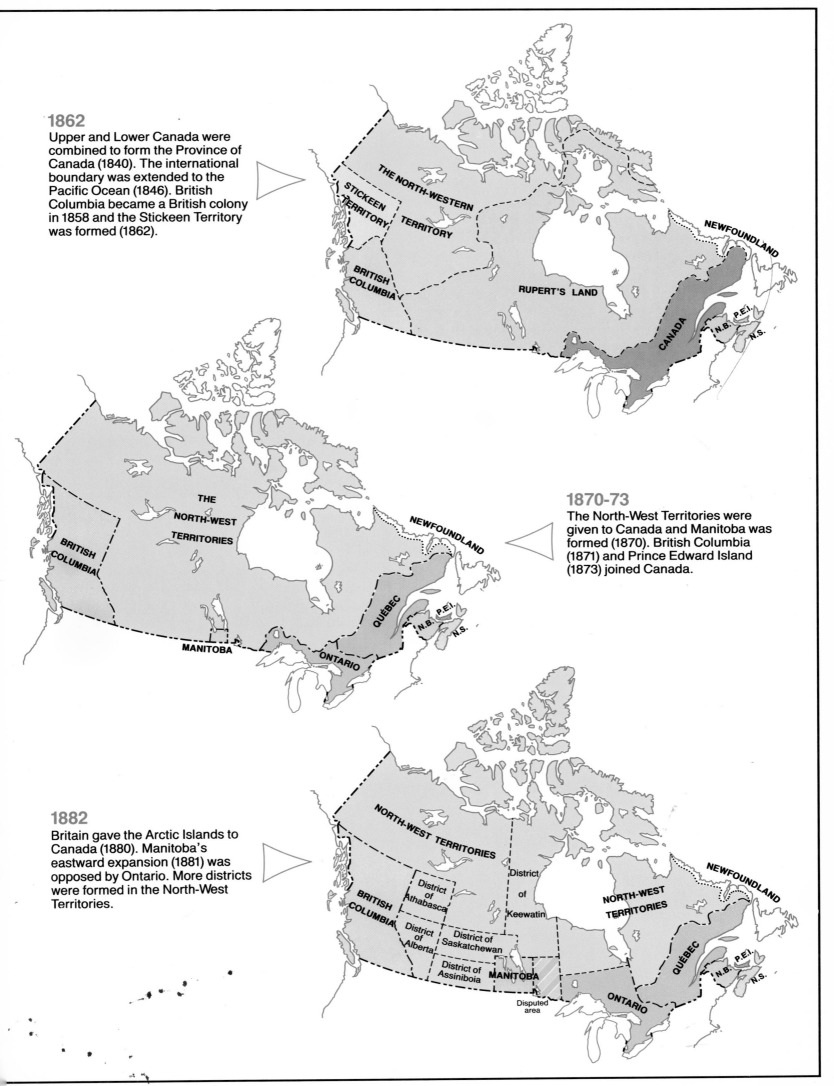

1862

Upper and Lower Canada were combined to form the Province of Canada (1840). The international boundary was extended to the Pacific Ocean (1846). British Columbia became a British colony in 1858 and the Stickeen Territory was formed (1862).

1870-73

The North-West Territories were given to Canada and Manitoba was formed (1870). British Columbia (1871) and Prince Edward Island (1873) joined Canada.

1882

Britain gave the Arctic Islands to Canada (1880). Manitoba's eastward expansion (1881) was opposed by Ontario. More districts were formed in the North-West Territories.

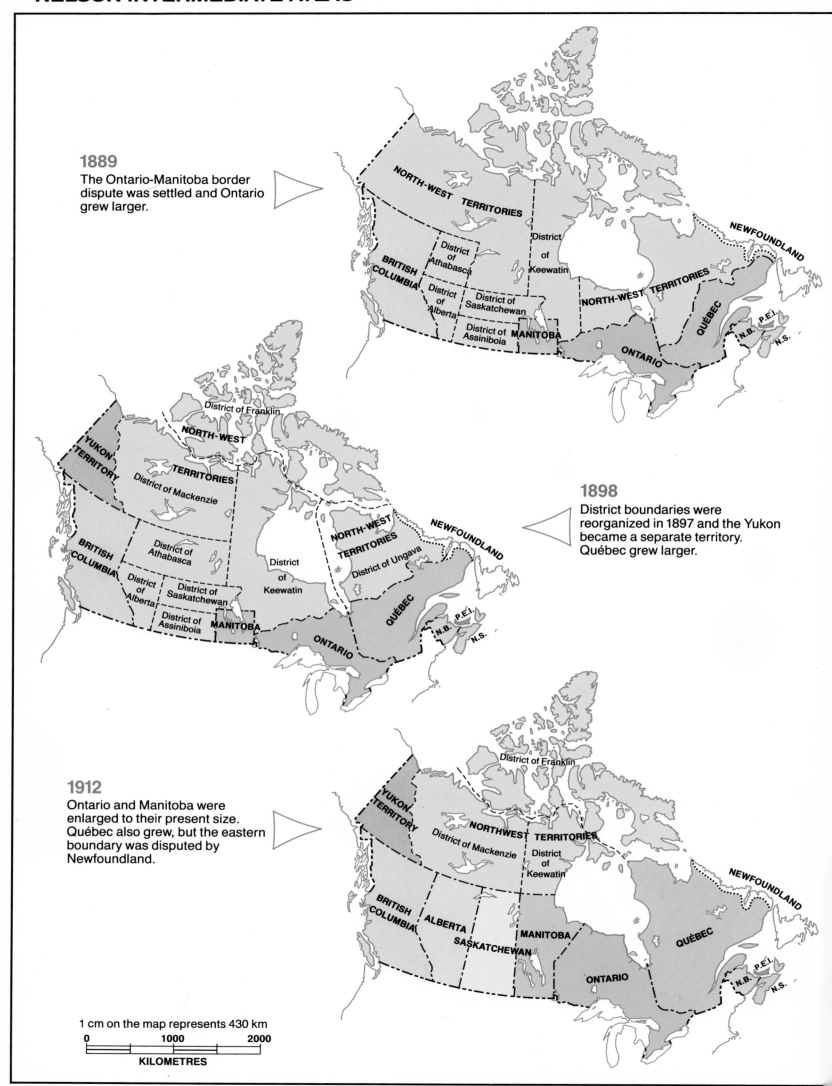

1889
The Ontario-Manitoba border dispute was settled and Ontario grew larger.

NORTH-WEST TERRITORIES

District of Athabasca

District of Keewatin

BRITISH COLUMBIA

District of Alberta

District of Saskatchewan

District of Assiniboia

MANITOBA

NORTH-WEST TERRITORIES

NEWFOUNDLAND

QUÉBEC

ONTARIO

N.B.

P.E.I.

N.S.

District of Franklin

NORTH-WEST TERRITORIES

YUKON TERRITORY

District of Mackenzie

BRITISH COLUMBIA

District of Athabasca

District of Alberta

District of Saskatchewan

District of Assiniboia

MANITOBA

District of Keewatin

NORTH-WEST TERRITORIES

District of Ungava

NEWFOUNDLAND

QUÉBEC

ONTARIO

N.B.

P.E.I.

N.S.

1898
District boundaries were reorganized in 1897 and the Yukon became a separate territory. Québec grew larger.

1912
Ontario and Manitoba were enlarged to their present size. Québec also grew, but the eastern boundary was disputed by Newfoundland.

District of Franklin

YUKON TERRITORY

NORTHWEST TERRITORIES

District of Mackenzie

District of Keewatin

BRITISH COLUMBIA

ALBERTA

SASKATCHEWAN

MANITOBA

NEWFOUNDLAND

QUÉBEC

ONTARIO

N.B.

P.E.I.

N.S.

1 cm on the map represents 430 km

0   1000   2000

KILOMETRES

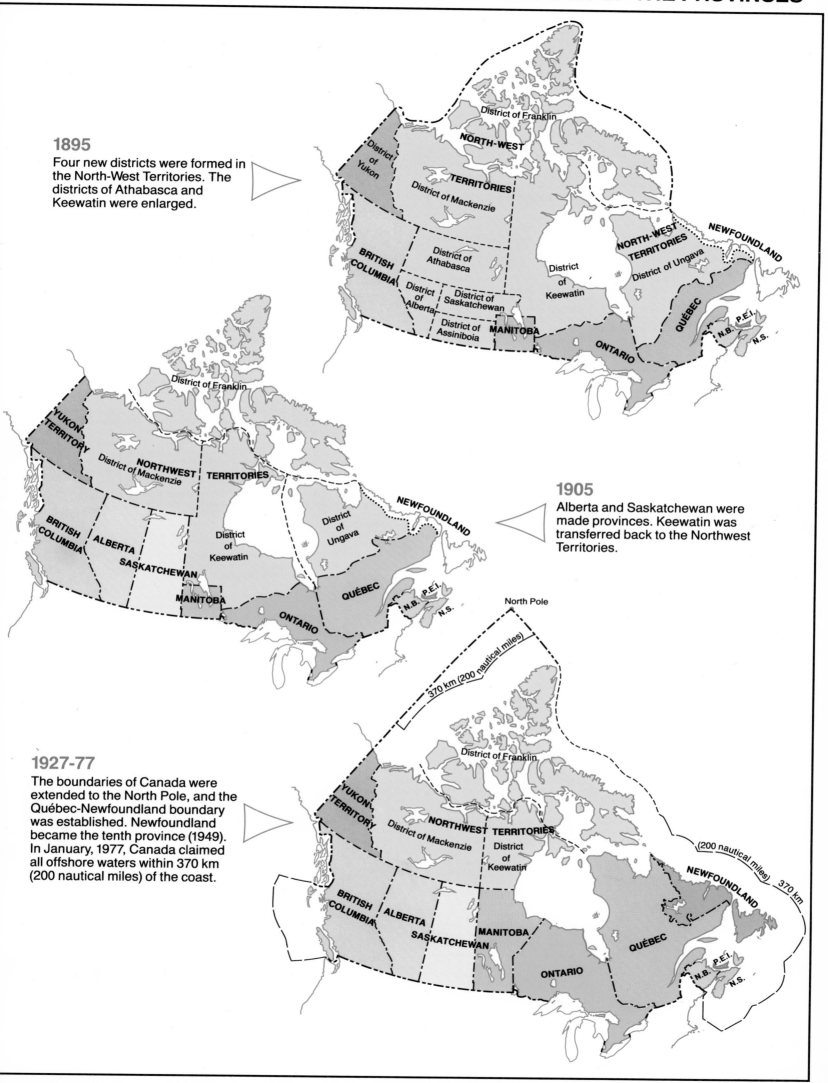

1895

Four new districts were formed in the North-West Territories. The districts of Athabasca and Keewatin were enlarged.

1905

Alberta and Saskatchewan were made provinces. Keewatin was transferred back to the Northwest Territories.

1927-77

The boundaries of Canada were extended to the North Pole, and the Québec-Newfoundland boundary was established. Newfoundland became the tenth province (1949). In January, 1977, Canada claimed all offshore waters within 370 km (200 nautical miles) of the coast.

ARCTIC OCEAN

QUEEN ELIZABETH ISLANDS

ARCTIC CIRCLE

BEAUFORT SEA

MELVILLE ISLAND

BANKS ISLAND

Kaujuitoq

PRINCE OF WALES ISLAND

VICTORIA ISLAND

ALASKA
(United States)

Tuktoyaktuk

Old Crow

Inuvik

Fort McPherson

Cambridge Bay

Coppermine

YUKON TERRITORY

Dawson

Norman Wells

Fort Franklin

NORTHWEST TERRITOR

Whitehorse

Faro

PACIFIC OCEAN

Atlin

Watson Lake

Yellowknife

Baker Lake

Fort Nelson

CANADA

QUEEN CHARLOTTE ISLANDS

Prince Rupert

Kitimat

BRITISH

Fort St John

Fort Vermilion

Churchill

Fort McMurray

Brochet

Ocean Falls

Prince George

COLUMBIA

Peace River

Grande Prairie

ALBERTA

SASKATCHEWAN

MANITO

Thompson

VANCOUVER ISLAND

Red Deer

Edmonton

Prince Albert

The Pas

Kamloops

Vancouver

Kelowna

Calgary

North Battleford

Saskatoon

Victoria

Lethbridge

Medicine Hat

Moose Jaw

Regina

Brandon

Winnipeg

UNITED STATES OF AMERICA

North latitude

West longitude

1 cm on the map represents 160 km

| 0 | 200 | 400 | 600 | 800 | 1000 |

KILOMETRES

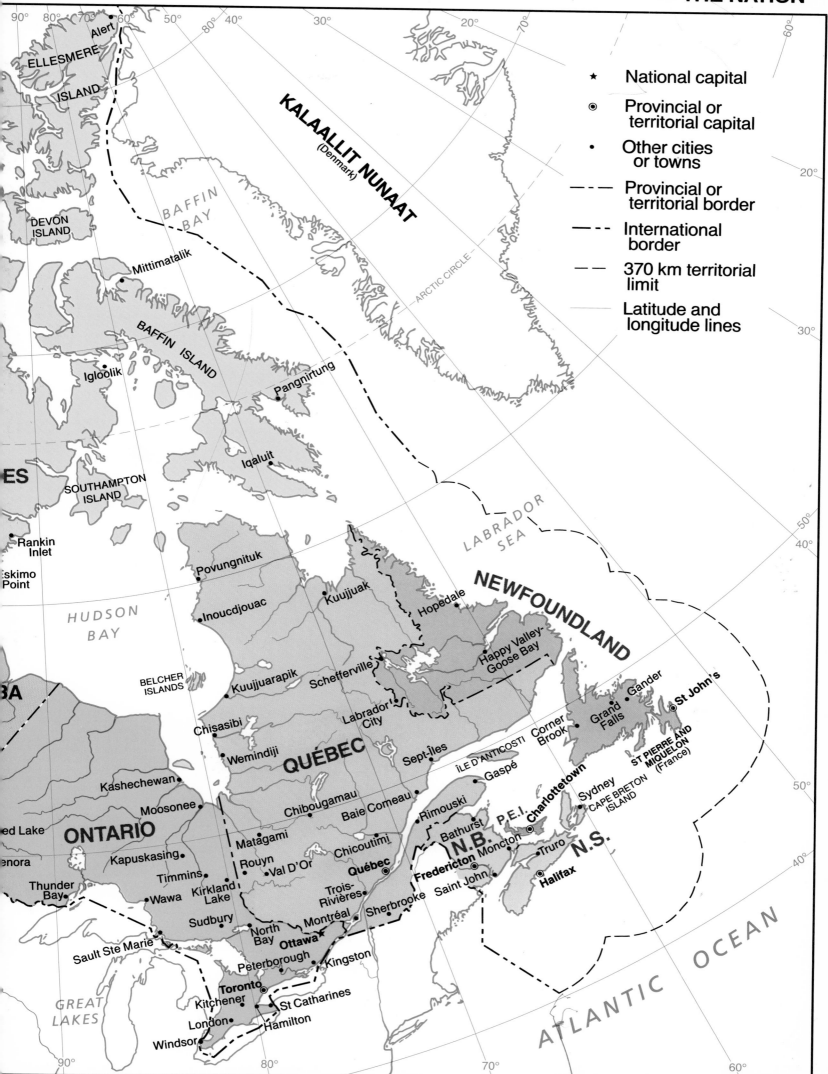

Legend:

★ National capital

⊙ Provincial or territorial capital

• Other cities or towns

–·– Provincial or territorial border

–··– International border

–– 370 km territorial limit

—— Latitude and longitude lines

ELLESMERE ISLAND

Alert

DEVON ISLAND

KALAALLIT NUNAAT (Denmark)

BAFFIN BAY

Mittimatalik

BAFFIN ISLAND

Igloolik

Pangnirtung

ARCTIC CIRCLE

Iqaluit

SOUTHAMPTON ISLAND

ES

Rankin Inlet

Eskimo Point

HUDSON BAY

BELCHER ISLANDS

BA

Povungnituk

Inoucdjouac

Kuujjuak

LABRADOR SEA

Hopedale

NEWFOUNDLAND

Happy Valley-Goose Bay

Kuujjuarapik

Schefferville

St John's

Gander

Grand Falls

Chisasibi

Labrador City

Corner Brook

ST PIERRE AND MIQUELON (France)

Wemindji

QUÉBEC

Sept-Îles

ÎLE D'ANTICOSTI

Gaspé

Kashechewan

Sydney

CAPE BRETON ISLAND

Moosonee

Chibougamau

Baie Comeau

Rimouski

Bathurst

P.E.I.

Charlottetown

Truro

N.S.

ONTARIO

Matagami

Chicoutimi

N.B.

Moncton

ed Lake

Kapuskasing

Rouyn

Val D'Or

Québec

Fredericton

Saint John

Halifax

enora

Timmins

Kirkland Lake

Trois-Rivières

Thunder Bay

Wawa

Sudbury

North Bay

Montréal

Sherbrooke

Sault Ste Marie

Ottawa

Peterborough

Kingston

GREAT LAKES

Toronto

Kitchener

St Catharines

London

Hamilton

Windsor

ATLANTIC OCEAN

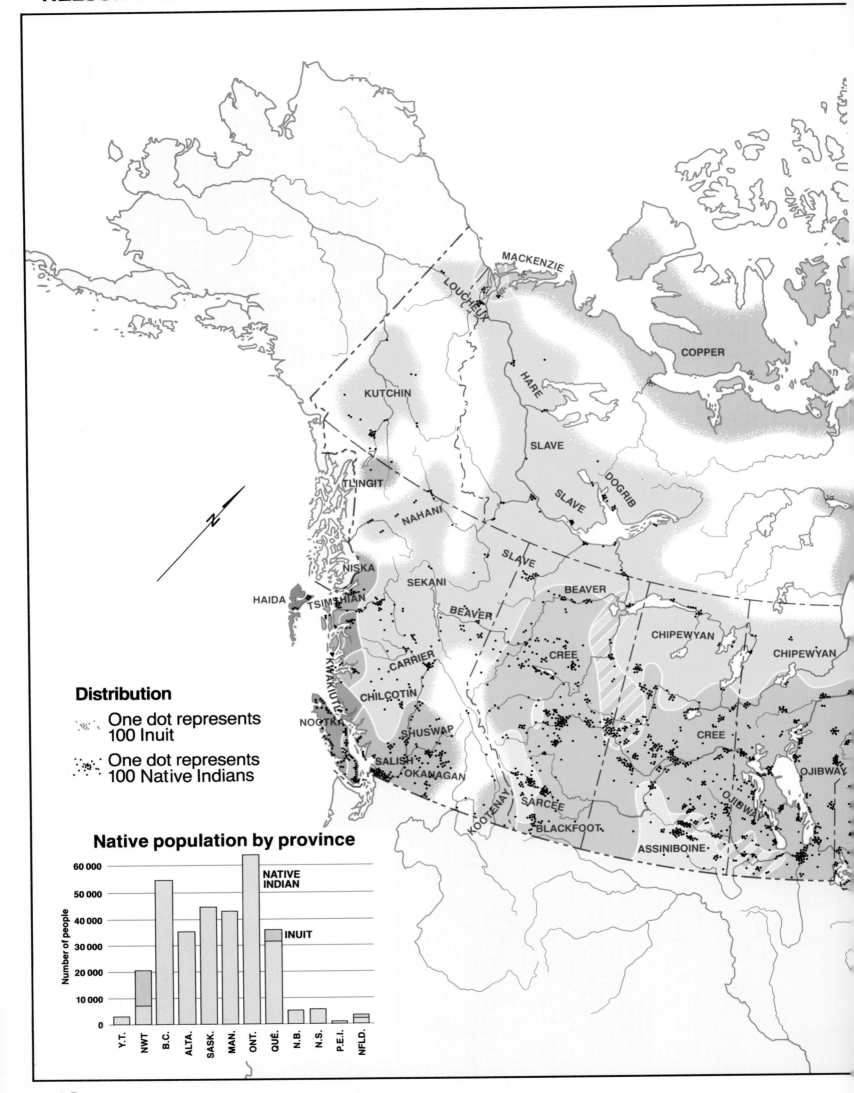

Distribution

One dot represents 100 Inuit

One dot represents 100 Native Indians

Native population by province

Number of people

NATIVE
INDIAN

INUIT

60 000
50 000
40 000
30 000
20 000
10 000
0

Y.T. NWT B.C. ALTA. SASK. MAN. ONT. QUÉ. N.B. N.S. P.E.I. NFLD.

Map labels:

MACKENZIE
LOUCHEUX
COPPER
KUTCHIN
HARE
SLAVE
DOGRIB
SLAVE
TLINGIT
NAHANI
SLAVE
NISKA
SEKANI
BEAVER
HAIDA
TSIMSHIAN
BEAVER
CHIPEWYAN
CHIPEWYAN
CARRIER
CREE
KWAKIUTL
CHILCOTIN
NOOTKA
SHUSWAP
CREE
SALISH
OKANAGAN
OJIBWAY
KOOTENAY
SARCEE
OJIBWAY
BLACKFOOT
ASSINIBOINE

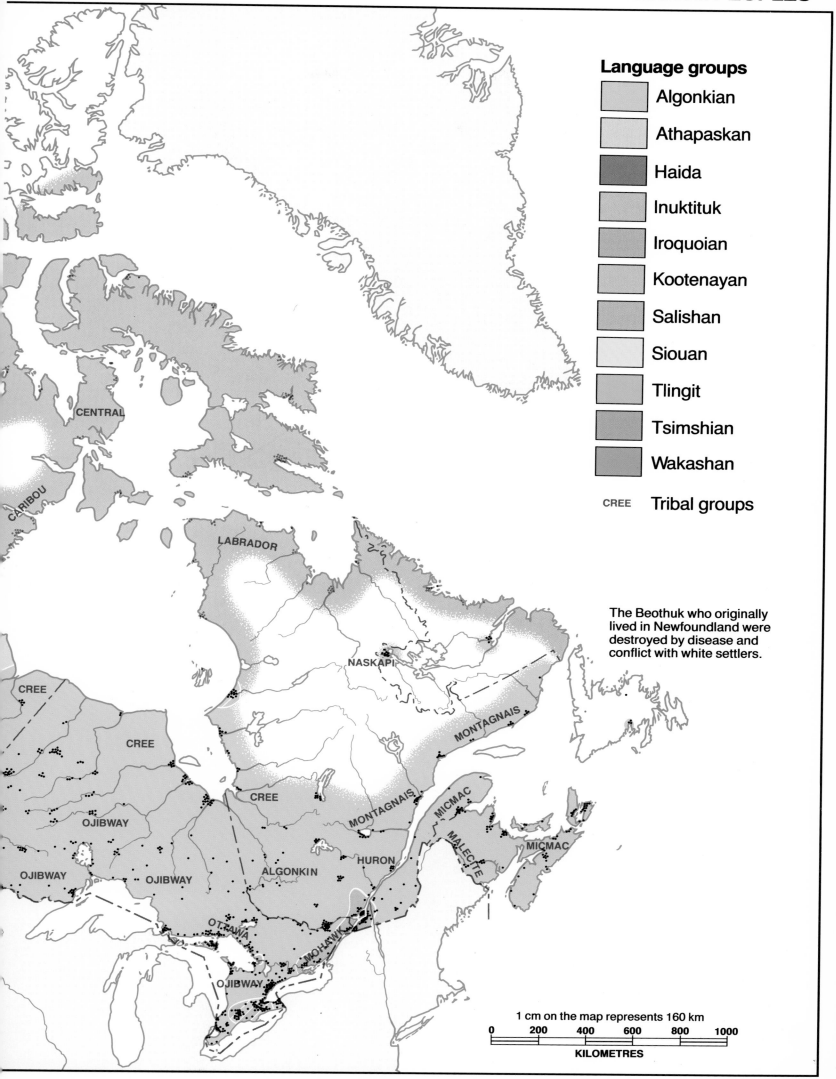

Language groups

Algonkian

Athapaskan

Haida

Inuktituk

Iroquoian

Kootenayan

Salishan

Siouan

Tlingit

Tsimshian

Wakashan

CREE Tribal groups

CENTRAL

CARIBOU

LABRADOR

The Beothuk who originally lived in Newfoundland were destroyed by disease and conflict with white settlers.

NASKAPI

CREE

CREE

CREE

MONTAGNAIS

MONTAGNAIS

OJIBWAY

MONTAGNAIS

MICMAC

OJIBWAY

OJIBWAY

ALGONKIN

HURON

MALECITE

MICMAC

OTTAWA

MOHAWK

OJIBWAY

1 cm on the map represents 160 km

0   200   400   600   800   1000

KILOMETRES

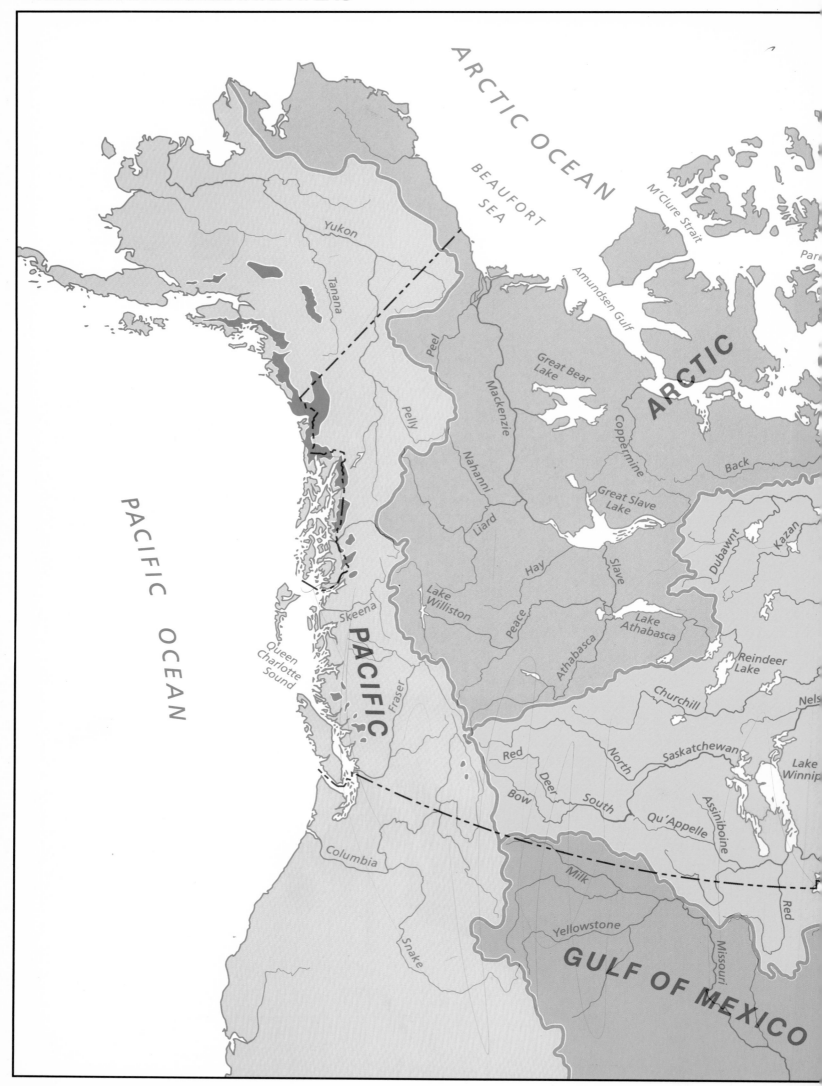

ARCTIC OCEAN

BEAUFORT SEA

M'Clure Strait

Par

Yukon

Tanana

Peel

Amundsen Gulf

ARCTIC

Great Bear Lake

Mackenzie

Coppermine

Back

Nahanni

Great Slave Lake

Dubawnt

Kazan

PACIFIC OCEAN

Pelly

Liard

Hay

Slave

Lake Williston

Peace

Lake Athabasca

Reindeer Lake

Skeena

PACIFIC

Athabasca

Churchill

Nels

Queen Charlotte Sound

Red

North

Saskatchewan

Lake Winnip

Fraser

Bow

Deer

South

Qu'Appelle

Assiniboine

Red

Columbia

Milk

Snake

Yellowstone

Missouri

GULF OF MEXICO

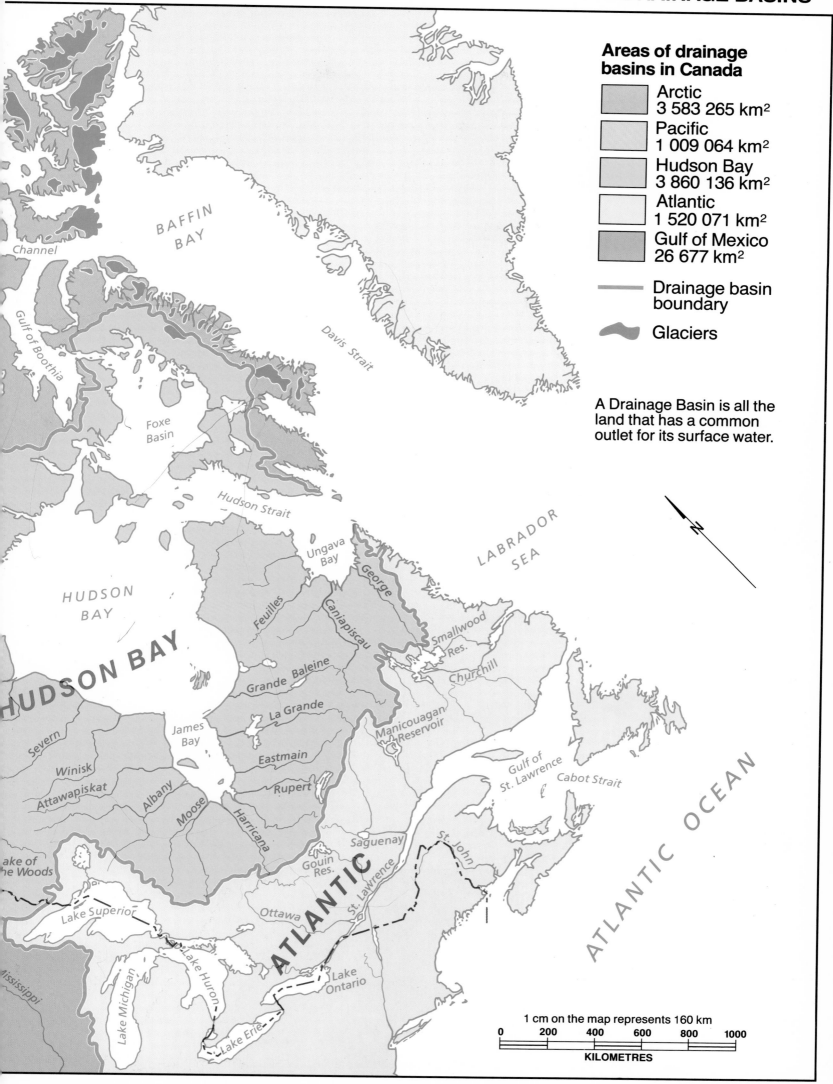

Areas of drainage basins in Canada

Arctic
3 583 265 km²

Pacific
1 009 064 km²

Hudson Bay
3 860 136 km²

Atlantic
1 520 071 km²

Gulf of Mexico
26 677 km²

Drainage basin boundary

Glaciers

A Drainage Basin is all the land that has a common outlet for its surface water.

BAFFIN BAY

Channel

Gulf of Boothia

Foxe Basin

Davis Strait

Hudson Strait

Ungava Bay

LABRADOR SEA

HUDSON BAY

George

Feuilles

Caniapiscau

Smallwood Res.

Grande Baleine

Churchill

La Grande

James Bay

Manicouagan Reservoir

Severn

Eastmain

Winisk

Rupert

Gulf of St. Lawrence

Cabot Strait

Attawapiskat

Albany

Moose

Harricana

Saguenay

St. John

ATLANTIC OCEAN

ake of he Woods

Lake Superior

Gouin Res.

St. Lawrence

Ottawa

ATLANTIC

St. Lawrence

Mississippi

Lake Michigan

Lake Huron

Lake Ontario

Lake Erie

1 cm on the map represents 160 km

0   200   400   600   800   1000

KILOMETRES

NELSON INTERMEDIATE ATLAS

Beef cattle ranch

Poultry farm

Orchard

Pig farm

Grain farm

YUKON TERRITORY

NORTHWEST TERRITORIES

BRITISH COLUMBIA

ALBERTA

SASKATCHEWAN

MANITOBA

1 cm on the map is equal to 160 km

0   200   400   600   800   1000

KILOMETRES

20

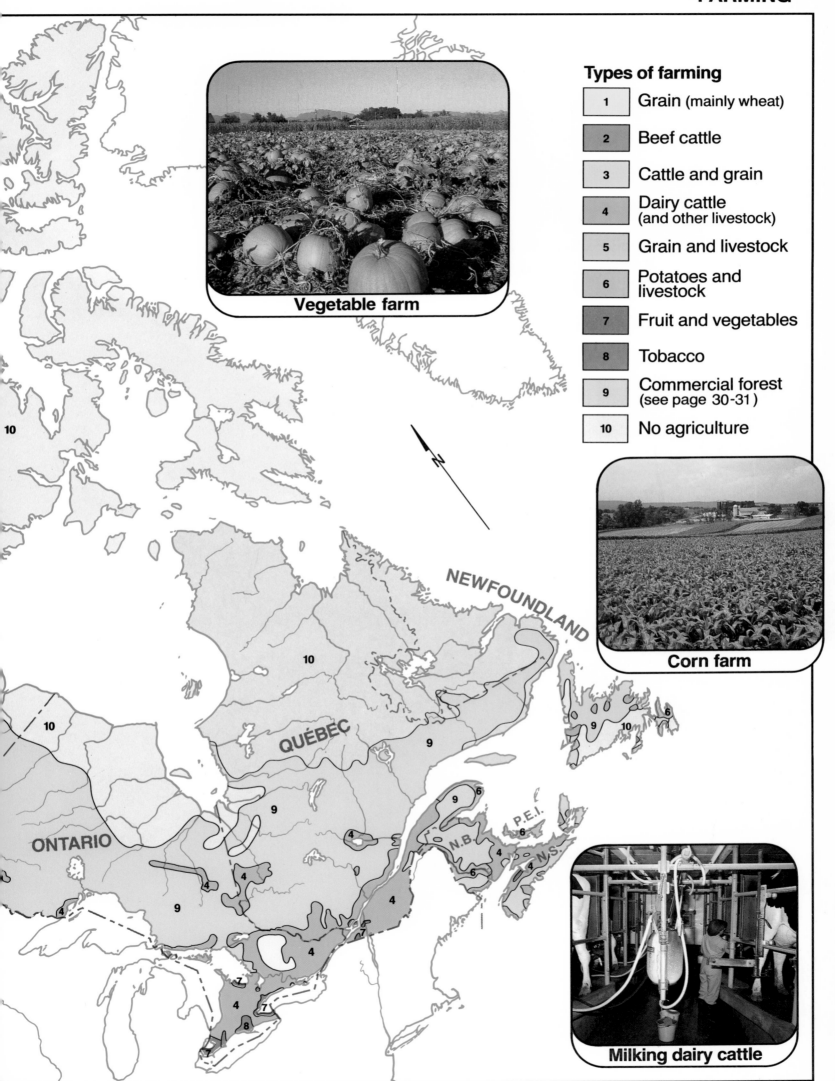

Vegetable farm

Types of farming

1	Grain (mainly wheat)
2	Beef cattle
3	Cattle and grain
4	Dairy cattle (and other livestock)
5	Grain and livestock
6	Potatoes and livestock
7	Fruit and vegetables
8	Tobacco
9	Commercial forest (see page 30-31)
10	No agriculture

Corn farm

Milking dairy cattle

NEWFOUNDLAND

QUÉBEC

ONTARIO

P.E.I.

N.B.

N.S.

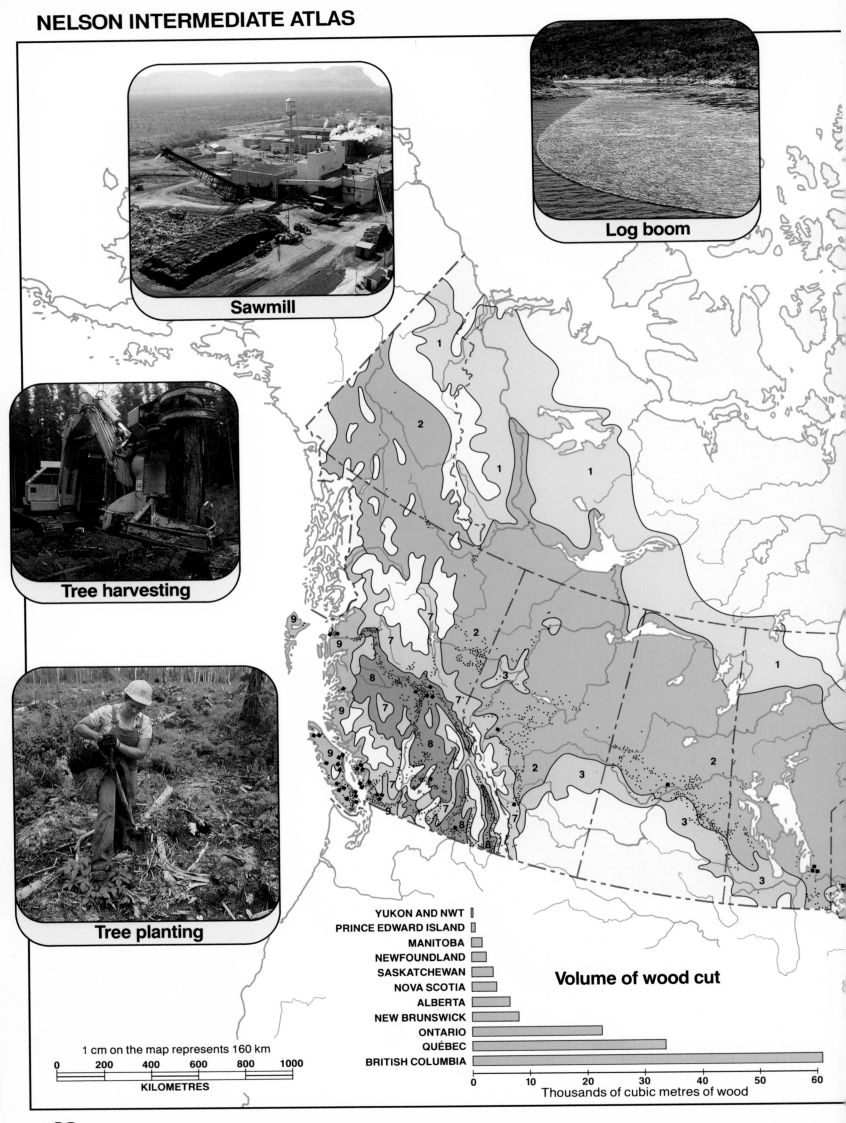

Sawmill

Log boom

Tree harvesting

Tree planting

1 cm on the map represents 160 km

0   200   400   600   800   1000

KILOMETRES

YUKON AND NWT

PRINCE EDWARD ISLAND

MANITOBA

NEWFOUNDLAND

SASKATCHEWAN

NOVA SCOTIA

ALBERTA

NEW BRUNSWICK

ONTARIO

QUÉBEC

BRITISH COLUMBIA

Volume of wood cut

0   10   20   30   40   50   60

Thousands of cubic metres of wood

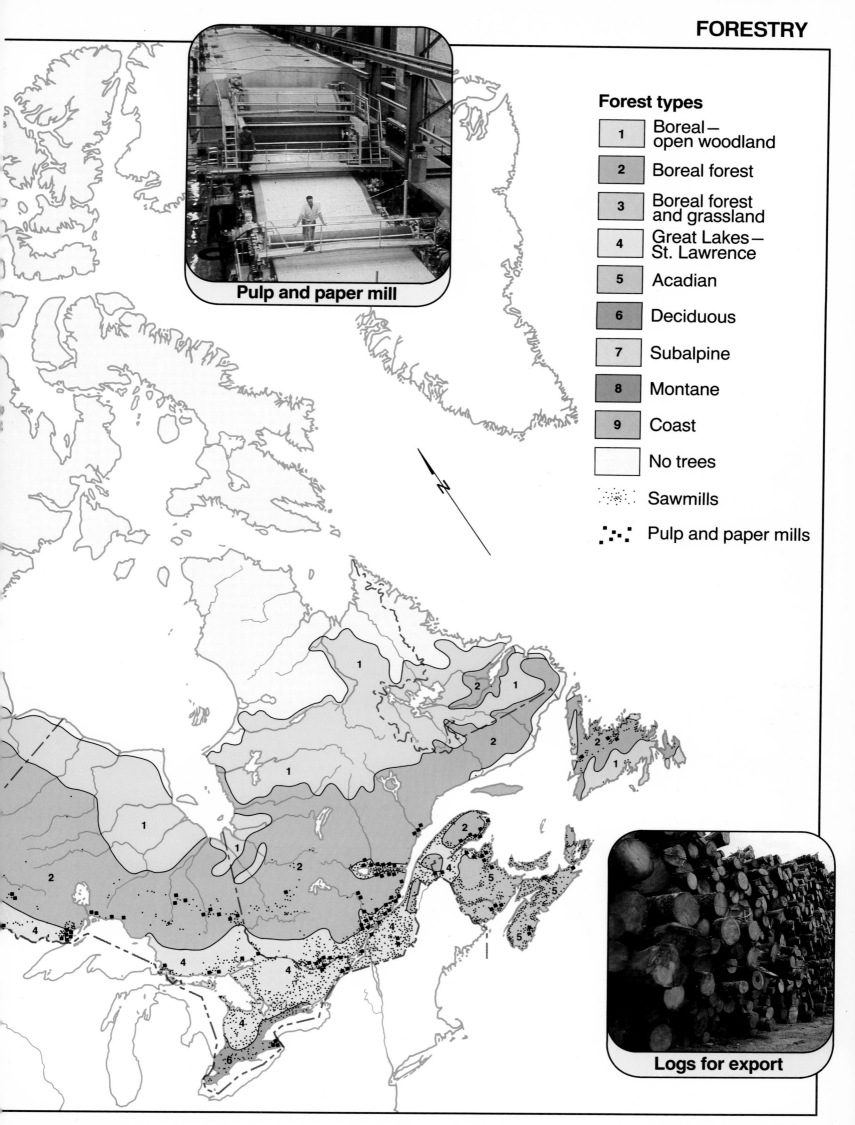

Pulp and paper mill

Forest types

1	Boreal — open woodland
2	Boreal forest
3	Boreal forest and grassland
4	Great Lakes — St. Lawrence
5	Acadian
6	Deciduous
7	Subalpine
8	Montane
9	Coast
	No trees
	Sawmills
	Pulp and paper mills

Logs for export

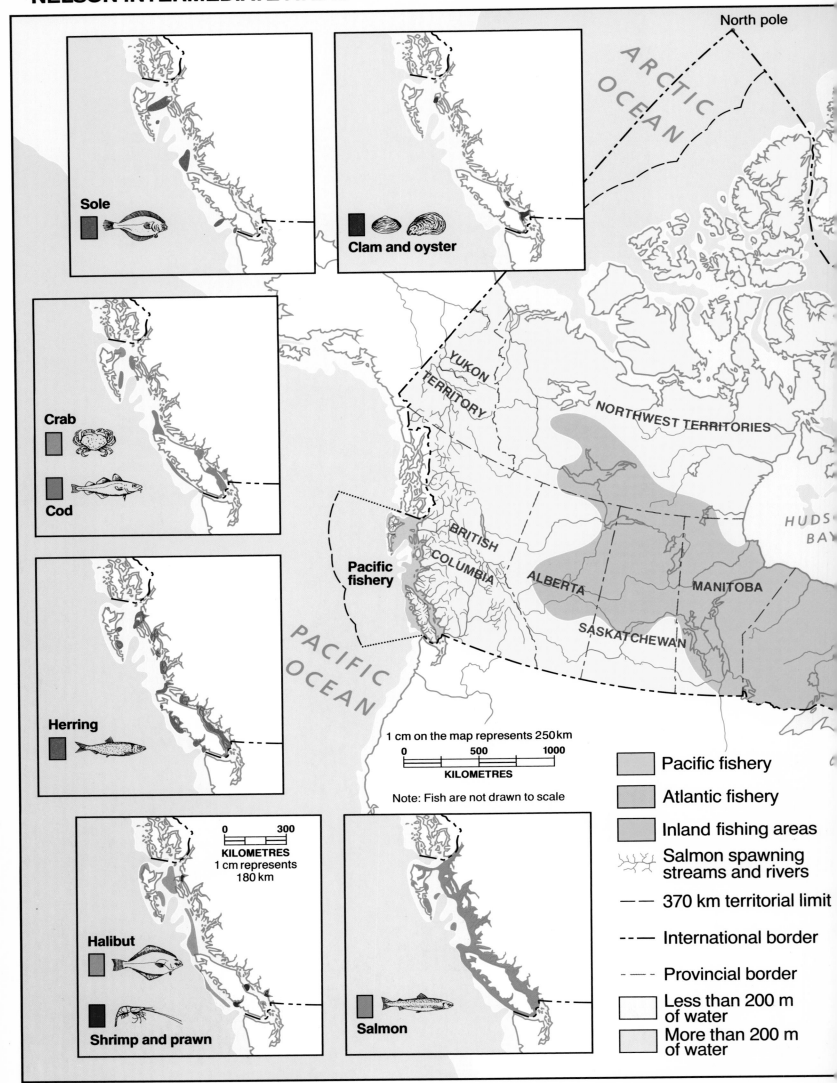

Sole

Clam and oyster

North pole

ARCTIC OCEAN

Crab

Cod

YUKON TERRITORY

NORTHWEST TERRITORIES

Herring

Pacific fishery

BRITISH COLUMBIA

ALBERTA

SASKATCHEWAN

MANITOBA

HUDSON BAY

PACIFIC OCEAN

1 cm on the map represents 250 km

0   500   1000

KILOMETRES

Note: Fish are not drawn to scale

0   300

KILOMETRES

1 cm represents 180 km

Halibut

Shrimp and prawn

Salmon

Pacific fishery

Atlantic fishery

Inland fishing areas

Salmon spawning streams and rivers

370 km territorial limit

International border

Provincial border

Less than 200 m of water

More than 200 m of water

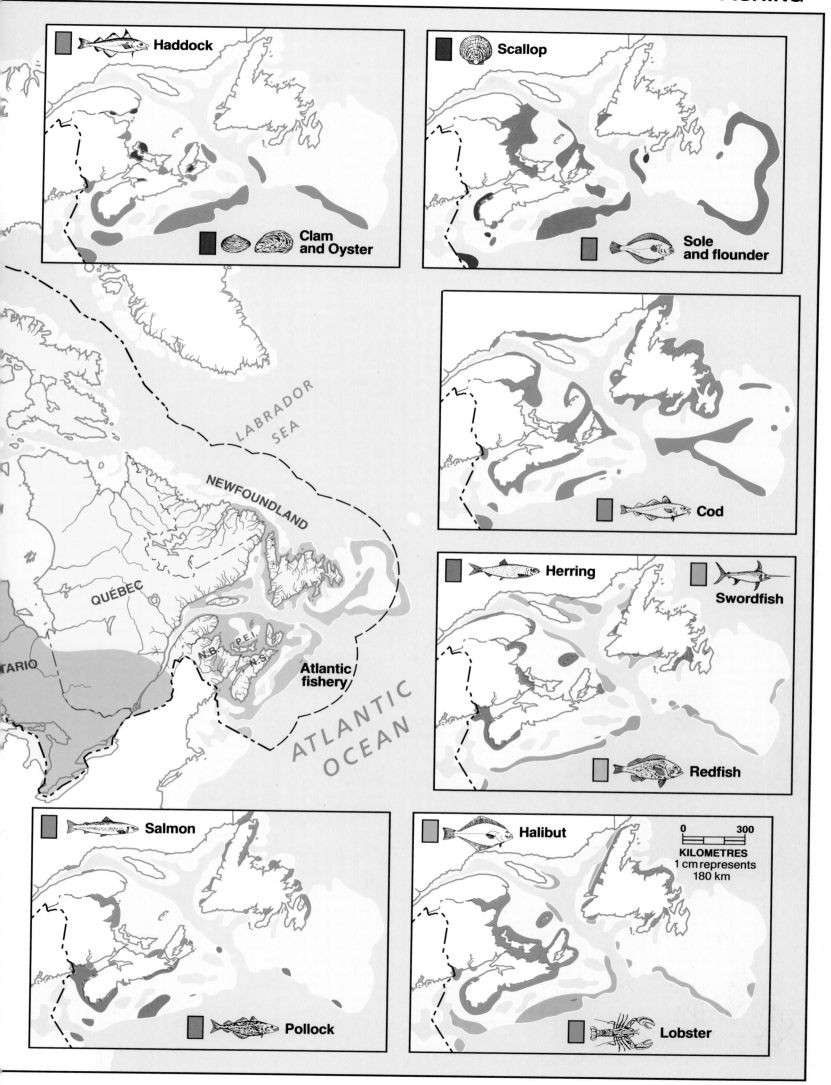

Haddock

Clam and Oyster

Scallop

Sole and flounder

Cod

Herring

Swordfish

Redfish

Salmon

Pollock

Halibut

Lobster

LABRADOR SEA

NEWFOUNDLAND

QUÉBEC

N.B.

P.E.I.

N.S.

ONTARIO

Atlantic fishery

ATLANTIC OCEAN

0   300
KILOMETRES
1 cm represents
180 km

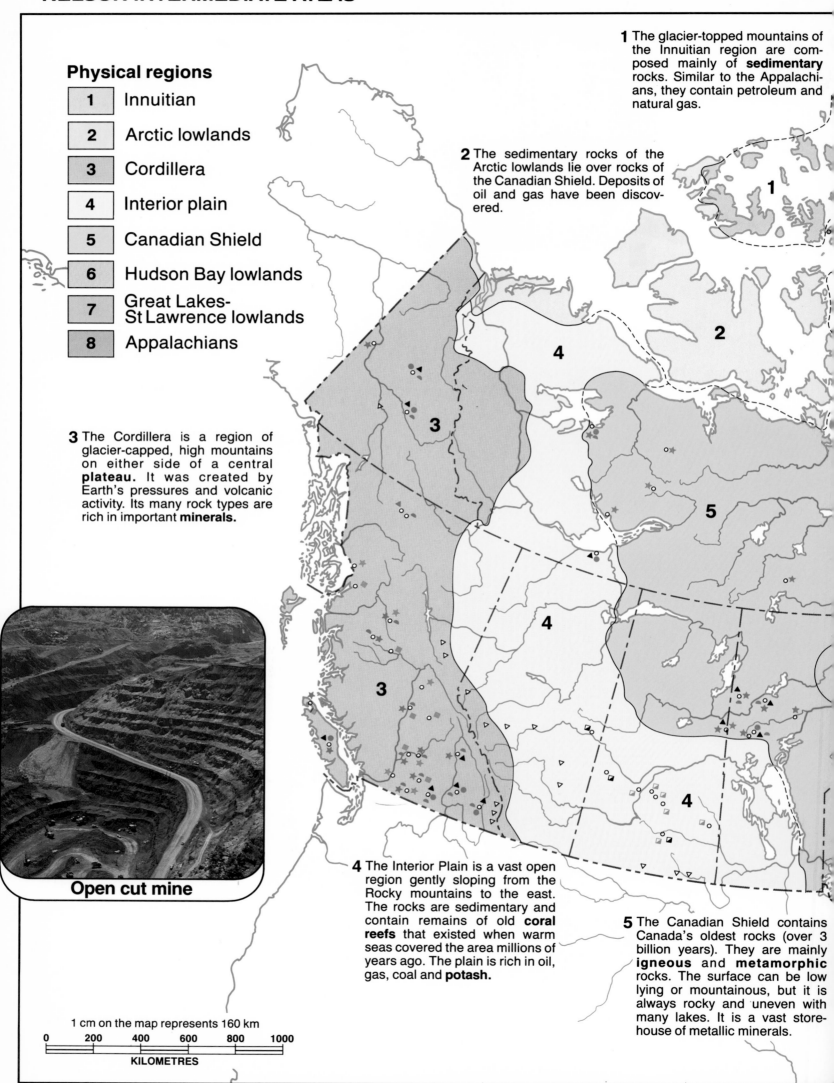

Physical regions

1	Innuitian
2	Arctic lowlands
3	Cordillera
4	Interior plain
5	Canadian Shield
6	Hudson Bay lowlands
7	Great Lakes-St Lawrence lowlands
8	Appalachians

1 The glacier-topped mountains of the Innuitian region are composed mainly of **sedimentary** rocks. Similar to the Appalachians, they contain petroleum and natural gas.

2 The sedimentary rocks of the Arctic lowlands lie over rocks of the Canadian Shield. Deposits of oil and gas have been discovered.

3 The Cordillera is a region of glacier-capped, high mountains on either side of a central **plateau.** It was created by Earth's pressures and volcanic activity. Its many rock types are rich in important **minerals.**

Open cut mine

4 The Interior Plain is a vast open region gently sloping from the Rocky mountains to the east. The rocks are sedimentary and contain remains of old **coral reefs** that existed when warm seas covered the area millions of years ago. The plain is rich in oil, gas, coal and **potash.**

5 The Canadian Shield contains Canada's oldest rocks (over 3 billion years). They are mainly **igneous** and **metamorphic** rocks. The surface can be low lying or mountainous, but it is always rocky and uneven with many lakes. It is a vast storehouse of metallic minerals.

1 cm on the map represents 160 km

0	200	400	600	800	1000

KILOMETRES

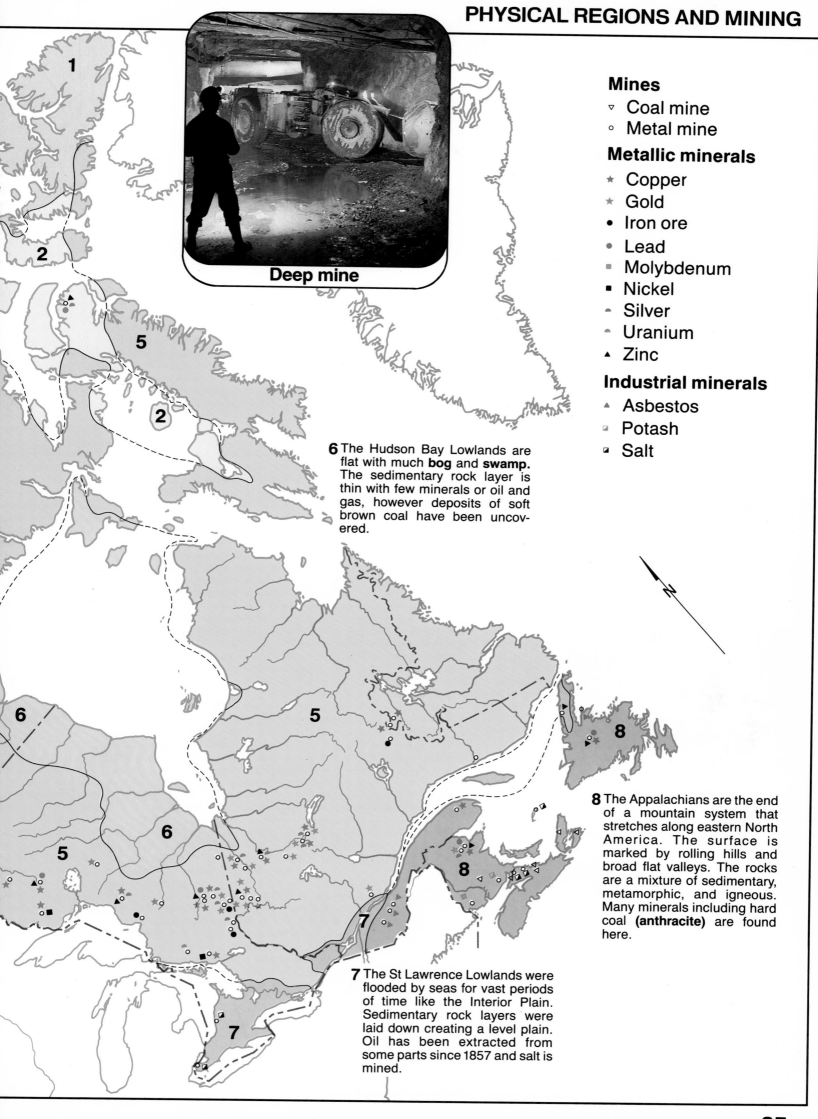

Deep mine

Mines
- ▽ Coal mine
- ○ Metal mine

Metallic minerals
- ★ Copper
- ☆ Gold
- • Iron ore
- • Lead
- ▪ Molybdenum
- ▪ Nickel
- ‐ Silver
- ‐ Uranium
- ▲ Zinc

Industrial minerals
- ▲ Asbestos
- ▫ Potash
- ▫ Salt

6 The Hudson Bay Lowlands are flat with much **bog** and **swamp.** The sedimentary rock layer is thin with few minerals or oil and gas, however deposits of soft brown coal have been uncovered.

8 The Appalachians are the end of a mountain system that stretches along eastern North America. The surface is marked by rolling hills and broad flat valleys. The rocks are a mixture of sedimentary, metamorphic, and igneous. Many minerals including hard coal **(anthracite)** are found here.

7 The St Lawrence Lowlands were flooded by seas for vast periods of time like the Interior Plain. Sedimentary rock layers were laid down creating a level plain. Oil has been extracted from some parts since 1857 and salt is mined.

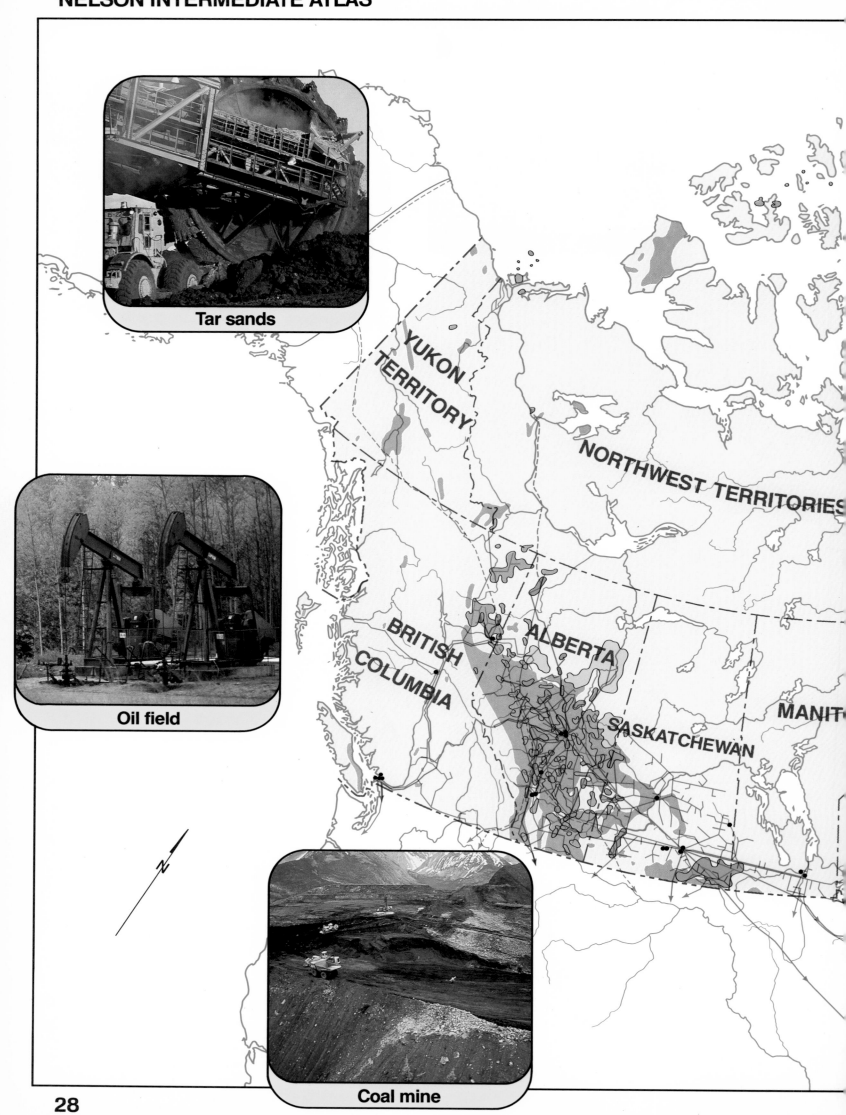

Tar sands

Oil field

Coal mine

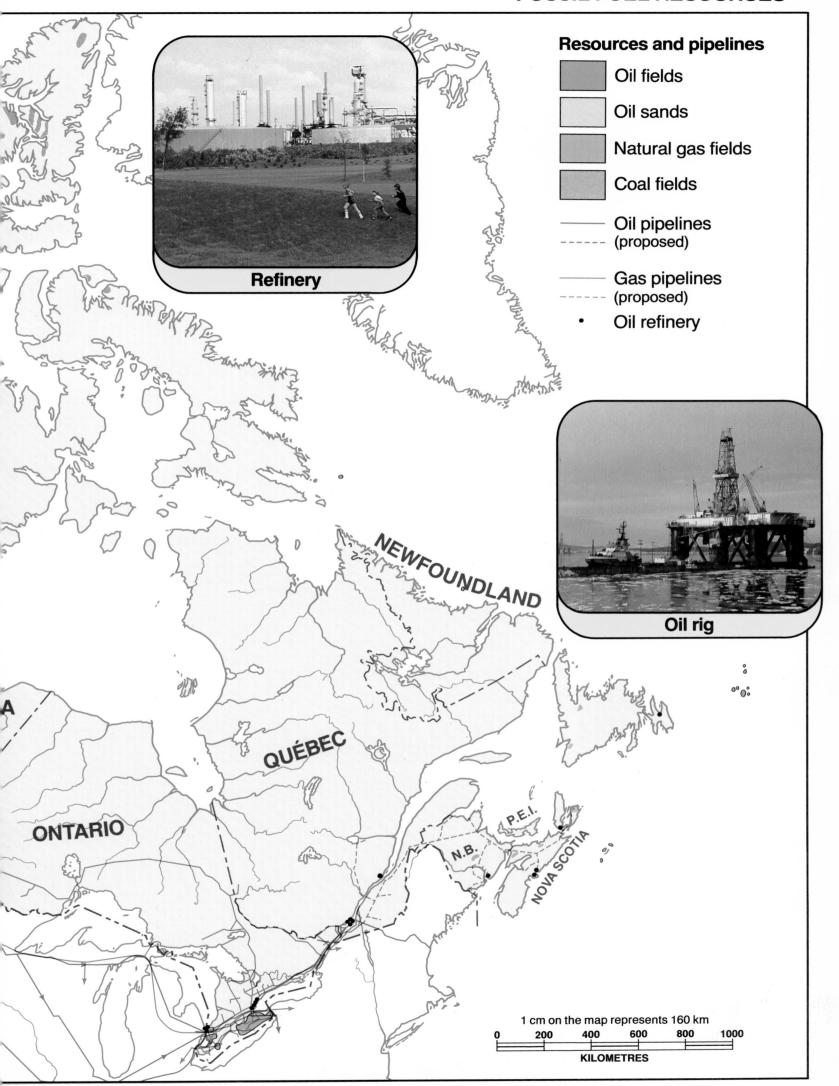

FOSSIL FUEL RESOURCES

Resources and pipelines

Oil fields

Oil sands

Natural gas fields

Coal fields

Oil pipelines
(proposed)

Gas pipelines
(proposed)

• Oil refinery

Refinery

Oil rig

NEWFOUNDLAND

QUÉBEC

ONTARIO

P.E.I.

N.B.

NOVA SCOTIA

1 cm on the map represents 160 km

0   200   400   600   800   1000
KILOMETRES

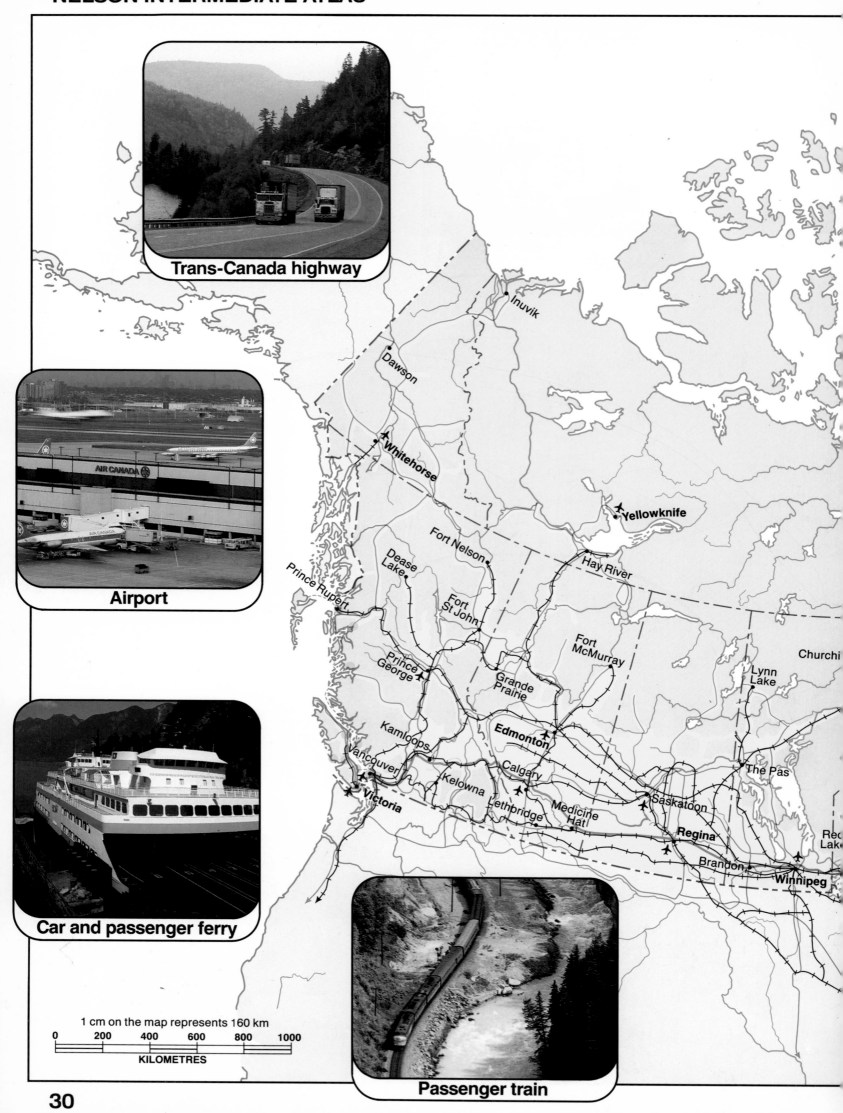

Trans-Canada highway

Airport

Car and passenger ferry

Passenger train

1 cm on the map represents 160 km

0   200   400   600   800   1000

KILOMETRES

Inuvik

Dawson

Whitehorse

Yellowknife

Fort Nelson

Hay River

Dease Lake

Prince Rupert

Fort St John

Fort McMurray

Churchi

Prince George

Grande Prairie

Lynn Lake

Kamloops

Edmonton

Vancouver

Calgary

The Pas

Victoria

Kelowna

Lethbridge

Medicine Hat

Saskatoon

Regina

Red Lak

Brandon

Winnipeg

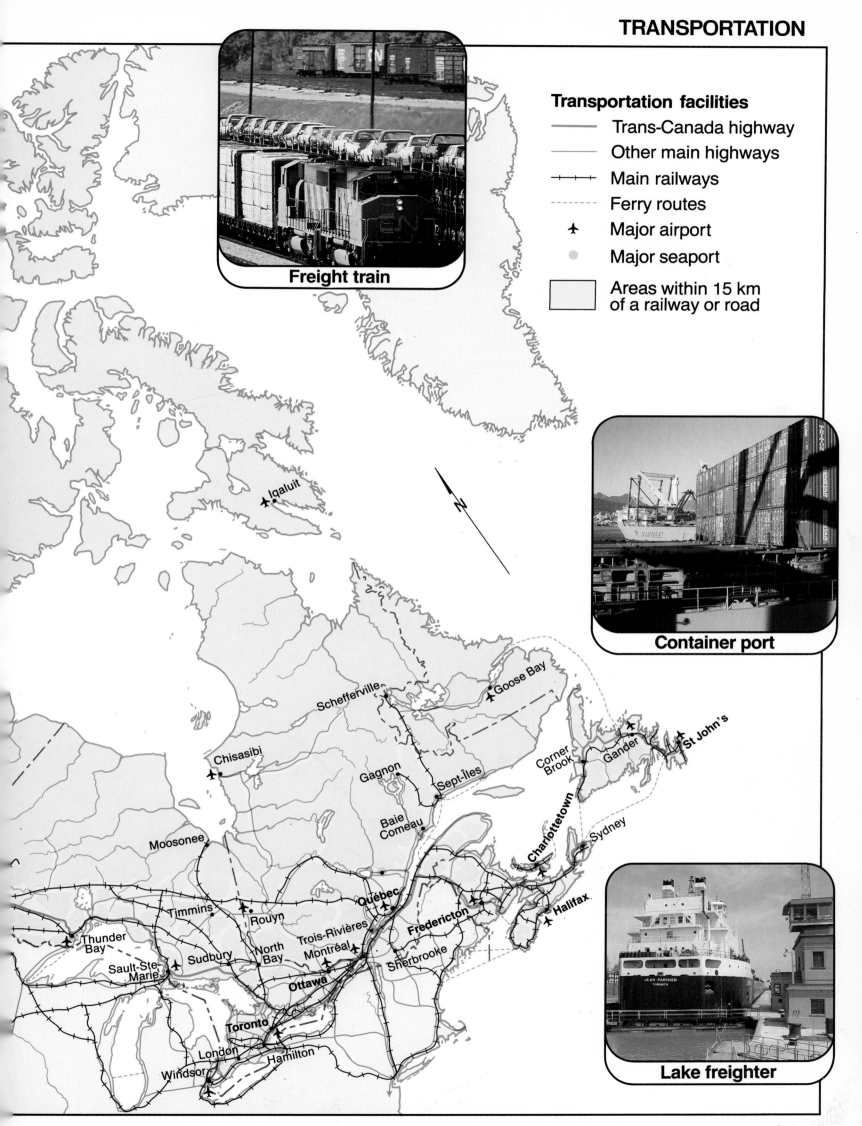

Freight train

Container port

Lake freighter

Transportation facilities

———	Trans-Canada highway
——	Other main highways
+‑+‑+	Main railways
‑ ‑ ‑	Ferry routes
✈	Major airport
●	Major seaport
▦	Areas within 15 km of a railway or road

N

Iqaluit

Scheffeville
Goose Bay
Chisasibi
Gagnon
Sept-Îles
Corner Brook
Gander
St John's
Baie Comeau
Charlottetown
Sydney
Moosonee
Québec
Halifax
Timmins
Rouyn
Trois-Rivières
Fredericton
Thunder Bay
North Bay
Montréal
Sherbrooke
Sudbury
Sault-Ste Marie
Ottawa
Toronto
London
Hamilton
Windsor

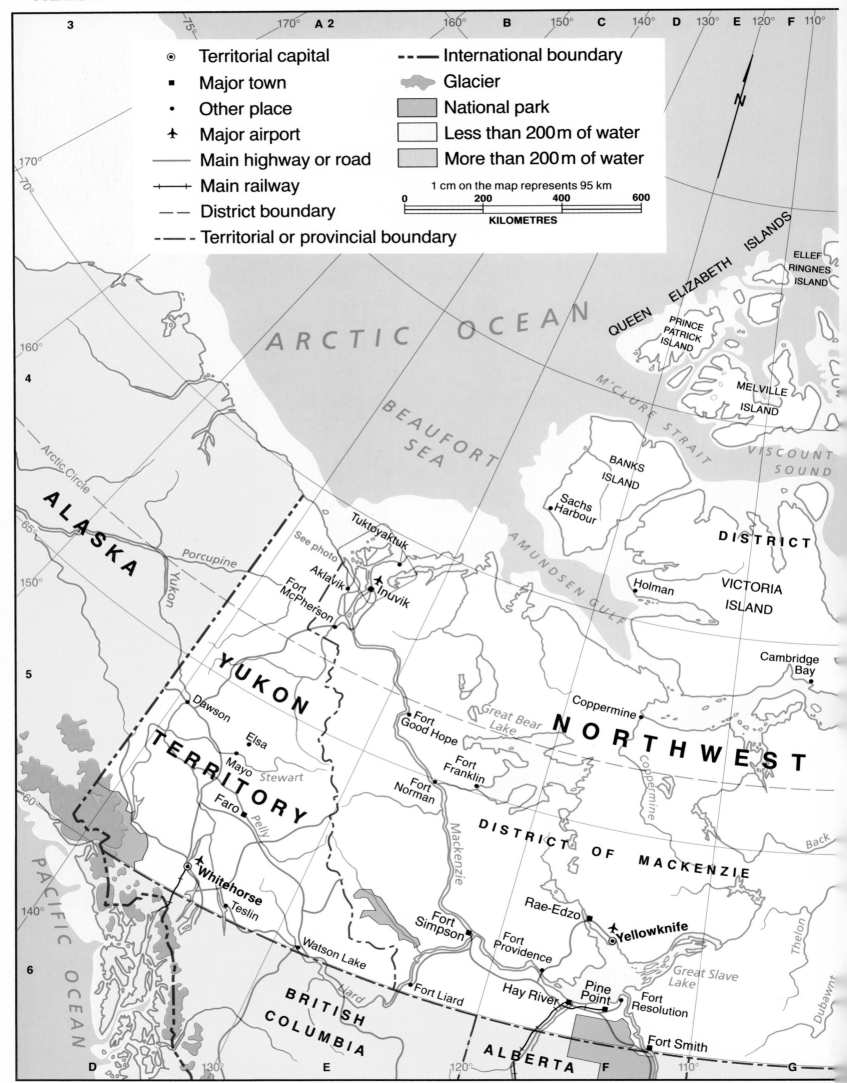

Territorial capital

Major town

Other place

Major airport

Main highway or road

Main railway

District boundary

Territorial or provincial boundary

International boundary

Glacier

National park

Less than 200m of water

More than 200m of water

1 cm on the map represents 95 km

0   200   400   600

KILOMETRES

ARCTIC OCEAN

QUEEN ELIZABETH ISLANDS

ELLEF RINGNES ISLAND

PRINCE PATRICK ISLAND

MELVILLE ISLAND

M'CLURE STRAIT

VISCOUNT SOUND

BEAUFORT SEA

BANKS ISLAND

DISTRICT

Sachs Harbour

AMUNDSEN GULF

Tuktoyaktuk

ALASKA

Arctic Circle

Porcupine

Yukon

See photo

Aklavik

Fort McPherson

Inuvik

Holman

VICTORIA ISLAND

Cambridge Bay

Dawson

Elsa

Mayo

Stewart

Faro

Pelly

YUKON

TERRITORY

Fort Good Hope

Great Bear Lake

Coppermine

NORTHWEST

Fort Franklin

Fort Norman

Coppermine

Mackenzie

DISTRICT OF MACKENZIE

Back

PACIFIC OCEAN

Whitehorse

Teslin

Watson Lake

Liard

Rae-Edzo

Fort Simpson

Fort Providence

Yellowknife

Hay River

Pine Point

Fort Resolution

Great Slave Lake

Thelon

BRITISH COLUMBIA

Fort Liard

ALBERTA

Fort Smith

Dubawnt

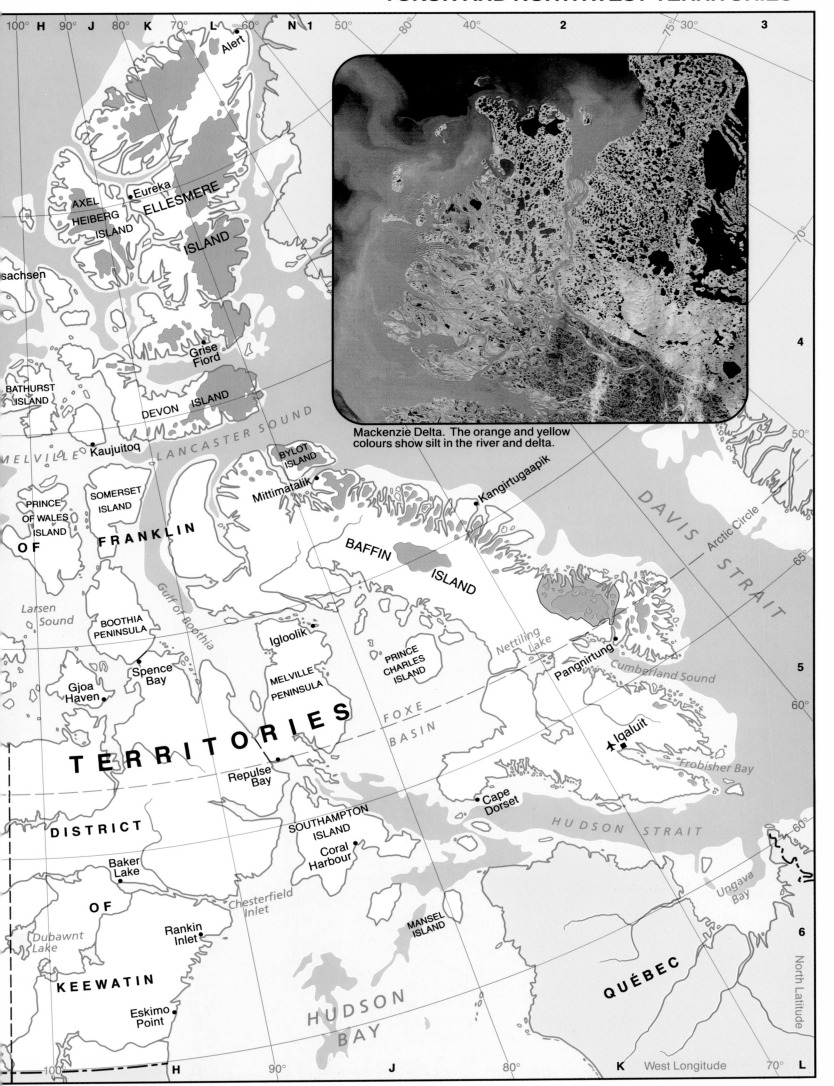

Mackenzie Delta. The orange and yellow colours show silt in the river and delta.

100° H 90° J 80° K 70° L 60° N 1 50° 80° 40° 2 75° 30° 3

Alert

AXEL HEIBERG ISLAND

Eureka

ELLESMERE

ISLAND

sachsen

70°

Grise Fiord

BATHURST ISLAND

DEVON ISLAND

4

MELVILLE Kaujuitoq

LANCASTER SOUND

50°

SOMERSET ISLAND

BYLOT ISLAND

Mittimatalik

Kangirtugaapik

Arctic Circle

PRINCE OF WALES ISLAND

OF FRANKLIN

BAFFIN

ISLAND

DAVIS

65°

Larsen Sound

BOOTHIA PENINSULA

Gulf of Boothia

Nettiling Lake

STRAIT

Igloolik

PRINCE CHARLES ISLAND

Pangnirtung

Cumberland Sound

5

Spence Bay

MELVILLE PENINSULA

60°

Gjoa Haven

TERRITORIES

FOXE

BASIN

Iqaluit

Frobisher Bay

Repulse Bay

Cape Dorset

HUDSON STRAIT

DISTRICT

SOUTHAMPTON ISLAND

60°

Baker Lake

Coral Harbour

Chesterfield Inlet

OF

Ungava Bay

Dubawnt Lake

Rankin Inlet

MANSEL ISLAND

6

KEEWATIN

QUÉBEC

North Latitude

Eskimo Point

HUDSON

BAY

100° H 90° J 80° K West Longitude 70° L

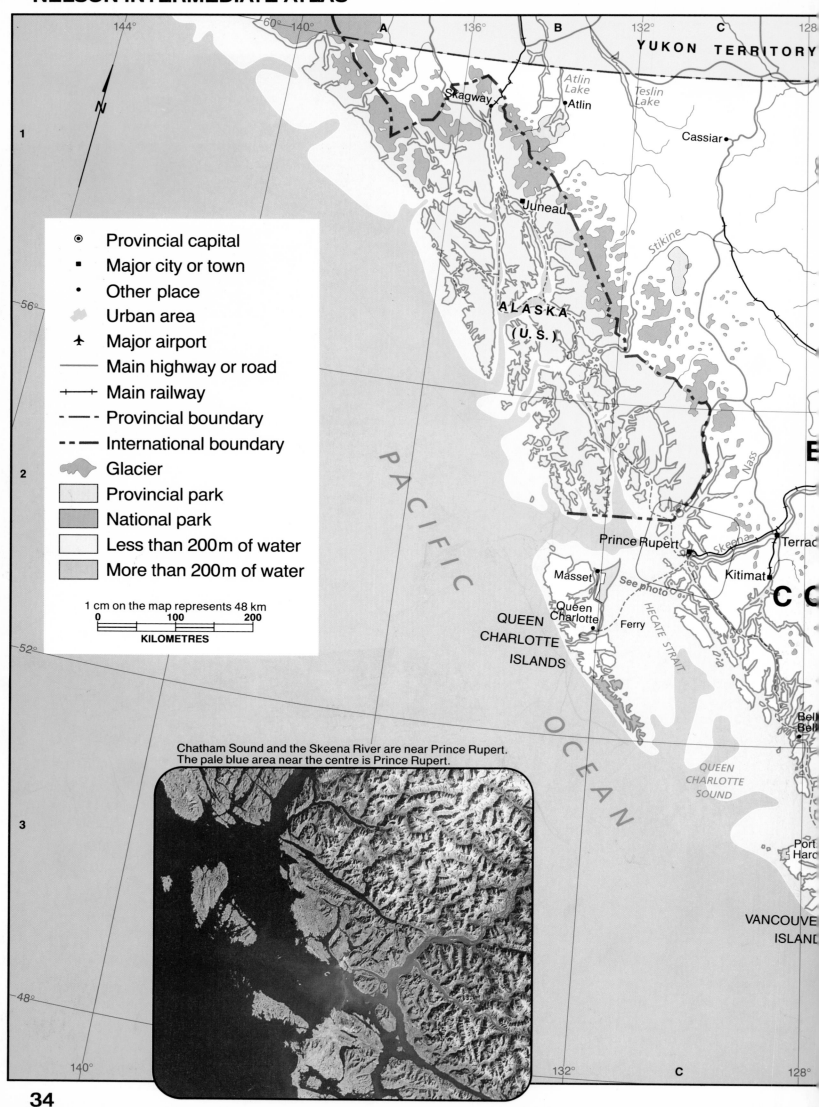

Legend:

- ⊙ Provincial capital
- ■ Major city or town
- • Other place
- Urban area
- ✈ Major airport
- — Main highway or road
- ┼┼┼ Main railway
- ─·─·─ Provincial boundary
- ▬·▬·▬ International boundary
- Glacier
- Provincial park
- National park
- Less than 200m of water
- More than 200m of water

1 cm on the map represents 48 km

0   100   200
KILOMETRES

YUKON TERRITORY

Skagway
Atlin Lake
Atlin
Teslin Lake
Cassiar

Juneau
Stikine

ALASKA
(U. S.)

PACIFIC

Nass

Prince Rupert
Skeena
Terrac
Masset
See photo
Kitimat
Queen Charlotte
Ferry
QUEEN
CHARLOTTE
ISLANDS
HECATE STRAIT

C O

Bel
Bel

QUEEN
CHARLOTTE
SOUND

OCEAN

Port
Hard

VANCOUVE
ISLAND

Chatham Sound and the Skeena River are near Prince Rupert.
The pale blue area near the centre is Prince Rupert.

D   124°   E   120°   F   116°   60°   G   112°

NORTHWEST TERRITORIES

1

Liard

Fort Nelson

Fort Nelson

Williston Lake

Finlay

Peace

Fort St John

56°

BRITISH

Takla Lake

DAM

Chetwynd

Dawson Creek

Babine Lake

Mackenzie

Smithers

Stuart Lake

Tumbler Ridge

Burns Lake

UMBIA

Nechako Reservoir

DAM

Prince George

Abraham Lake is the dark blue shape in the lower right. The Columbia Icefield is near the centre, west of the curve in the lake.

2

See photo

52°

Quesnel

Quesnel Lake

McNaughton Lake

ALBERTA

Bella Coola

Williams Lake

Chilcotin

100 Mile House

Columbia

DAM

Calgary

Banff

Chilko Lake

Shuswap Lake

Golden

Revelstoke

Cache Creek

Chase

3

Lillooet

N Thompson

Salmon Arm

Arrow Lakes

Nakusp

Kootenay Lake

Kimberley

Kamloops

Merritt

Vernon

Fraser

Okanagan Lake

Kelowna

Whistler

Cranbrook

Fernie

Campbell River

Powell River

Nelson

Castlegar

Lake Koocanusa

Princeton

Summerland

Gold River

Comox

Squamish

Penticton

Trail

Creston

Courtenay

Parksville

Vancouver

Hope

Kootenay

North Latitude

Port Alberni

Nanaimo

Chilliwack

Oliver

Matsqui

48°

Ucluelet

UNITED STATES

Sidney

Victoria

D   124°   E   120°   F   116° West Longitude   G

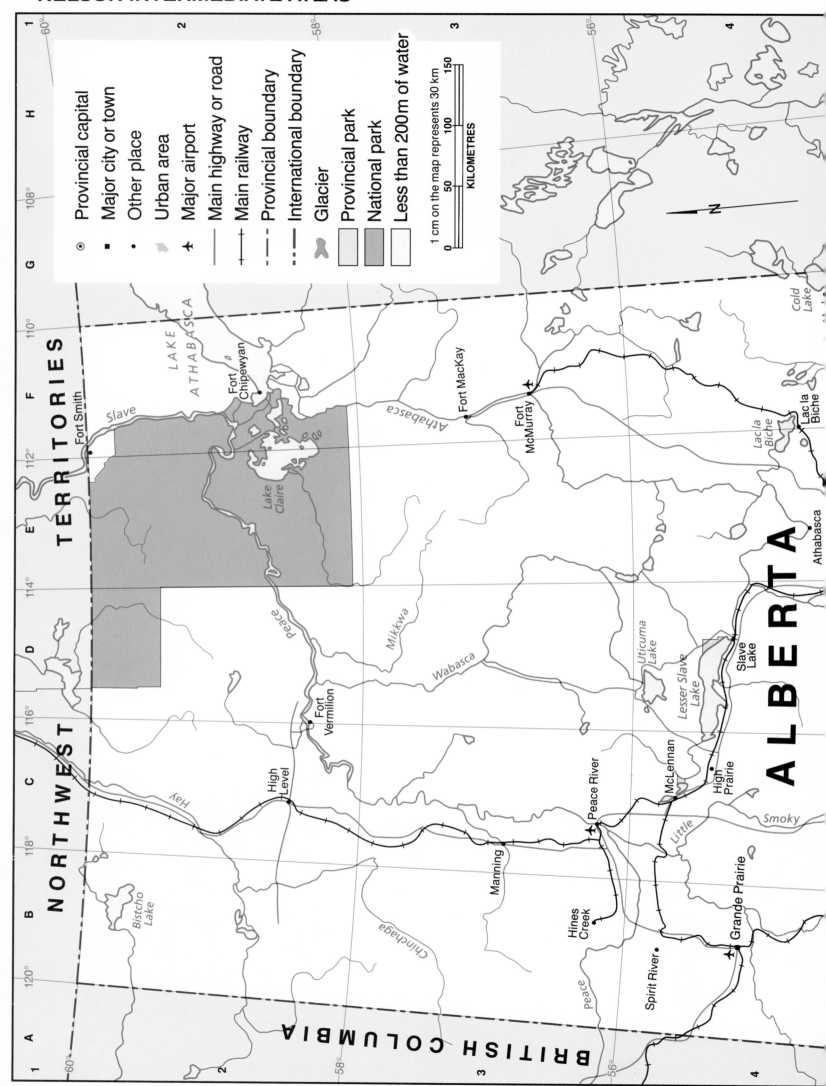

BRITISH COLUMBIA

ALBERTA

NORTHWEST TERRITORIES

LAKE ATHABASCA

Fort Smith

Fort Chipewyan

Lake Claire

Slave

Peace

Hay

Chinchaga

Bistcho Lake

High Level

Fort Vermilion

Mikkwa

Wabasca

Manning

Hines Creek

Spirit River

Grande Prairie

Peace River

McLennan

High Prairie

Peace

Little

Smoky

Uticuma Lake

Lesser Slave Lake

Slave Lake

Fort MacKay

Fort McMurray

Athabasca

Lac la Biche

Lac la Biche

Cold Lake

Athabasca

Legend:

- ◎ Provincial capital
- ■ Major city or town
- ● Other place
- Urban area
- ✈ Major airport
- —— Main highway or road
- —+— Main railway
- —·—· Provincial boundary
- —··—·· International boundary
- Glacier
- Provincial park
- National park
- Less than 200m of water

1 cm on the map represents 30 km

KILOMETRES
0   50   100   150

N

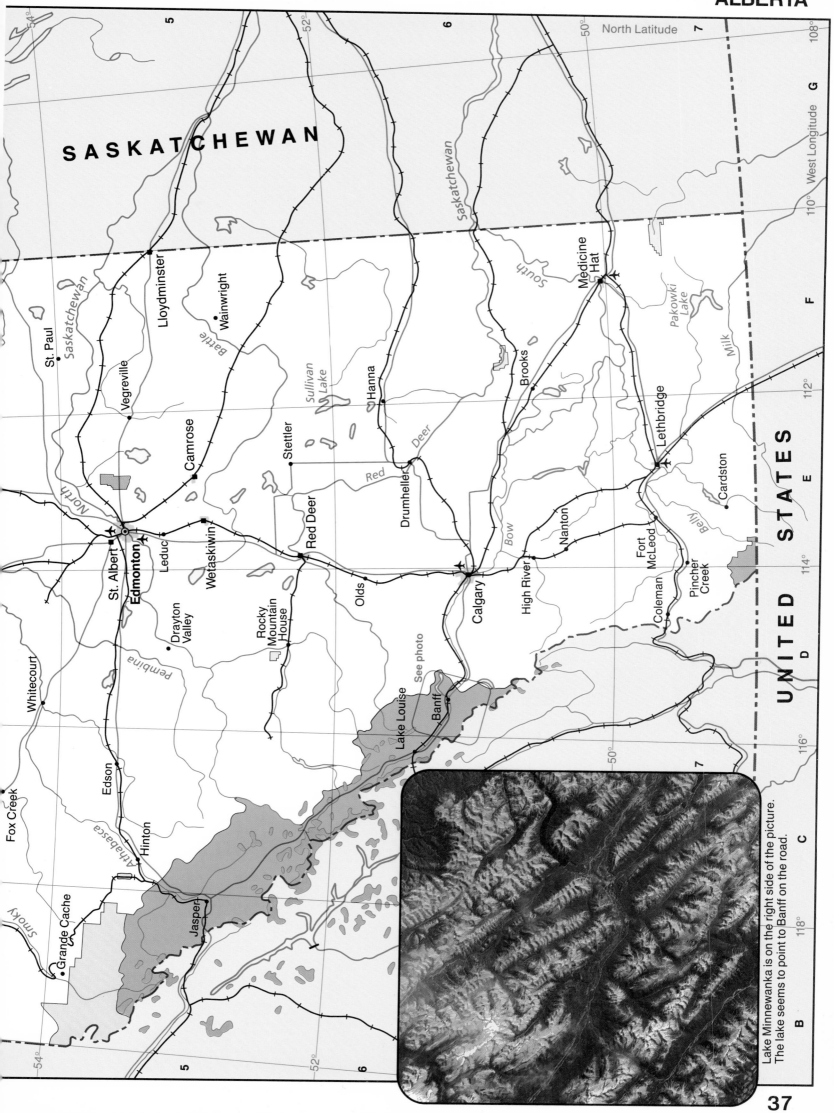

North Latitude

7

50°

G

West Longitude

108°

F

110°

S A S K A T C H E W A N

Saskatchewan

South

112°

Medicine Hat

Pakowki Lake

Milk

Lloydminster

Wainwright

Battle

Hanna

Brooks

Lethbridge

E

St. Paul

Saskatchewan

Vegreville

Camrose

Stettler

Sullivan Lake

Deer

Red

Drumheller

Cardston

114°

North

Edmonton

St. Albert

Leduc

Wetaskiwin

Red Deer

Olds

Nanton

Calgary

High River

Fort McLeod

Coleman

Pincher Creek

Bow

Bow

Belly

U N I T E D   S T A T E S

Drayton Valley

Rocky Mountain House

Pembina

See photo

Banff

Lake Louise

116°

50°

D

7

Whitecourt

Edson

Hinton

Athabasca

118°

Fox Creek

Smoky

Grande Cache

Jasper

C

B

Lake Minnewanka is on the right side of the picture. The lake seems to point to Banff on the road.

5

52°

6

7

5

52°

6

7

54°

54°

50°

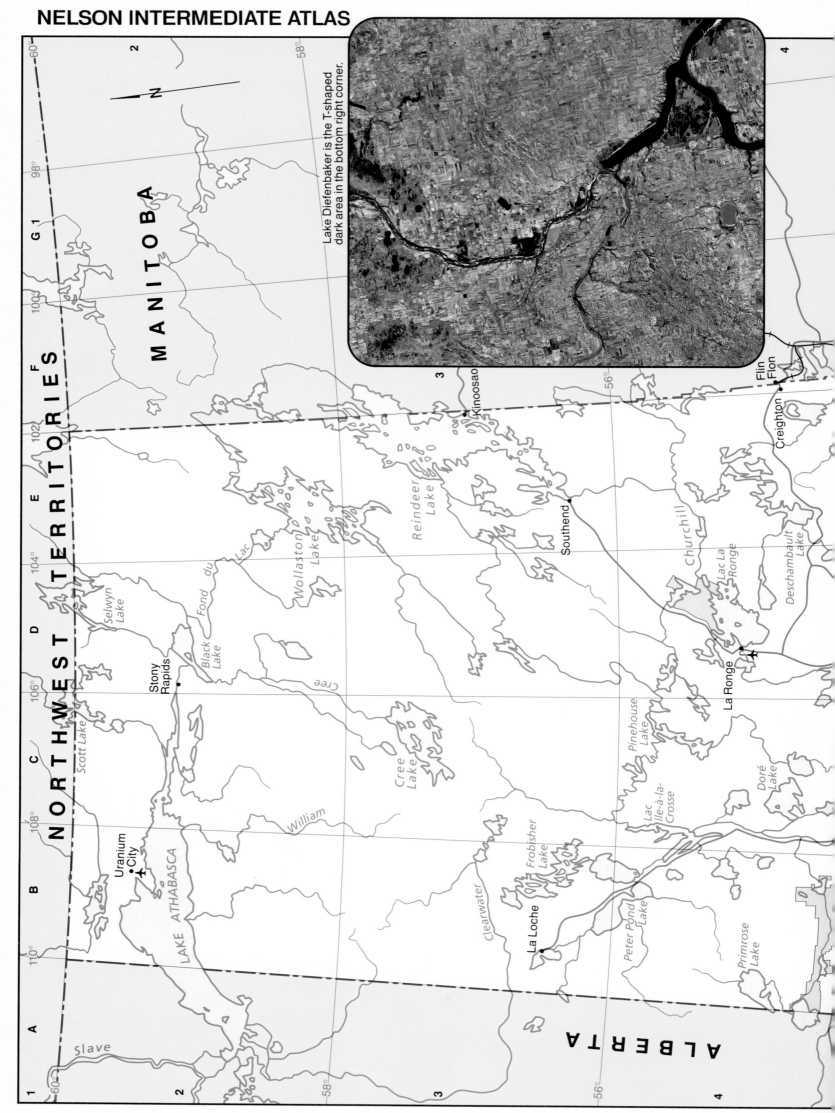

Lake Diefenbaker is the T-shaped dark area in the bottom right corner.

N

MANITOBA

NORTHWEST TERRITORIES

ALBERTA

Slave

LAKE ATHABASCA

Uranium City

Scott Lake

Selwyn Lake

Fond du Lac

Black Lake

Stony Rapids

Wollaston Lake

Cree

William

Cree Lake

Clearwater

Frobisher Lake

La Loche

Peter Pond Lake

Lac Île-à-la-Crosse

Primrose Lake

Pinehouse Lake

Doré Lake

La Ronge

Lac La Ronge

Churchill

Deschambault Lake

Southend

Reindeer Lake

Kinoosao

Flin Flon

Creighton

60°

58°

56°

110°

108°

106°

104°

102°

100°

98°

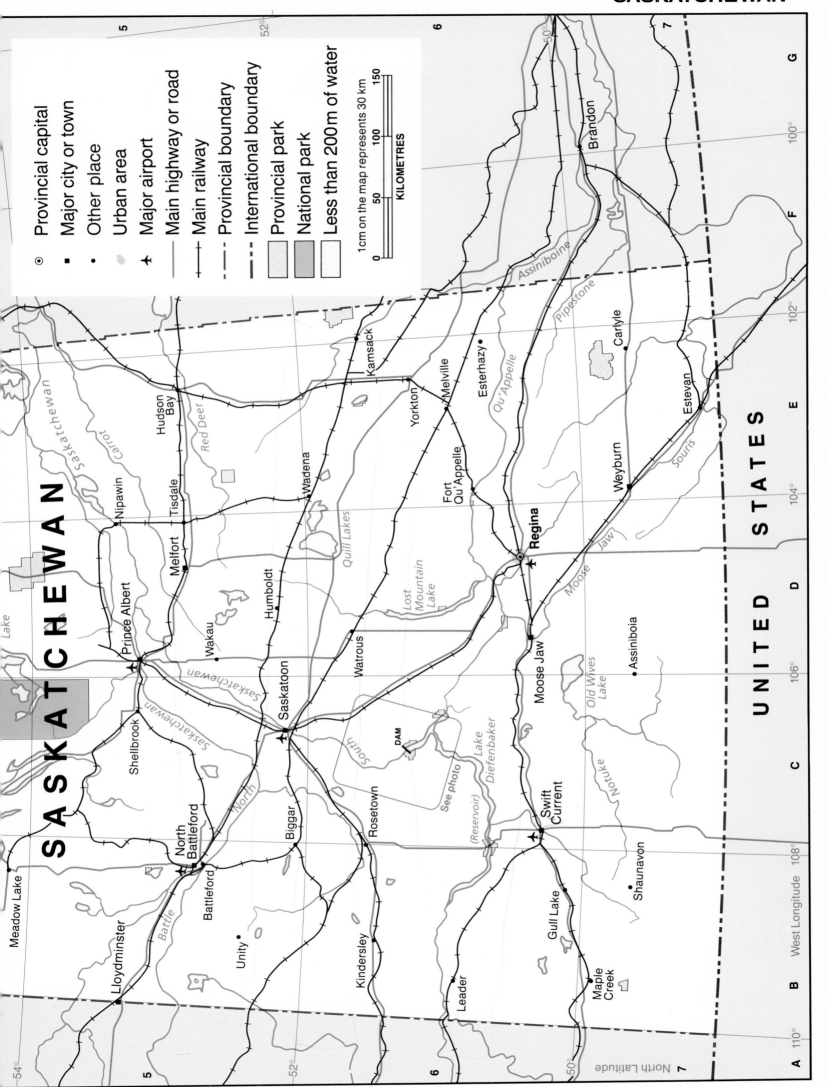

SASKATCHEWAN

SASKATCHEWAN

UNITED STATES

Legend:
- ⊙ Provincial capital
- ■ Major city or town
- • Other place
- Urban area
- ✈ Major airport
- —— Main highway or road
- ┼┼ Main railway
- —·— Provincial boundary
- —··— International boundary
- Provincial park
- National park
- Less than 200m of water

1cm on the map represents 30 km

KILOMETRES

0   50   100   150

Places:
Meadow Lake, Lloydminster, North Battleford, Battleford, Shellbrook, Prince Albert, Nipawin, Tisdale, Melfort, Hudson Bay, Wakau, Humboldt, Saskatoon, Biggar, Unity, Kindersley, Rosetown, Watrous, Wadena, Kamsack, Yorkton, Melville, Esterhazy, Fort Qu'Appelle, Regina, Moose Jaw, Swift Current, Gull Lake, Maple Creek, Shaunavon, Leader, Assiniboia, Weyburn, Estevan, Carlyle, Brandon

Rivers and lakes:
Saskatchewan, Carrot, Red Deer, Quill Lakes, Lost Mountain Lake, South Saskatchewan, North Saskatchewan, Battle, Lake Diefenbaker (Reservoir), Old Wives Lake, Notuke, Moose Jaw, Souris, Qu'Appelle, Assiniboine, Pipestone

DAM

See photo

North Latitude

West Longitude

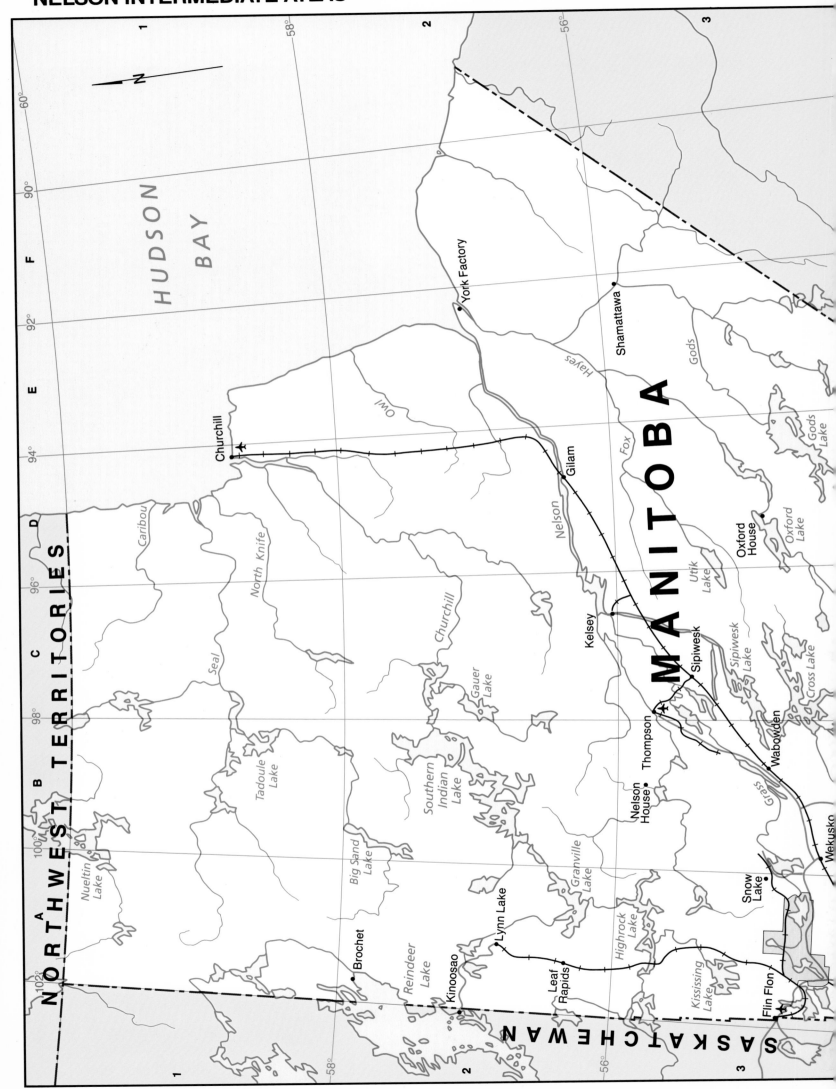

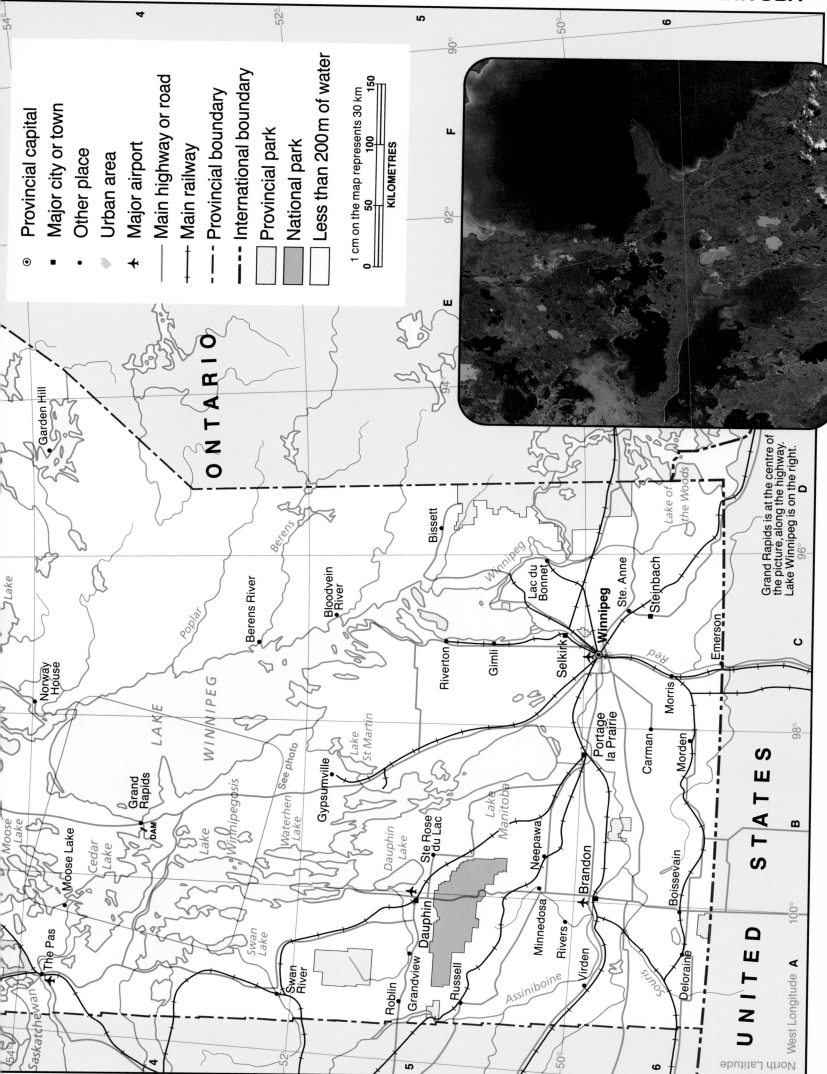

Legend

- ⊙ Provincial capital
- ■ Major city or town
- • Other place
- ◆ Urban area
- ✈ Major airport
- —— Main highway or road
- —+— Main railway
- —·— Provincial boundary
- —··— International boundary
- ▢ Provincial park
- ▢ National park
- ▢ Less than 200 m of water

1 cm on the map represents 30 km

0   50   100   150
KILOMETRES

ONTARIO

Garden Hill

Norway House

The Pas

Moose Lake

Moose Lake

Cedar Lake

Grand Rapids
DAM

WINNIPEG LAKE

Berens River

Bloodvein River

Berens

Poplar

Winnipegosis

Lake Winnipegosis

Waterhen Lake

See photo

Lake St Martin

Gypsumville

Roblin

Grandview

Swan River

Swan Lake

Russell

Dauphin

Ste Rose du Lac

Dauphin Lake

Lake Manitoba

Neepawa

Minnedosa

Rivers

Virden

Brandon

Portage la Prairie

Carman

Morden

Boissevain

Deloraine

Assiniboine

Souris

Bissett

Lac du Bonnet

Winnipeg

Riverton

Gimli

Selkirk

Winnipeg

Ste. Anne

Steinbach

Morris

Emerson

Red

Lake of the Woods

UNITED STATES

West Longitude

North Latitude

Grand Rapids is at the centre of the picture, along the highway. Lake Winnipeg is on the right.

Thunder Bay is the pale blue area
at the lower centre of the picture.
The dark brown colour shows forests.

1 · A · 96° · B · 92° · C · 88° · D

56°

M A N I T O B A

Fort
Severn

Winisk

Sachigo

Severn

Winisk

Fawn

2

Big Trout
Lake

*Big
Trout Lake*

*Sachigo
Lake*

Sandy
Lake

Sandy Lake

Weagamow
Lake

*Wunnummin
Lake*

Attawapiskat

52°

L A K E

W I N N I P E G

Berens

North
Caribou Lake

Pikangikum

Trout Lake

O N T A R I O

*Red
Lake*

Balmertown

Red
Lake

*Lake
St Joseph*

*Ogoki
Reservoir*

Ogoki

3

Ear Falls

Grassy
Narrows

*Lac
Seul*

Armstrong

Nakina

Kenogam

Winnipeg

Keewatin

Kenora

Dryden

Sioux
Lookout

*Lake
Nipigon*

Geraldton

Longlac

*Eagle
Lake*

Beardmore

*Lake of
the Woods*

Ignace

*Long
Lake*

Manitouwadge

*Rainy
Lake*

Rainy
River

Fort
Frances

Atikokan

*Lac des
Mille Lacs*

Nipigon
Red Rock

Schreiber

Marathon

Emo

48°

See photo

Thunder
Bay

Terrace
Bay

White River

U N I T E D

S T A T E S

4

L A K E   S U P E R I O R

North Latitude

96° · West Longitude · B · 92° · C · 88° · D

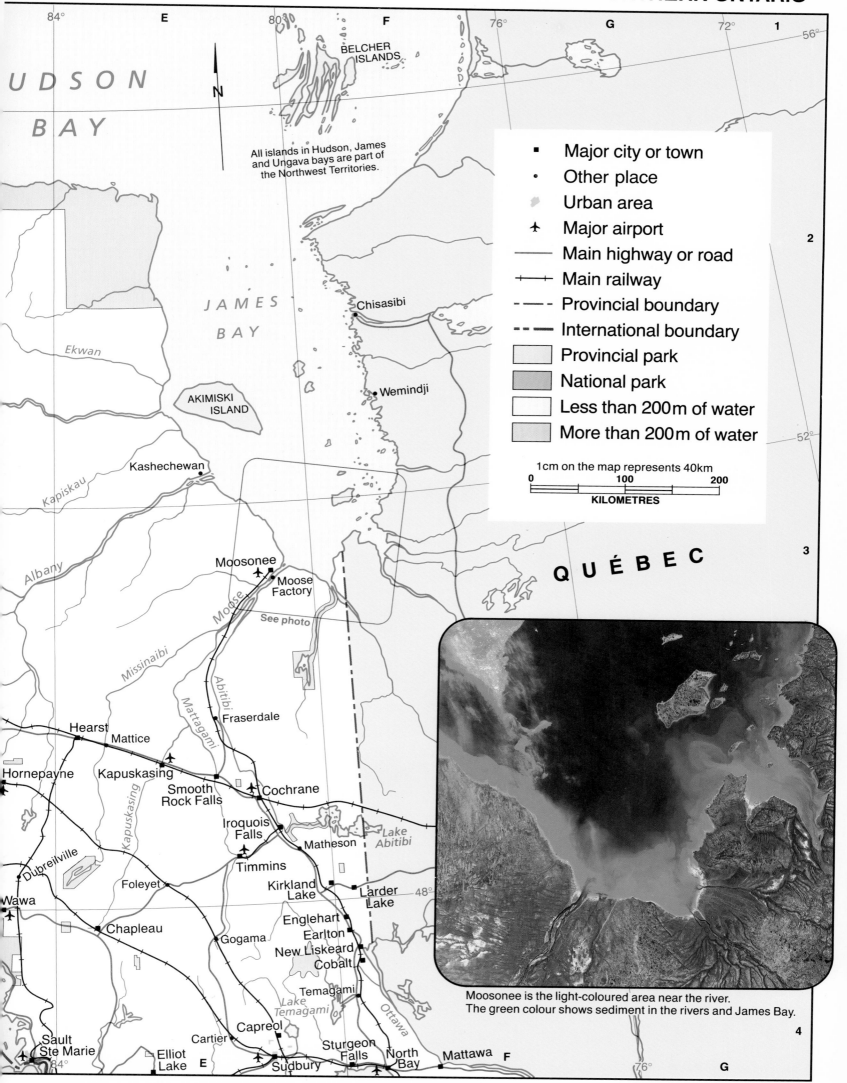

HUDSON BAY

BELCHER ISLANDS

All islands in Hudson, James and Ungava bays are part of the Northwest Territories.

N

JAMES BAY

Ekwan

Chisasibi

AKIMISKI ISLAND

Wemindji

Kapiskau

Kashechewan

Albany

Moosonee
Moose Factory

Moose

See photo

Missinaibi

Abitibi

Mattagami

Fraserdale

Hearst
Mattice

Kapuskasing

Hornepayne

Kapuskasing

Smooth Rock Falls

Cochrane

Dubreuilville

Iroquois Falls

Matheson

Lake Abitibi

Timmins

Foleyet

Kirkland Lake

Larder Lake

Wawa

Englehart

Chapleau

Gogama

Earlton

New Liskeard

Cobalt

Temagami

Lake Temagami

Ottawa

Sault Ste Marie

Cartier

Capreol

Sturgeon Falls

Elliot Lake

Sudbury

North Bay

Mattawa

QUÉBEC

Legend

- ■ Major city or town
- • Other place
- Urban area
- ✈ Major airport
- Main highway or road
- +—+ Main railway
- — ⋅ — Provincial boundary
- — ⋅⋅ — International boundary
- Provincial park
- National park
- Less than 200m of water
- More than 200m of water

1cm on the map represents 40km

0   100   200
KILOMETRES

Moosonee is the light-coloured area near the river.
The green colour shows sediment in the rivers and James Bay.

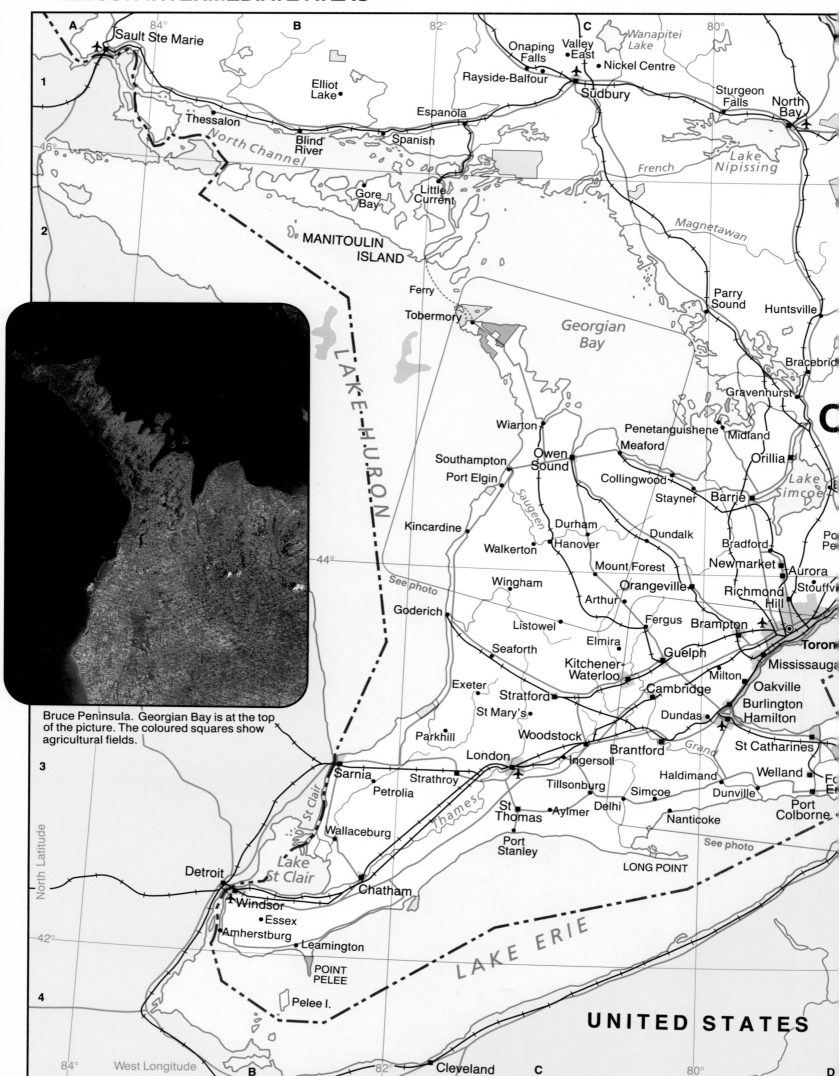

Bruce Peninsula. Georgian Bay is at the top of the picture. The coloured squares show agricultural fields.

A · Sault Ste Marie

B

82°

C · Onaping Falls · Valley East · Nickel Centre

Wanapitei Lake

80°

Elliot Lake

Rayside-Balfour

Sturgeon Falls · North Bay

46°

Thessalon

Blind River · Spanish

Espanola

Sudbury

Lake Nipissing

French

North Channel

Gore Bay · Little Current

Magnetawan

2

MANITOULIN ISLAND

Ferry

Tobermory

Parry Sound · Huntsville

Georgian Bay

Bracebrid

Gravenhurst

Wiarton

Penetanguishene · Midland

Gravenhurst

Southampton · Port Elgin

Owen Sound

Meaford

Orillia

Collingwood

Lake Simcoe

Saugeen

Stayner · Barrie

Kincardine

Durham

Dundalk

Bradford

Walkerton · Hanover

Mount Forest

Newmarket · Aurora

44°

Wingham

Orangeville

Richmond Hill · Stouffvi

See photo

Arthur

Listowel

Fergus · Brampton

Goderich

Seaforth

Elmira

Guelph · Toron

Kitchener-Waterloo

Mississauga

Exeter

Stratford

Cambridge

Milton · Oakville

St Mary's

Dundas

Burlington · Hamilton

Parkhill

Woodstock

Brantford

St Catharines

LAKE HURON

London

Ingersoll

Grand

3

Sarnia

Strathroy

Tillsonburg

Haldimand

Welland · Fo En

St Clair

Petrolia

Simcoe

Dunville

Port Colborne

Thames

St Thomas

Aylmer · Delhi

Nanticoke

Wallaceburg

Port Stanley

See photo

Detroit

Lake St Clair

LONG POINT

North Latitude

Chatham

42°

Windsor · Essex

Amherstburg · Leamington

LAKE ERIE

POINT PELEE

4

Pelee I.

UNITED STATES

84° West Longitude

82° · Cleveland

C

80°

D

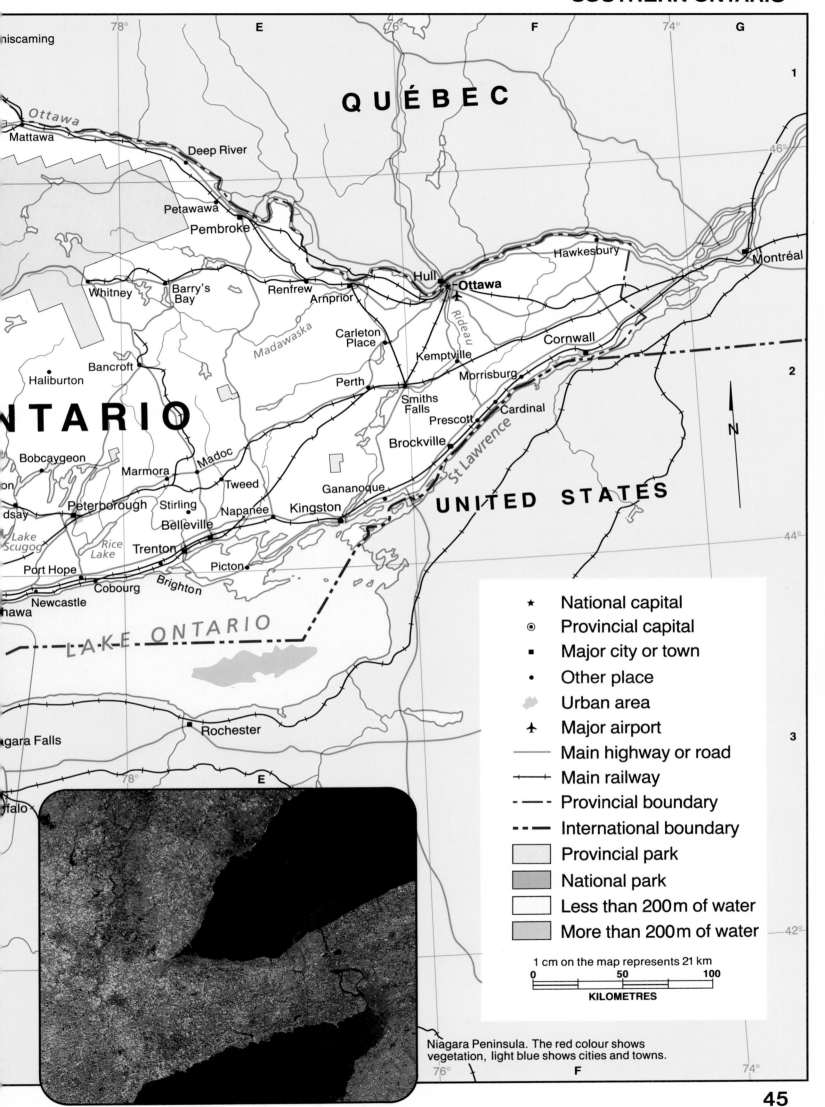

Q U É B E C

Ottawa

Mattawa

Deep River

Petawawa

Pembroke

Hawkesbury

Montréal

Whitney

Barry's Bay

Renfrew

Arnprior

Hull

Ottawa

Haliburton

Bancroft

Carleton Place

Kemptville

Cornwall

O N T A R I O

Madawaska

Rideau

Perth

Morrisburg

Bobcaygeon

Marmora

Madoc

Smiths Falls

Prescott

Cardinal

Peterborough

Stirling

Tweed

Brockville

U N I T E D   S T A T E S

St Lawrence

N

dsay

Napanee

Gananoque

Belleville

Kingston

Lake Scugog

Rice Lake

Trenton

Port Hope

Picton

Cobourg

Brighton

Newcastle

hawa

L A K E   O N T A R I O

gara Falls

Rochester

ffalo

★	National capital
◉	Provincial capital
■	Major city or town
•	Other place
	Urban area
✈	Major airport
——	Main highway or road
┼┼┼	Main railway
— · —	Provincial boundary
— ·· —	International boundary
	Provincial park
	National park
	Less than 200 m of water
	More than 200 m of water

1 cm on the map represents 21 km

0   50   100

KILOMETRES

Niagara Peninsula. The red colour shows
vegetation, light blue shows cities and towns.

45

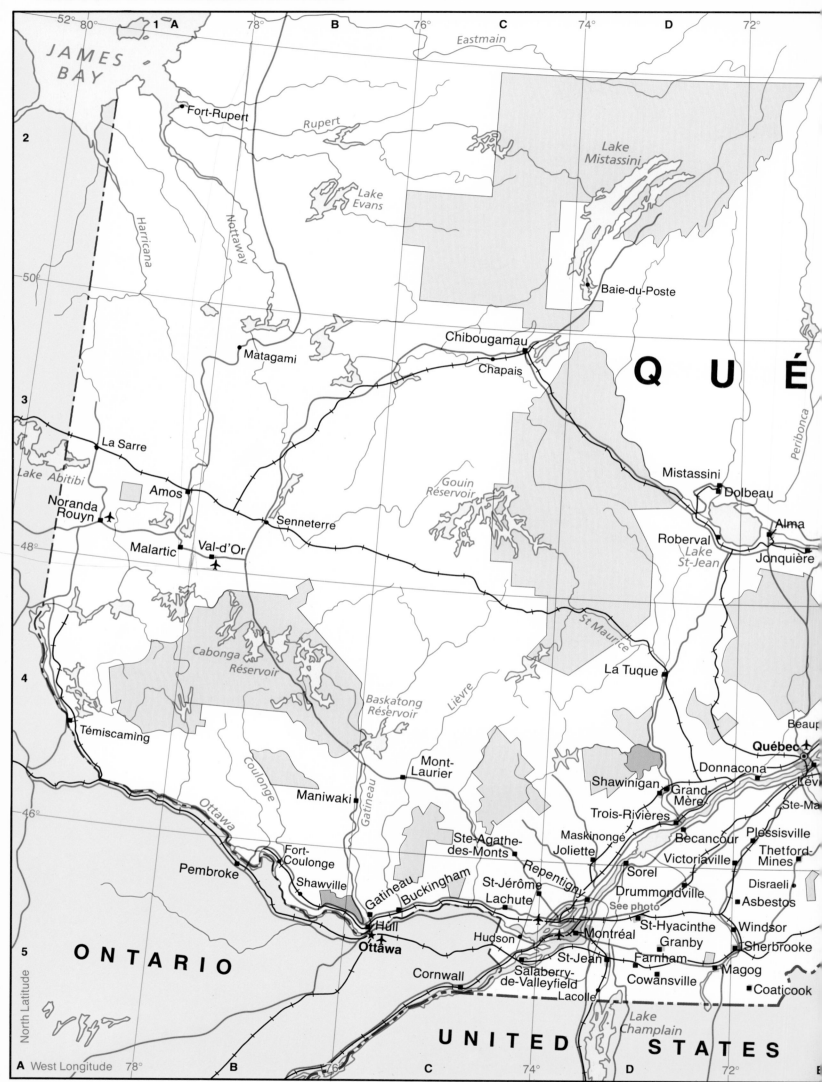

JAMES BAY

Fort-Rupert

Rupert

Eastmain

Harricana

Nottaway

Lake Evans

Lake Mistassini

Baie-du-Poste

Matagami

Chibougamau

Chapais

QUÉ

Peribonca

La Sarre

Lake Abitibi

Amos

Senneterre

Gouin Réservoir

Mistassini

Dolbeau

Alma

Noranda Rouyn

Malartic

Val-d'Or

Roberval

Lake St-Jean

Jonquière

Cabonga Réservoir

Baskatong Réservoir

Lièvre

St Maurice

La Tuque

Témiscaming

Coulonge

Mont-Laurier

Maniwaki

Gatineau

Beaup

Québec

Lév

Ottawa

Fort-Coulonge

Pembroke

Shawville

Gatineau

Buckingham

Ste-Agathe-des-Monts

Repentigny

Donnacona

Shawinigan

Grand-Mère

Trois-Rivières

Ste-Ma

Plessisville

Maskinongé

Joliette

Becancour

Victoriaville

Thetford-Mines

Sorel

Drummondville

Disraeli

Asbestos

St-Jérôme

Lachute

See photo

Montréal

St-Hyacinthe

Granby

Windsor

Sherbrooke

Hudson

St-Jean

Farnham

Magog

Hull

Ottawa

Cornwall

Salaberry-de-Valleyfield

Cowansville

Coaticook

Lacolle

ONTARIO

North Latitude

Lake Champlain

UNITED STATES

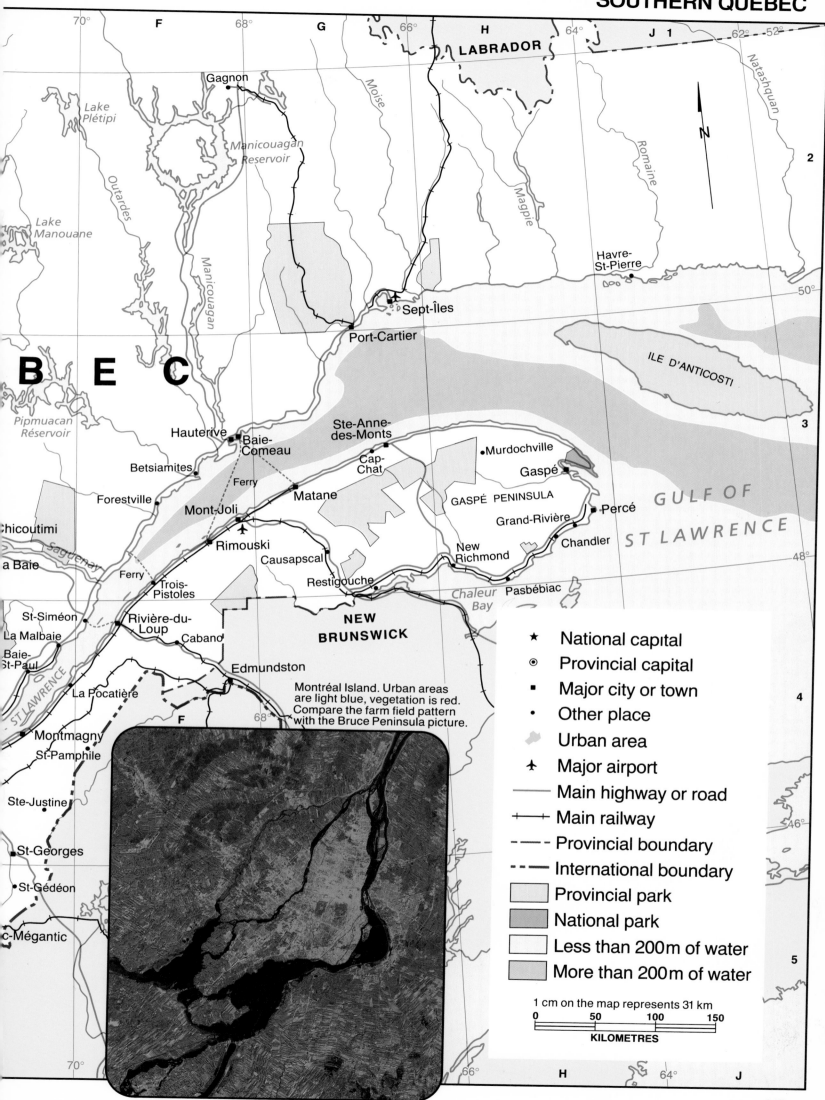

Montréal Island. Urban areas are light blue, vegetation is red. Compare the farm field pattern with the Bruce Peninsula picture.

LABRADOR

Gagnon

Lake Plétipi

Manicouagan Reservoir

Moise

Romaine

Natashquan

Magpie

Outardes

Lake Manouane

Manicouagan

Havre-St-Pierre

B E C

Sept-Îles

Port-Cartier

ILE D'ANTICOSTI

Pipmuacan Réservoir

Hauterive

Baie-Comeau

Ste-Anne-des-Monts

Murdochville

Betsiamites

Cap-Chat

Gaspé

Ferry

GASPÉ PENINSULA

GULF OF

Forestville

Matane

Grand-Rivière

Percé

Chicoutimi

Mont-Joli

ST LAWRENCE

a Baie

Rimouski

Causapscal

New Richmond

Chandler

Sagueñar

Restigouche

Pasbébiac

Ferry

Trois-Pistoles

Chaleur Bay

St-Siméon

Rivière-du-Loup

La Malbaie

Cabano

NEW BRUNSWICK

Baie-St-Paul

Edmundston

ST LAWRENCE

La Pocatière

Montmagny

St-Pamphile

Ste-Justine

St-Georges

St-Gédéon

C-Mégantic

Legend

★ National capital

◉ Provincial capital

■ Major city or town

• Other place

Urban area

✈ Major airport

— Main highway or road

+—+ Main railway

– – – Provincial boundary

▪ ▪ ▪ International boundary

Provincial park

National park

Less than 200m of water

More than 200m of water

1 cm on the map represents 31 km

0   50   100   150

KILOMETRES

47

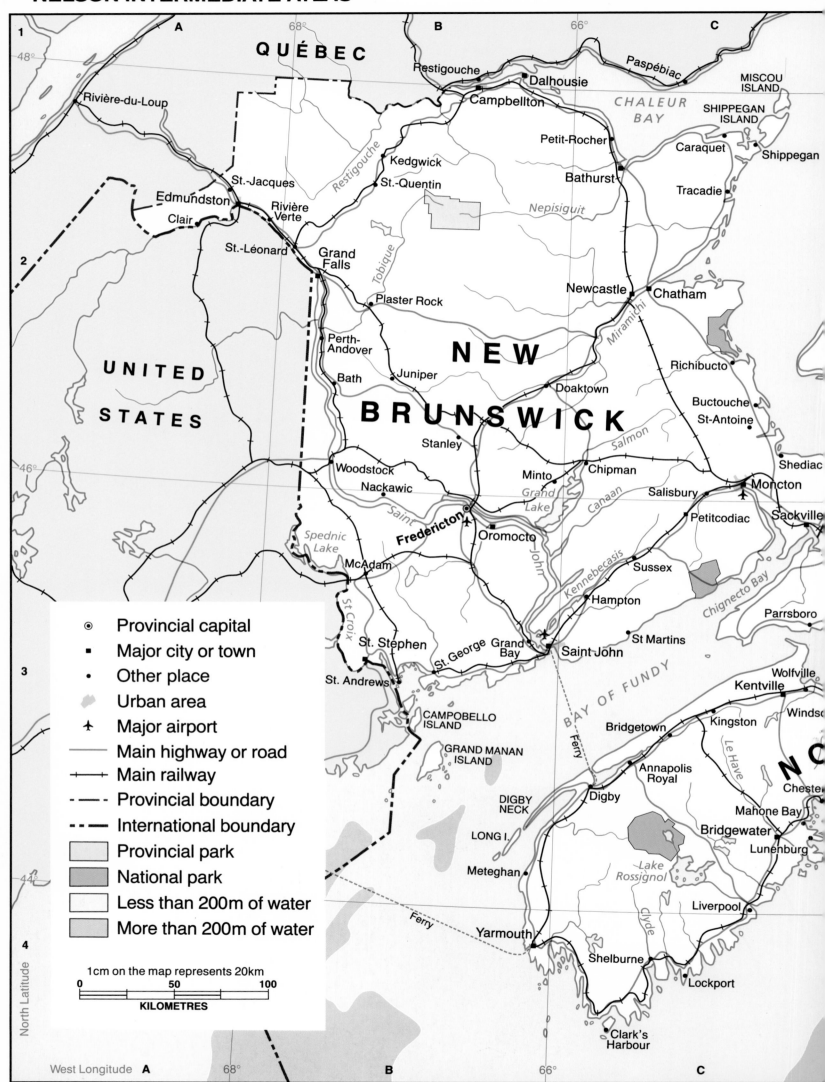

QUÉBEC

Rivière-du-Loup

Restigouche

Paspébiac

Dalhousie

MISCOU
ISLAND

Campbellton

CHALEUR
BAY

SHIPPEGAN
ISLAND

St.-Jacques

Kedgwick

Petit-Rocher

Caraquet

Edmundston

St.-Quentin

Shippegan

Clair

Rivière
Verte

Bathurst

Tracadie

St.-Léonard

Grand
Falls

Nepisiguit

Plaster Rock

Newcastle

Chatham

UNITED

Perth-
Andover

Miramichi

STATES

Bath

Juniper

Richibucto

Doaktown

Buctouche

NEW

St-Antoine

Stanley

Salmon

Shediac

Woodstock

Minto

Chipman

Salisbury

Moncton

Nackawic

BRUNSWICK

Grand
Lake

Canaan

Petitcodiac

Sackville

Spednic
Lake

Fredericton

Oromocto

John

Kennebecasis

Sussex

Chignecto Bay

Parrsboro

McAdam

Saint
Croix

Hampton

St Martins

St. Stephen

St. George

Grand
Bay

Saint John

Wolfville

Kentville

St. Andrews

BAY OF FUNDY

Ferry

Bridgetown

Kingston

Windsor

CAMPOBELLO
ISLAND

GRAND MANAN
ISLAND

Annapolis
Royal

Le Have

NO

Chester

DIGBY
NECK

Digby

Mahone Bay

LONG I.

Lake
Rossignol

Bridgewater

Lunenburg

Meteghan

Clyde

Liverpool

Ferry

Yarmouth

Shelburne

Lockport

Clark's
Harbour

Legend

- ⊙ Provincial capital
- ■ Major city or town
- • Other place
- Urban area
- ✈ Major airport
- —— Main highway or road
- +++ Main railway
- —·— Provincial boundary
- —··— International boundary
- Provincial park
- National park
- Less than 200m of water
- More than 200m of water

1cm on the map represents 20km

0   50   100

KILOMETRES

North Latitude

West Longitude **A**

48

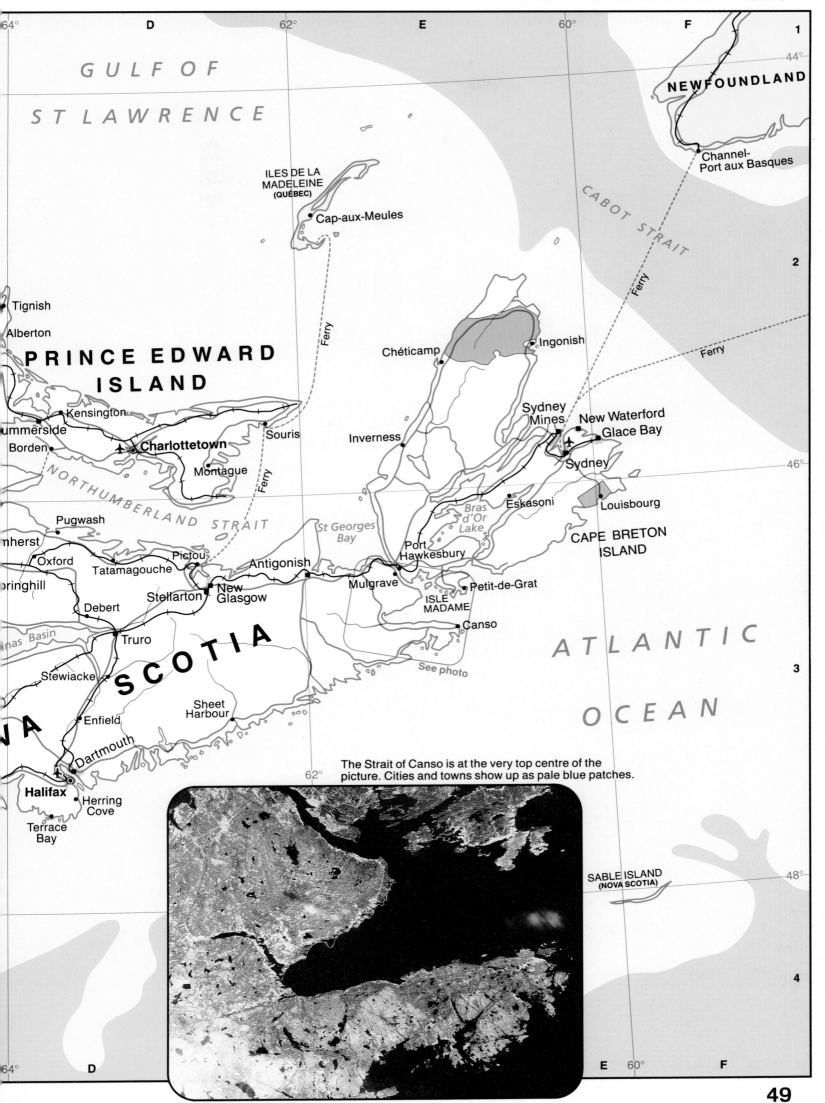

GULF OF ST LAWRENCE

64°
D
62°
E
60°
F
1
44°

NEWFOUNDLAND

Channel-Port aux Basques

ILES DE LA MADELEINE (QUÉBEC)

Cap-aux-Meules

CABOT STRAIT

2

Tignish

Alberton

Ferry

PRINCE EDWARD ISLAND

Chéticamp

Ingonish

Ferry

Ferry

Kensington

Souris

Inverness

Sydney Mines

New Waterford
Glace Bay

ummerside

Borden

Charlottetown

Sydney

46°

Montague

NORTHUMBERLAND STRAIT

Bras d'Or Lake

Eskasoni

Louisbourg

Pugwash

St Georges Bay

CAPE BRETON ISLAND

mherst

Oxford

Pictou

Antigonish

Port Hawkesbury

ringhill

Tatamagouche

Mulgrave

Petit-de-Grat

Stellarton

New Glasgow

ISLE MADAME

Debert

A T L A N T I C

inas Basin

Truro

SCOTIA

Canso

Stewiacke

O C E A N

NA SCOTIA

Sheet Harbour

See photo

3

Enfield

Dartmouth

Halifax

Herring Cove

62°

SABLE ISLAND (NOVA SCOTIA)

48°

Terrace Bay

The Strait of Canso is at the very top centre of the picture. Cities and towns show up as pale blue patches.

64°
D
60°
E
F
4

Port au Port Peninsula is at the centre of the picture.
Clouds are over the Gulf of St. Lawrence.

QUÉBEC

LABRADOR

Red Bay

STRAIT OF BELLE ISLE

Main Brook

Roddickton

Engle

Port au Choix

Hawke's Bay

Daniel's Harbour

Fleur de Ly

Jackson's Arm

White Bay

Baie Verte

Norris Point

Hampden

Springdale

See photo

Bay of Islands

Deer Lake

Cox's Cove

Grand Lake

Badger

Corner Brook

Buchans

Exploits

ILE D'ANTICOSTI (QUÉBEC)

Red Indian Lake

DAM

NEWFOUND

Lourdes

Stephenville

GULF OF

ST LAWRENCE

St George's Bay

St. George's

Victoria Lake

DAM

Meelpaeg Lake

48°

DAM

ILES DE LA MADELEINE (QUEBEC)

Grey

St. Alban's

Isle aux Morts

Channel-Port aux Basques

Rose Blanche

Burgeo

Seal Cove

CABOT

Ramea

Harbou Breto

STRAIT

Grand Ban Fortune

MIQUELON (FRANCE)

Ferry

CAPE BRETON ISLAND (NOVA SCOTIA)

ST. PIERRE (FRANCE)

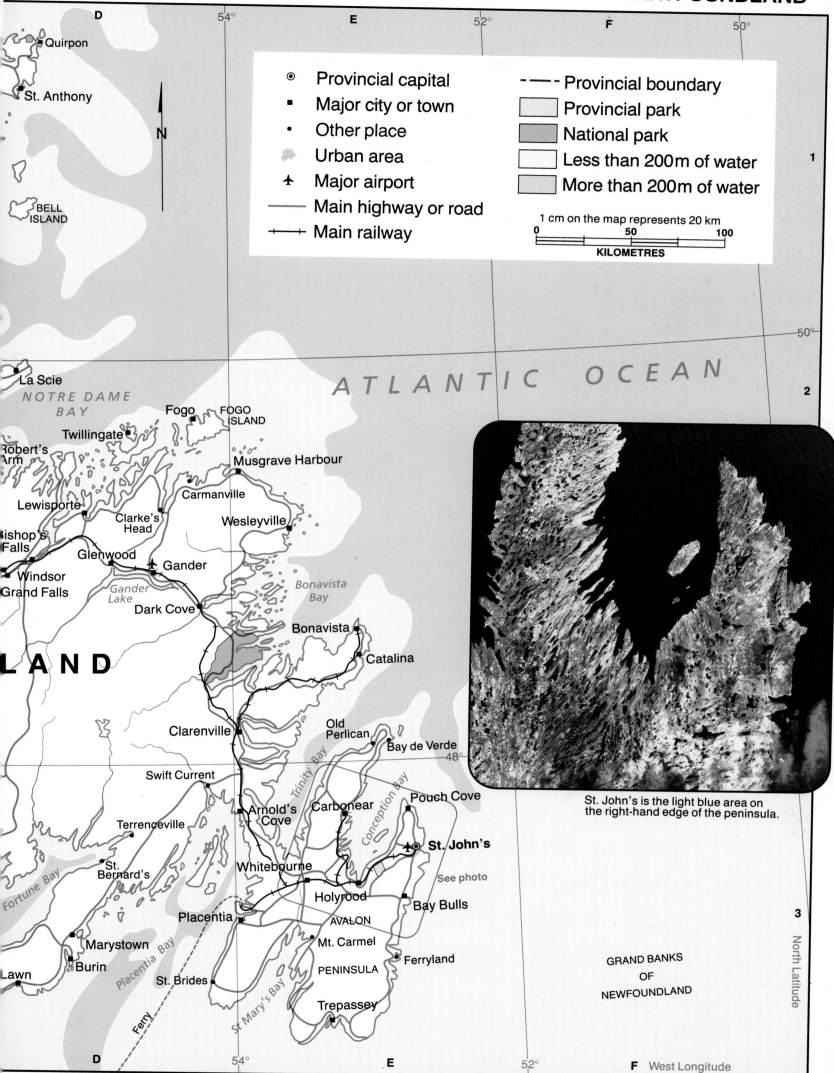

Legend

◉ Provincial capital
■ Major city or town
• Other place
Urban area
✈ Major airport
Main highway or road
Main railway

- - - Provincial boundary
Provincial park
National park
Less than 200m of water
More than 200m of water

1 cm on the map represents 20 km

0   50   100
KILOMETRES

N

Quirpon
St. Anthony
BELL ISLAND

D   54°   E   52°   F   50°

ATLANTIC OCEAN

La Scie
NOTRE DAME BAY
Fogo   FOGO ISLAND
Twillingate
Robert's Arm
Musgrave Harbour
Lewisporte   Carmanville
Clarke's Head
Wesleyville
Bishop's Falls
Glenwood   Gander
Windsor   Gander Lake
Grand Falls   Bonavista Bay
Dark Cove

L A N D   Bonavista
Catalina

Clarenville   Old Perlican
Bay de Verde
Swift Current
Pouch Cove
Terrenceville   Arnold's Cove   Carbonear
Conception Bay
Trinity Bay
St. John's
St. Bernard's   Whitebourne   See photo
Fortune Bay   Holyrood   Bay Bulls
Placentia   AVALON
Marystown   Mt. Carmel   Ferryland
Burin   Placentia Bay   PENINSULA
Lawn   St. Brides
St. Mary's Bay   Trepassey

Ferry

1
50°
2
48°
3

St. John's is the light blue area on the right-hand edge of the peninsula.

GRAND BANKS OF NEWFOUNDLAND

North Latitude

West Longitude

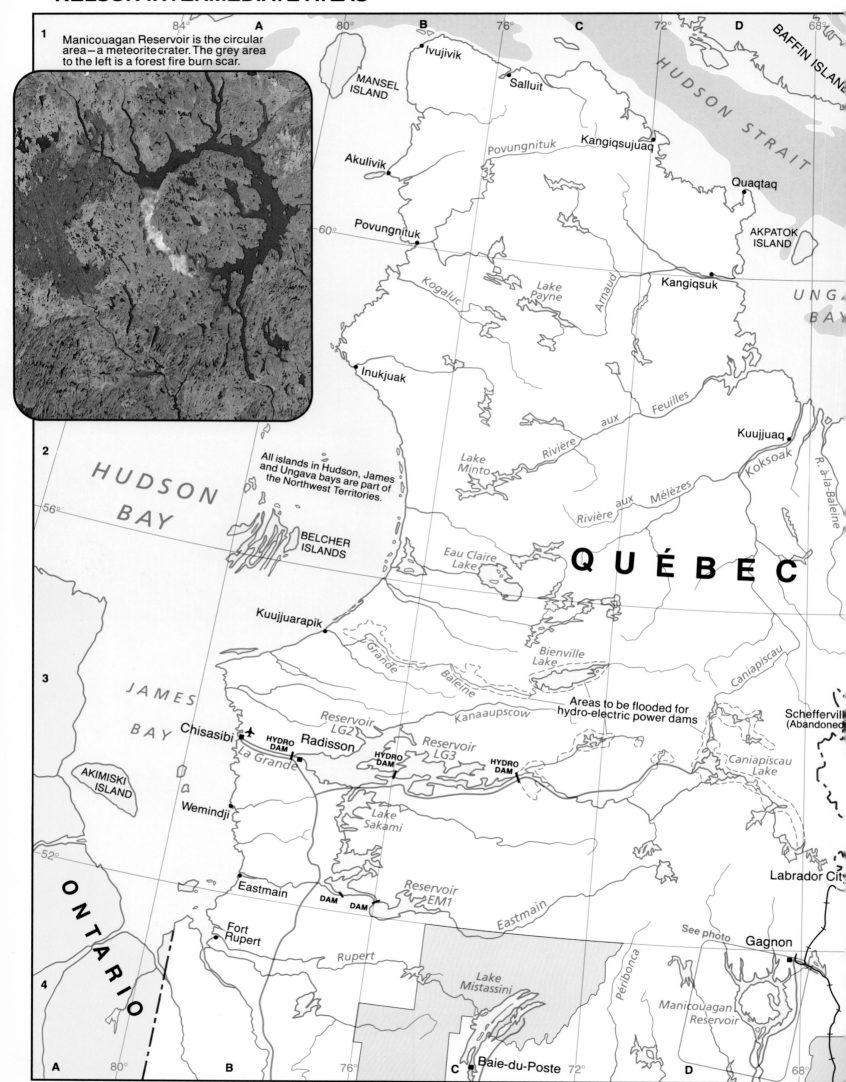

Manicouagan Reservoir is the circular area—a meteorite crater. The grey area to the left is a forest fire burn scar.

All islands in Hudson, James and Ungava bays are part of the Northwest Territories.

HUDSON STRAIT

BAFFIN ISLAND

Ivujivik

Salluit

MANSEL ISLAND

Povungnituk

Kangiqsujuaq

Quaqtaq

Akulivik

AKPATOK ISLAND

Povungnituk

Lake Payne

Arnaud

Kangiqsuk

UNGAVA BAY

Inukjuak

Rivière

aux

Feuilles

Kuujjuaq

Lake Minto

Koksoak

R. à-la-Baleine

Rivière aux Mélèzes

HUDSON BAY

BELCHER ISLANDS

Eau Claire Lake

QUÉBEC

Kuujjuarapik

Bienville Lake

Caniapiscau

Grande

Baleine

JAMES BAY

Reservoir LG2

Kanaaupscow

Areas to be flooded for hydro-electric power dams

Schefferville (Abandoned)

Chisasibi

HYDRO DAM

Radisson

HYDRO DAM

Reservoir LG3

HYDRO DAM

Caniapiscau Lake

La Grande

AKIMISKI ISLAND

Wemindji

Lake Sakami

Eastmain

DAM   DAM

Reservoir EM1

Eastmain

Labrador City

ONTARIO

Fort Rupert

Rupert

Péribonca

See photo

Gagnon

Lake Mistassini

Manicouagan Reservoir

Baie-du-Poste

84°   80°   76°   72°   68°

60°

56°

52°

80°   76°   72°   68°

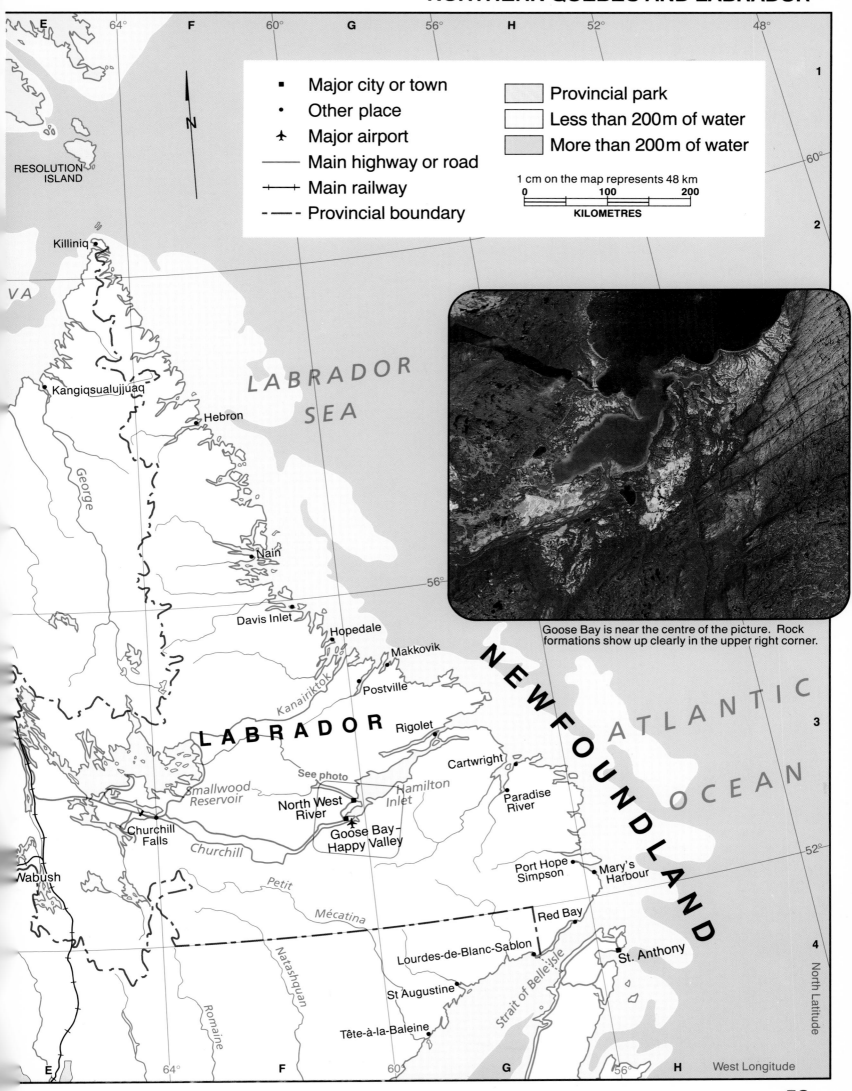

Legend

- ■ Major city or town
- • Other place
- ✈ Major airport
- —— Main highway or road
- +++ Main railway
- -·-· Provincial boundary

- Provincial park
- Less than 200m of water
- More than 200m of water

1 cm on the map represents 48 km

0   100   200
KILOMETRES

Goose Bay is near the centre of the picture. Rock formations show up clearly in the upper right corner.

RESOLUTION ISLAND

VA

Killiniq

Kangiqsualujjuaq

Hebron

George

LABRADOR SEA

Nain

Davis Inlet

Hopedale

Makkovik

Postville

Kanairiktok

LABRADOR

Rigolet

NEWFOUNDLAND

ATLANTIC

OCEAN

Cartwright

See photo

Smallwood Reservoir

Hamilton Inlet

North West River

Paradise River

Churchill Falls

Goose Bay – Happy Valley

Churchill

Wabush

Petit

Port Hope Simpson

Mary's Harbour

Mécatina

Red Bay

Natashquan

Lourdes-de-Blanc-Sablon

Strait of Belle Isle

St. Anthony

Romaine

St Augustine

Tête-à-la-Baleine

North Latitude

West Longitude

180° 150° 120° 90° 60° 30° 0°

PRIME MERIDIAN

BEAUFORT SEA

NORWEGIAN SEA

BAFFIN BAY

NORTH SEA

60°

CANADA

HUDSON BAY

LABRADOR SEA

GULF OF ALASKA

NORTH

GREAT LAKES

AMERICA

30°

GULF OF MEXICO

TROPIC OF CANCER

ATLANTIC

CARIBBEAN SEA

PACIFIC

OCEAN

GULF OF GUINEA

0°

OCEAN

SOUTH

AMERICA

TROPIC OF CAPRICORN

30°

Ocean currents
(Northern hemisphere winter)

→ Warm current
→ Cold current

Antarctica, the seventh continent is not shown on this map.

150° 120° 90° 60° West longitude 30° 0°

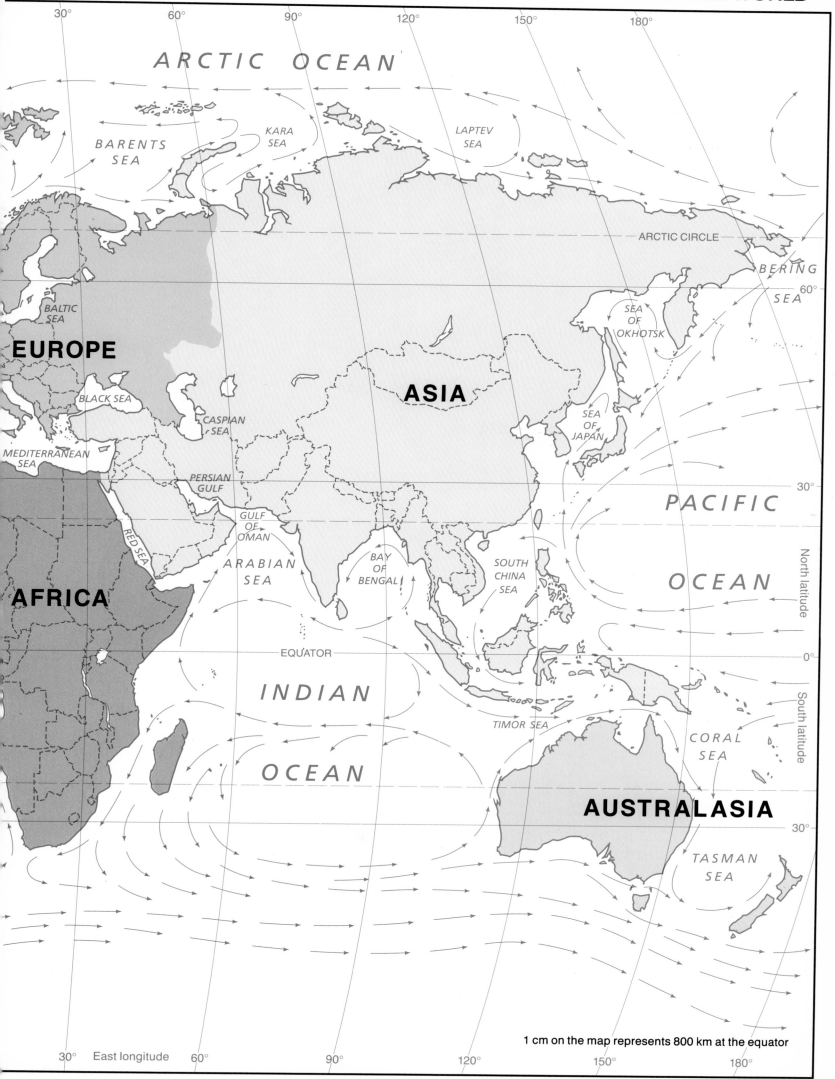

30°   60°   90°   120°   150°   180°

ARCTIC OCEAN

BARENTS
SEA

KARA
SEA

LAPTEV
SEA

ARCTIC CIRCLE

BERING
SEA

60°

BALTIC
SEA

SEA
OF
OKHOTSK

EUROPE

BLACK SEA

CASPIAN
SEA

ASIA

SEA
OF
JAPAN

MEDITERRANEAN
SEA

PERSIAN
GULF

30°

PACIFIC

RED SEA

GULF
OF
OMAN

OCEAN

North latitude

AFRICA

ARABIAN
SEA

BAY
OF
BENGAL

SOUTH
CHINA
SEA

EQUATOR

0°

INDIAN

TIMOR SEA

South latitude

OCEAN

CORAL
SEA

AUSTRALASIA

30°

TASMAN
SEA

1 cm on the map represents 800 km at the equator

30°   East longitude   60°   90°   120°   150°   180°

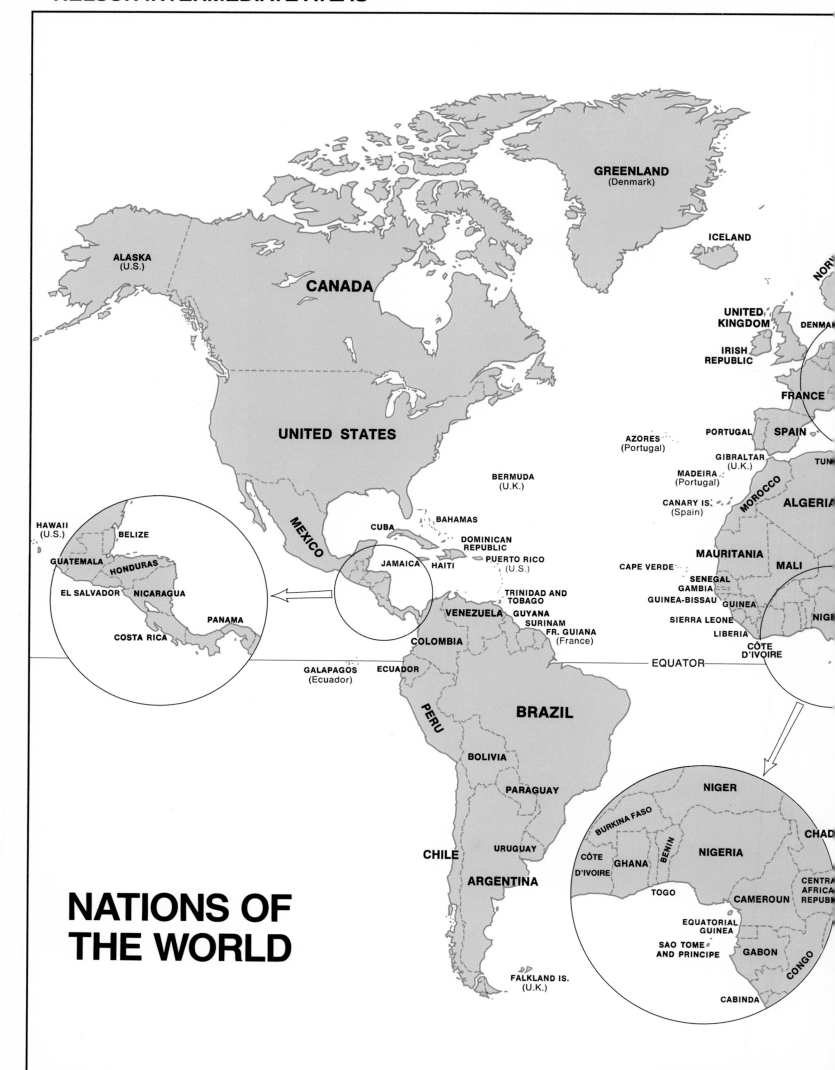

GREENLAND
(Denmark)

ICELAND

NOR

ALASKA
(U.S.)

UNITED
KINGDOM

DENMA

CANADA

IRISH
REPUBLIC

FRANCE

AZORES
(Portugal)

PORTUGAL

SPAIN

GIBRALTAR
(U.K.)

TUN

BERMUDA
(U.K.)

MADEIRA
(Portugal)

MOROCCO

ALGERIA

CANARY IS.
(Spain)

HAWAII
(U.S.)

BELIZE

BAHAMAS

CUBA

MEXICO

DOMINICAN
REPUBLIC

MAURITANIA

MALI

GUATEMALA

JAMAICA

HAITI

PUERTO RICO
(U.S.)

CAPE VERDE

HONDURAS

SENEGAL
GAMBIA

EL SALVADOR

NICARAGUA

GUINEA-BISSAU

GUINEA

TRINIDAD AND
TOBAGO

NIG

SIERRA LEONE

COSTA RICA

PANAMA

VENEZUELA

GUYANA

LIBERIA

SURINAM

FR. GUIANA
(France)

CÔTE
D'IVOIRE

COLOMBIA

EQUATOR

GALAPAGOS
(Ecuador)

ECUADOR

PERU

BRAZIL

BOLIVIA

NIGER

PARAGUAY

BURKINA FASO

CHAD

CÔTE
D'IVOIRE

GHANA

BENIN

NIGERIA

CHILE

URUGUAY

CENTRAL
AFRICA
REPUBL

ARGENTINA

TOGO

CAMEROUN

NATIONS OF
THE WORLD

EQUATORIAL
GUINEA

SAO TOME
AND PRINCIPE

GABON

CONGO

FALKLAND IS.
(U.K.)

CABINDA

UNION OF SOVIET SOCIALIST REPUBLICS

Inset (top) — Europe:

NETHERLANDS
BELGIUM
LUXEMBOURG
EAST GERMANY
WEST GERMANY
POLAND
U.S.S.R.
CZECHOSLOVAKIA
SWITZERLAND
AUSTRIA
HUNGARY
FRANCE
ROMANIA
ITALY
YUGOSLAVIA
BULGARIA
CORSICA (France)
ALBANIA
SARDINIA (Italy)
GREECE
SICILY (Italy)

Main map labels:

SVALBARD (Norway)
SWEDEN
FINLAND
POLAND
ITALY
MALTA
CYPRUS
LEBANON
ISRAEL
SYRIA
IRAQ
IRAN
TURKEY
AFGHAN-ISTAN
PAKISTAN
JORDAN
SAUDI ARABIA
LIBYA
EGYPT
CHAD
SUDAN
C.A.R.
ETHIOPIA
SOMALIA
UGANDA
KENYA
RWANDA
BURUNDI
ZAIRE
TANZANIA
NGOLA
ZAMBIA
MALAWI
MOZAMBIQUE
NAMIBIA
BOTSWANA
ZIMBABWE
SOUTH AFRICA
SWAZILAND
LESOTHO
MADAGASCAR
MAURITIUS
REUNION
SEYCHELLES
MALDIVES
MONGOLIA
CHINA
NORTH KOREA
SOUTH KOREA
JAPAN
NEPAL
BHUTAN
BANGLADESH
INDIA
BURMA
TAIWAN
HONG KONG (U.K.)
LAOS
THAILAND
VIETNAM
KAMPUCHEA
ANDAMAN IS. (India)
SRI LANKA
PHILIPPINES
BRUNEI
MALAYSIA
SINGAPORE
INDONESIA
PAPUA-NEW GUINEA
SOLOMON IS.
NEW HEBRIDES (France & U.K.)
NEW CALEDONIA (France)
AUSTRALIA
NEW ZEALAND

Inset (bottom) — Arabian Peninsula:

IRAQ
IRAN
KUWAIT
BAHRAIN
QATAR
SAUDI ARABIA
UNITED ARAB EMIRATES
OMAN
P.D.R. OF YEMEN
YEMEN
ETHIOPIA
DJIBOUTI
SOMALIA

1 cm on the map is equal to 800 km at the equator

GREENLAND
(Denmark)

ICELAND

ALASKA
(U.S.)

CANADA

1 DENMARK
2 NETHERLANDS
3 BELGIUM
4 LUXEMBOURG
5 WEST GERMANY
6 EAST GERMANY
7 POLAND
8 CZECHOSLOVAKIA
9 SWITZERLAND
10 AUSTRIA
11 ITALY
12 YUGOSLAVIA
13 HUNGARY
14 ROMANIA
15 BULGARIA
16 ALBANIA
17 GREECE

NORW

UNITED
KINGDOM

IRISH
REPUBLIC

FRANCE

UNITED STATES

AZORES
(Portugal)

PORTUGAL SPAIN

GIBRALTAR
(U.K.)

•BERMUDA
(U.K.)

MADEIRA
(Portugal)

TUNIS

CANARY IS.
(Spain)

MOROCCO

ALGERIA

BAHAMAS

HAWAII
(U.S.)

MEXICO

CUBA

DOMINICAN
REPUBLIC

PUERTO RICO

JAMAICA HAITI

MAURITANIA

CAPE VERDE

SENEGAL
GAMBIA
GUINEA-BISSAU

MALI

N

1 BELIZE
2 GUATEMALA
3 HONDURAS
4 EL SALVADOR
5 NICARAGUA
6 COSTA RICA
7 PANAMA

1
2 3
4 5
6
7

TRINIDAD AND
TOBAGO

GUINEA

SIERRA LEONE

LIBERIA

CÔTE
D'IVOIRE

2
3 4
NIG

VENEZUELA

GUYANA
SURINAM

FR. GUIANA
(France)

COLOMBIA

GALAPAGOS IS.
(Ecuador)

ECUADOR

EQUATOR

1 BURKINA FASO
2 GHANA
3 TOGO
4 BENIN
5 CAMEROON
6 CENTRAL AFRICAN REP.
7 EQUATORIAL GUINEA
8 GABON
9 CONGO
10 SAO TOME & PRINCIPE
11 CABINDA

10

PERU

BRAZIL

MAJOR
INTERNATIONAL
ORGANIZATIONS

BOLIVIA

PARAGUAY

Commonwealth of Nations

European Economic Community*

CHILE

URUGUAY

Organization of American States

Arab League

ARGENTINA

Communist states

FALKLAND IS.
(U.K.)

Nations not members of the above organizations

*(E.E.C. or Common market)

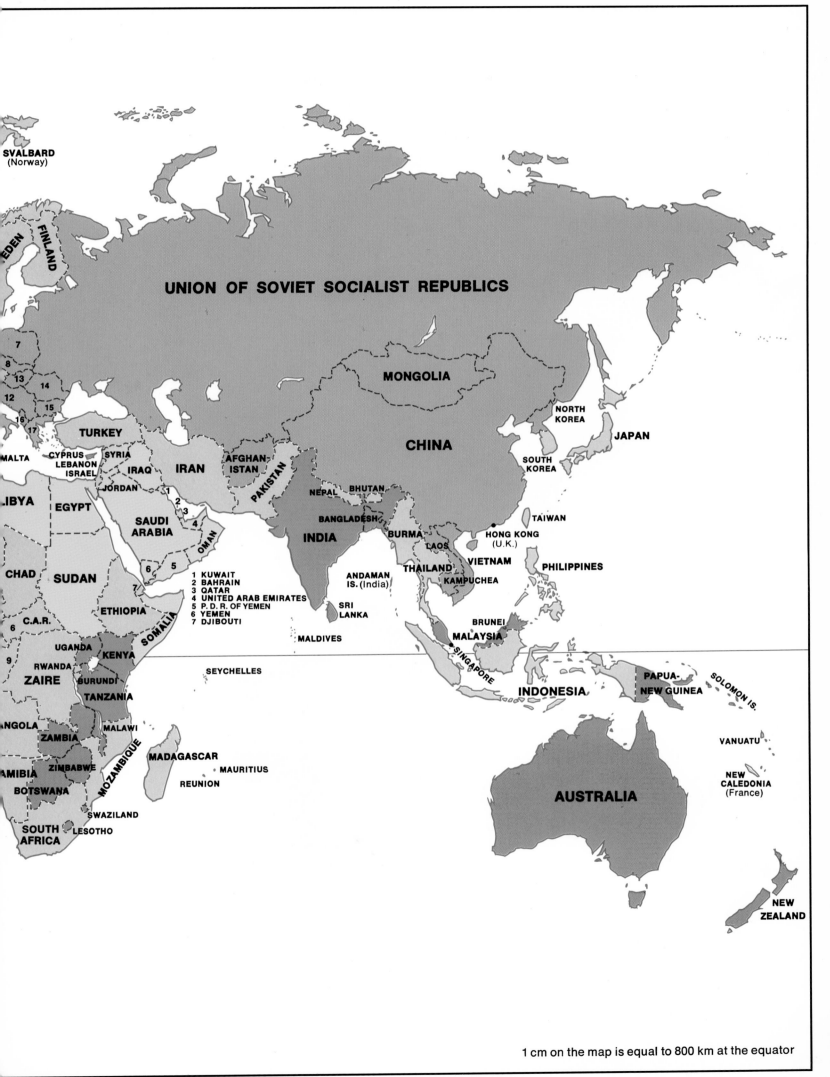

SVALBARD
(Norway)

EDEN

FINLAND

UNION OF SOVIET SOCIALIST REPUBLICS

7

8

13   14

12

15

16

17

TURKEY

MALTA

CYPRUS
LEBANON
ISRAEL

SYRIA

IRAQ

JORDAN

IRAN

AFGHAN-
ISTAN

PAKISTAN

MONGOLIA

NORTH
KOREA

JAPAN

CHINA

SOUTH
KOREA

IBYA

EGYPT

SAUDI
ARABIA

OMAN

1
2
3

4

6   5

1 KUWAIT
2 BAHRAIN
3 QATAR
4 UNITED ARAB EMIRATES
5 P. D. R. OF YEMEN
6 YEMEN
7 DJIBOUTI

NEPAL

BHUTAN

BANGLADESH

INDIA

BURMA

LAOS

THAILAND

KAMPUCHEA

ANDAMAN
IS. (India)

SRI
LANKA

MALDIVES

TAIWAN

HONG KONG
(U.K.)

VIETNAM

PHILIPPINES

CHAD

SUDAN

ETHIOPIA

C.A.R.

6

SOMALIA

UGANDA

RWANDA

KENYA

9

ZAIRE

BURUNDI

TANZANIA

SEYCHELLES

BRUNEI

MALAYSIA

SINGAPORE

INDONESIA

PAPUA-
NEW GUINEA

SOLOMON IS.

NGOLA

ZAMBIA

MALAWI

MOZAMBIQUE

MADAGASCAR

MAURITIUS

REUNION

VANUATU

NEW
CALEDONIA
(France)

AMIBIA

ZIMBABWE

BOTSWANA

SWAZILAND

SOUTH
AFRICA

LESOTHO

AUSTRALIA

NEW
ZEALAND

1 cm on the map is equal to 800 km at the equator

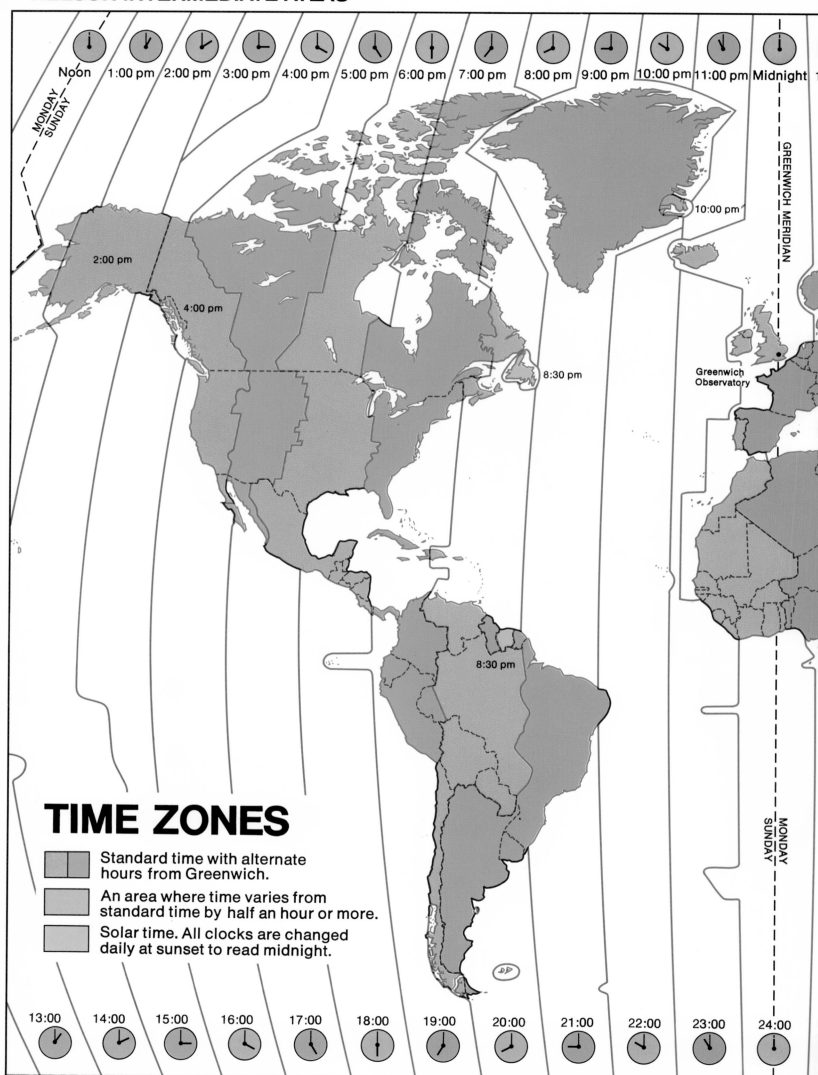

Noon | 1:00 pm | 2:00 pm | 3:00 pm | 4:00 pm | 5:00 pm | 6:00 pm | 7:00 pm | 8:00 pm | 9:00 pm | 10:00 pm | 11:00 pm | Midnight

MONDAY / SUNDAY

GREENWICH MERIDIAN

2:00 pm

4:00 pm

10:00 pm

8:30 pm

Greenwich
Observatory

8:30 pm

MONDAY / SUNDAY

TIME ZONES

Standard time with alternate hours from Greenwich.

An area where time varies from standard time by half an hour or more.

Solar time. All clocks are changed daily at sunset to read midnight.

13:00 | 14:00 | 15:00 | 16:00 | 17:00 | 18:00 | 19:00 | 20:00 | 21:00 | 22:00 | 23:00 | 24:00

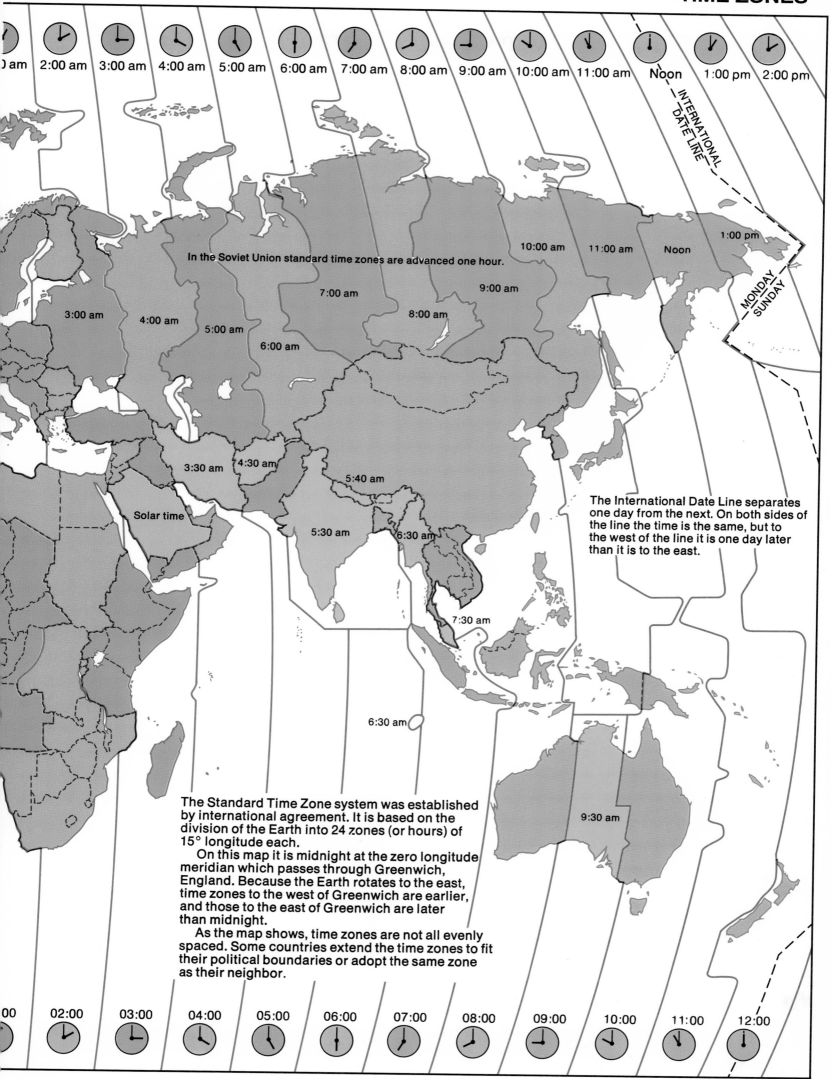

2:00 am 3:00 am 4:00 am 5:00 am 6:00 am 7:00 am 8:00 am 9:00 am 10:00 am 11:00 am Noon 1:00 pm 2:00 pm

INTERNATIONAL DATE LINE

In the Soviet Union standard time zones are advanced one hour.

10:00 am 11:00 am Noon 1:00 pm

MONDAY / SUNDAY

7:00 am 9:00 am

3:00 am 4:00 am 8:00 am

5:00 am

6:00 am

3:30 am 4:30 am

5:40 am

Solar time

5:30 am 6:30 am

The International Date Line separates one day from the next. On both sides of the line the time is the same, but to the west of the line it is one day later than it is to the east.

7:30 am

6:30 am

9:30 am

The Standard Time Zone system was established by international agreement. It is based on the division of the Earth into 24 zones (or hours) of 15° longitude each.

On this map it is midnight at the zero longitude meridian which passes through Greenwich, England. Because the Earth rotates to the east, time zones to the west of Greenwich are earlier, and those to the east of Greenwich are later than midnight.

As the map shows, time zones are not all evenly spaced. Some countries extend the time zones to fit their political boundaries or adopt the same zone as their neighbor.

02:00 03:00 04:00 05:00 06:00 07:00 08:00 09:00 10:00 11:00 12:00

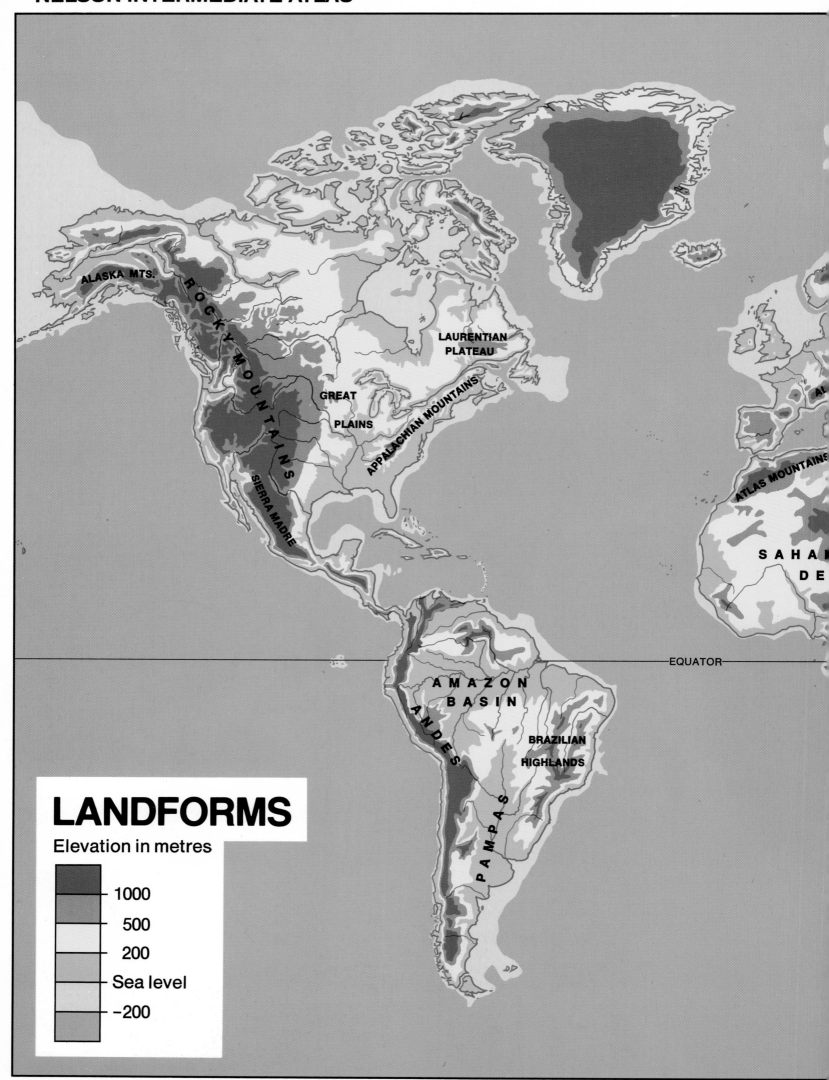

ALASKA MTS.

ROCKY MOUNTAINS

GREAT PLAINS

LAURENTIAN PLATEAU

APPALACHIAN MOUNTAINS

SIERRA MADRE

ATLAS MOUNTAINS

SAHA
DE

EQUATOR

AMAZON BASIN

ANDES

BRAZILIAN HIGHLANDS

PAMPAS

LANDFORMS

Elevation in metres

1000

500

200

Sea level

-200

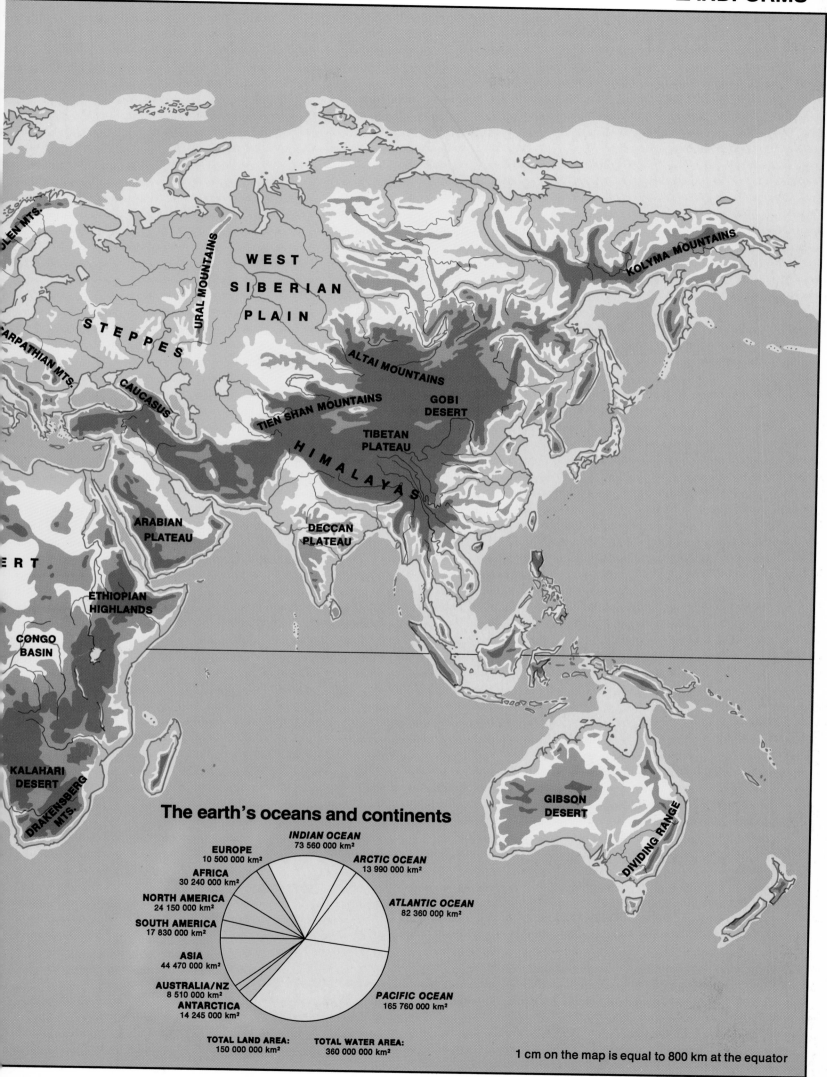

KOLYMA MOUNTAINS

WEST SIBERIAN PLAIN

URAL MOUNTAINS

STEPPES

CARPATHIAN MTS.

CAUCASUS

ALTAI MOUNTAINS

TIEN SHAN MOUNTAINS

GOBI DESERT

TIBETAN PLATEAU

HIMALAYAS

ARABIAN PLATEAU

DECCAN PLATEAU

ETHIOPIAN HIGHLANDS

CONGO BASIN

KALAHARI DESERT

DRAKENSBERG MTS.

GIBSON DESERT

DIVIDING RANGE

The earth's oceans and continents

EUROPE
10 500 000 km²

AFRICA
30 240 000 km²

NORTH AMERICA
24 150 000 km²

SOUTH AMERICA
17 830 000 km²

ASIA
44 470 000 km²

AUSTRALIA/NZ
8 510 000 km²

ANTARCTICA
14 245 000 km²

INDIAN OCEAN
73 560 000 km²

ARCTIC OCEAN
13 990 000 km²

ATLANTIC OCEAN
82 360 000 km²

PACIFIC OCEAN
165 760 000 km²

TOTAL LAND AREA:
150 000 000 km²

TOTAL WATER AREA:
360 000 000 km²

1 cm on the map is equal to 800 km at the equator

63

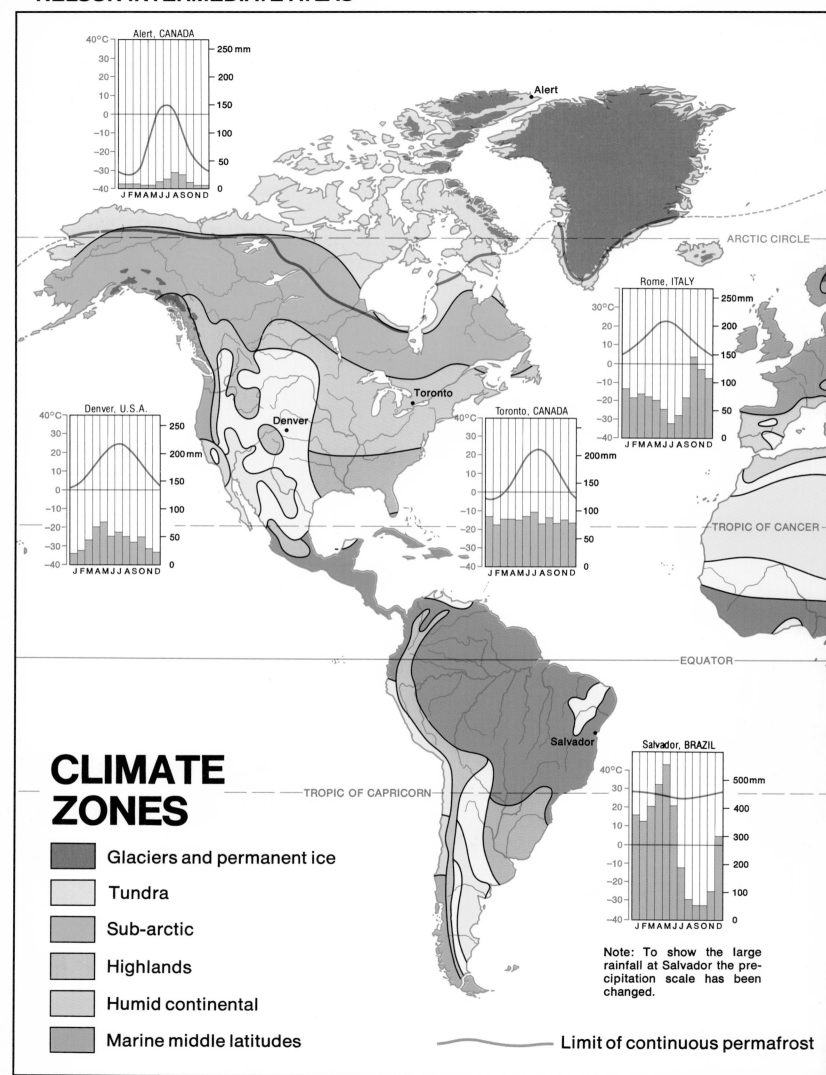

Alert, CANADA

Denver, U.S.A.

Toronto, CANADA

Rome, ITALY

Salvador, BRAZIL

Alert

Toronto

Denver

Salvador

ARCTIC CIRCLE

TROPIC OF CANCER

EQUATOR

TROPIC OF CAPRICORN

CLIMATE ZONES

Glaciers and permanent ice

Tundra

Sub-arctic

Highlands

Humid continental

Marine middle latitudes

Note: To show the large rainfall at Salvador the precipitation scale has been changed.

Limit of continuous permafrost

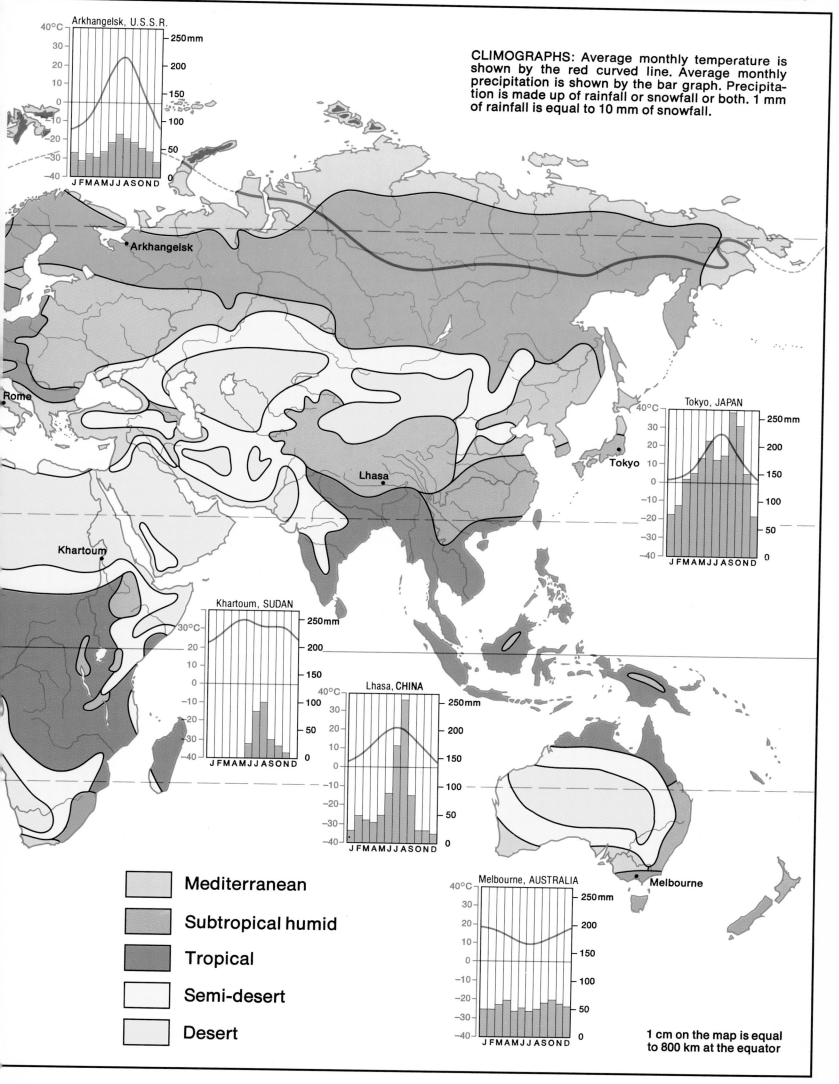

CLIMOGRAPHS: Average monthly temperature is shown by the red curved line. Average monthly precipitation is shown by the bar graph. Precipitation is made up of rainfall or snowfall or both. 1 mm of rainfall is equal to 10 mm of snowfall.

Arkhangelsk, U.S.S.R.

Tokyo, JAPAN

Khartoum, SUDAN

Lhasa, CHINA

Melbourne, AUSTRALIA

Mediterranean

Subtropical humid

Tropical

Semi-desert

Desert

1 cm on the map is equal to 800 km at the equator

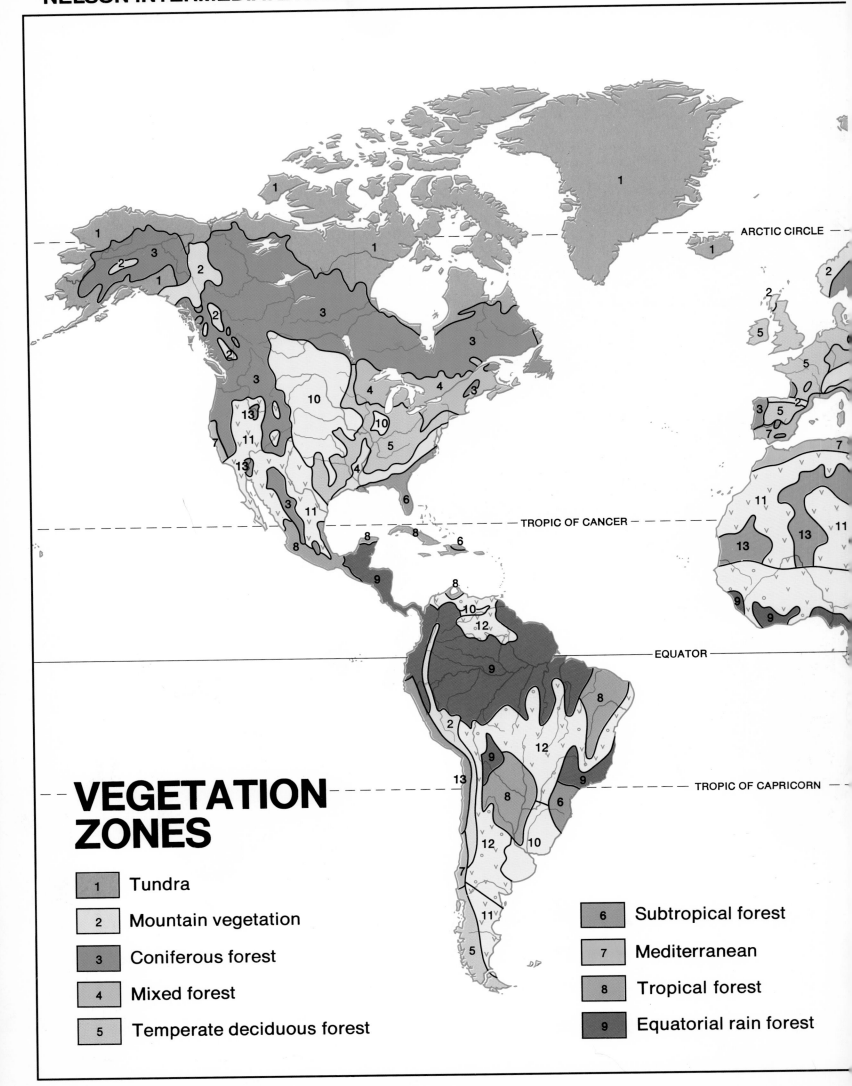

VEGETATION ZONES

1	Tundra
2	Mountain vegetation
3	Coniferous forest
4	Mixed forest
5	Temperate deciduous forest
6	Subtropical forest
7	Mediterranean
8	Tropical forest
9	Equatorial rain forest

ARCTIC CIRCLE

TROPIC OF CANCER

EQUATOR

TROPIC OF CAPRICORN

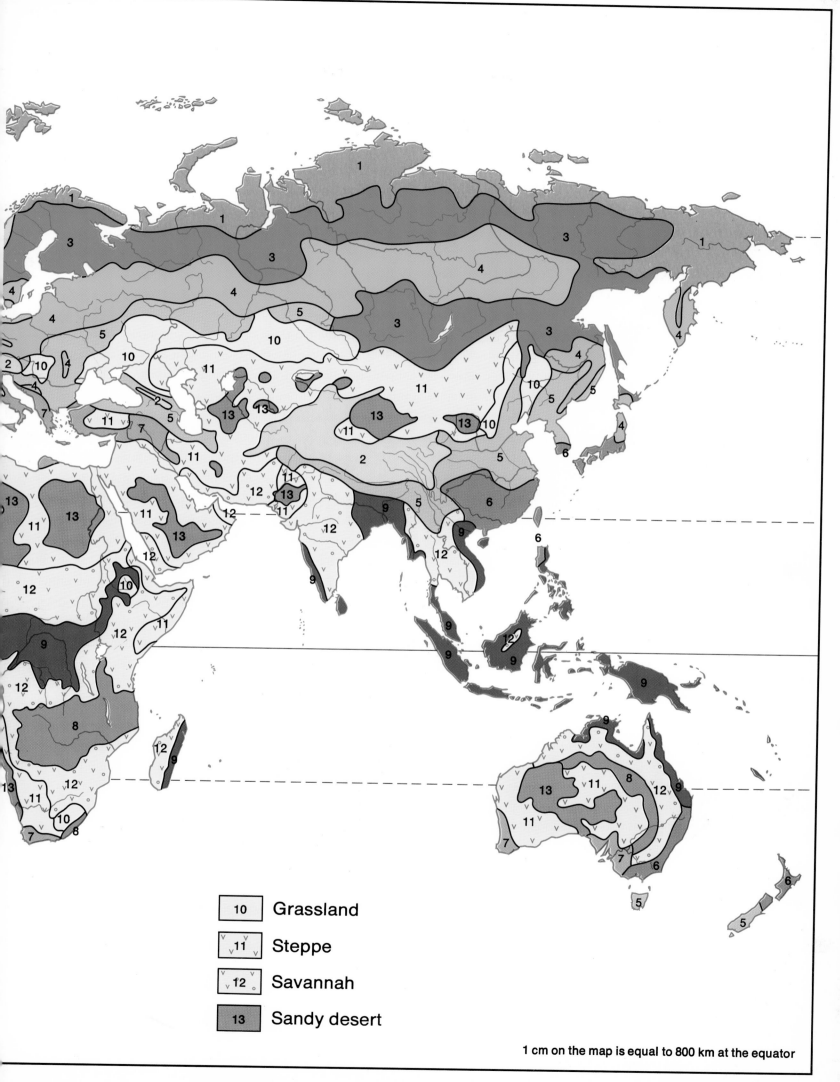

10 Grassland

11 Steppe

12 Savannah

13 Sandy desert

1 cm on the map is equal to 800 km at the equator

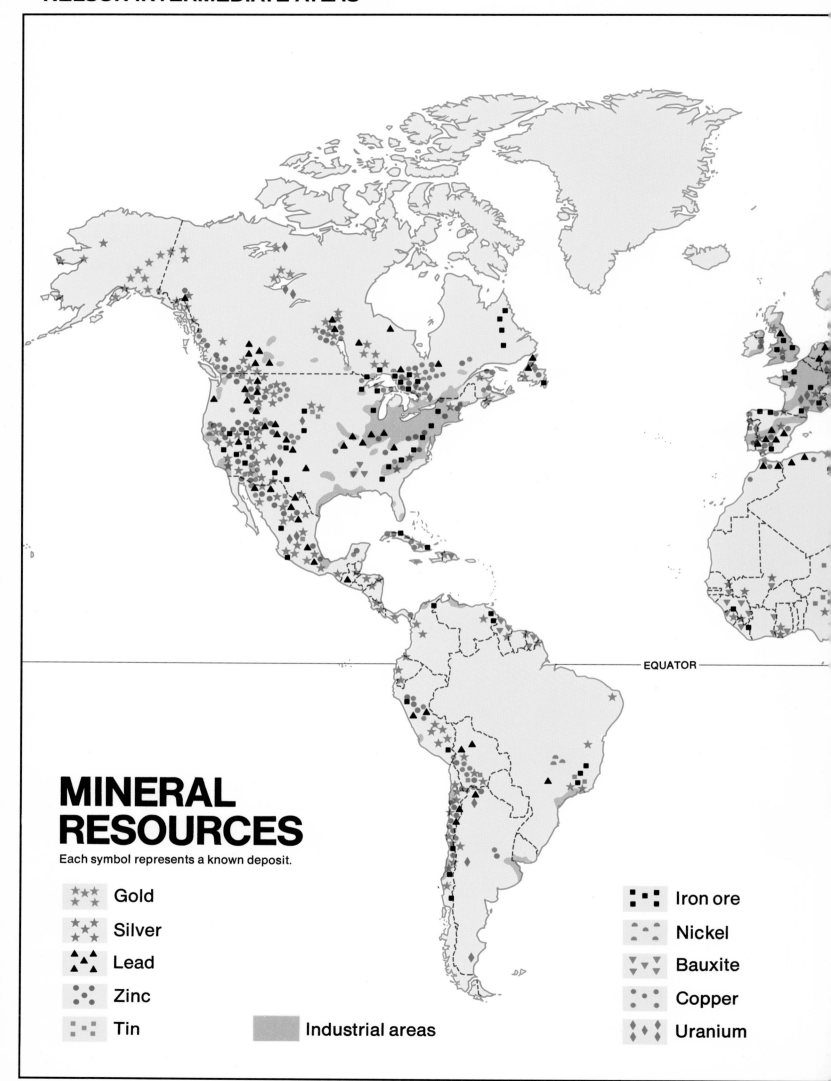

MINERAL RESOURCES

Each symbol represents a known deposit.

Gold

Silver

Lead

Zinc

Tin

Industrial areas

Iron ore

Nickel

Bauxite

Copper

Uranium

EQUATOR

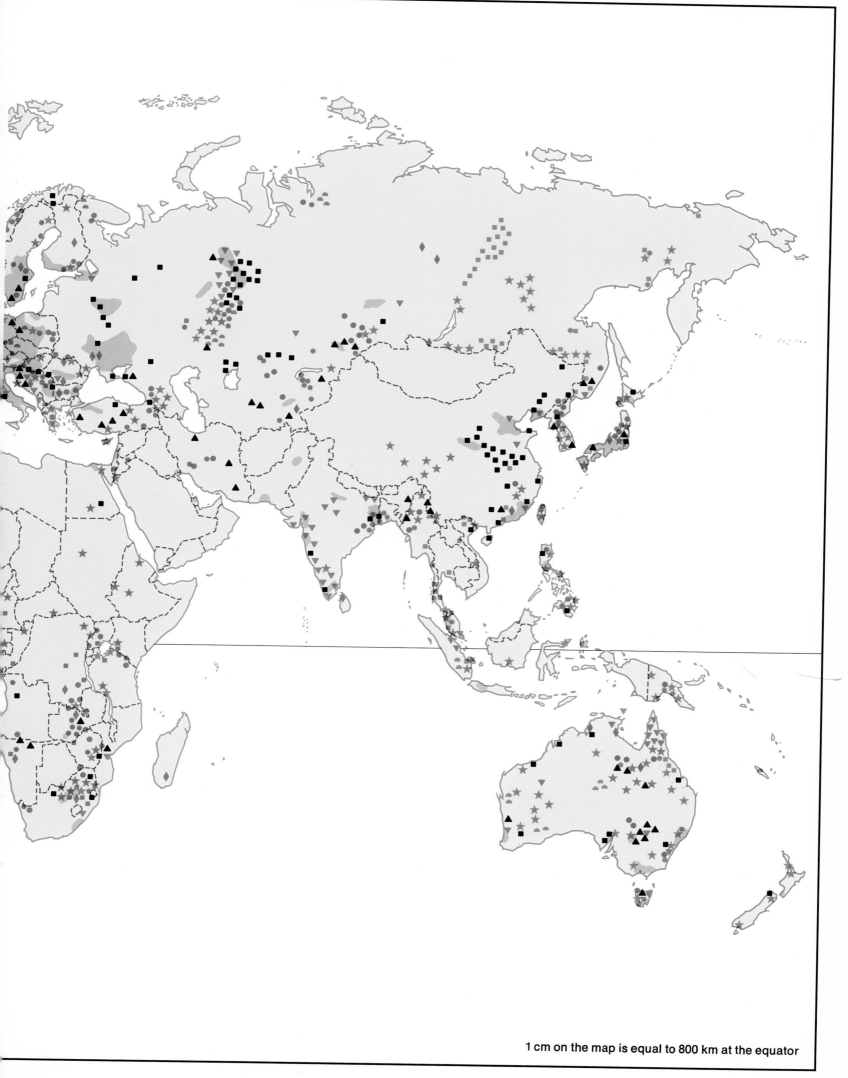

1 cm on the map is equal to 800 km at the equator

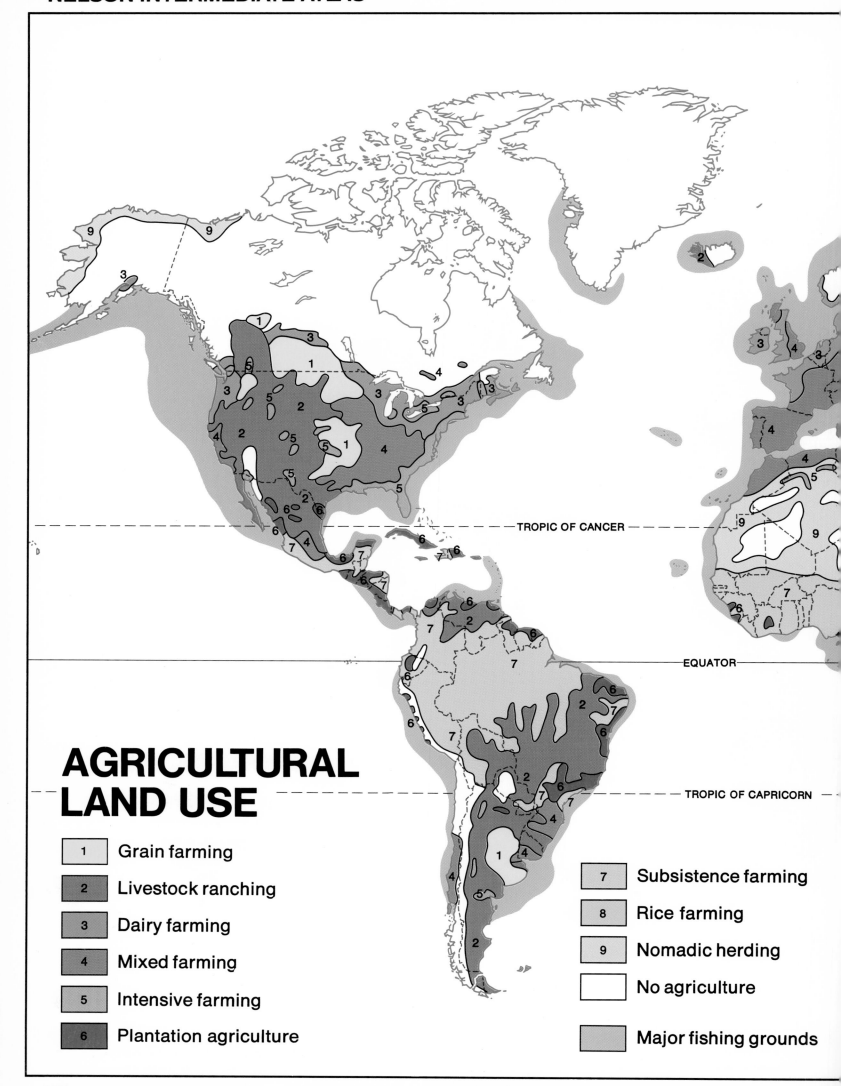

AGRICULTURAL LAND USE

TROPIC OF CANCER

EQUATOR

TROPIC OF CAPRICORN

1	Grain farming
2	Livestock ranching
3	Dairy farming
4	Mixed farming
5	Intensive farming
6	Plantation agriculture

7	Subsistence farming
8	Rice farming
9	Nomadic herding
	No agriculture
	Major fishing grounds

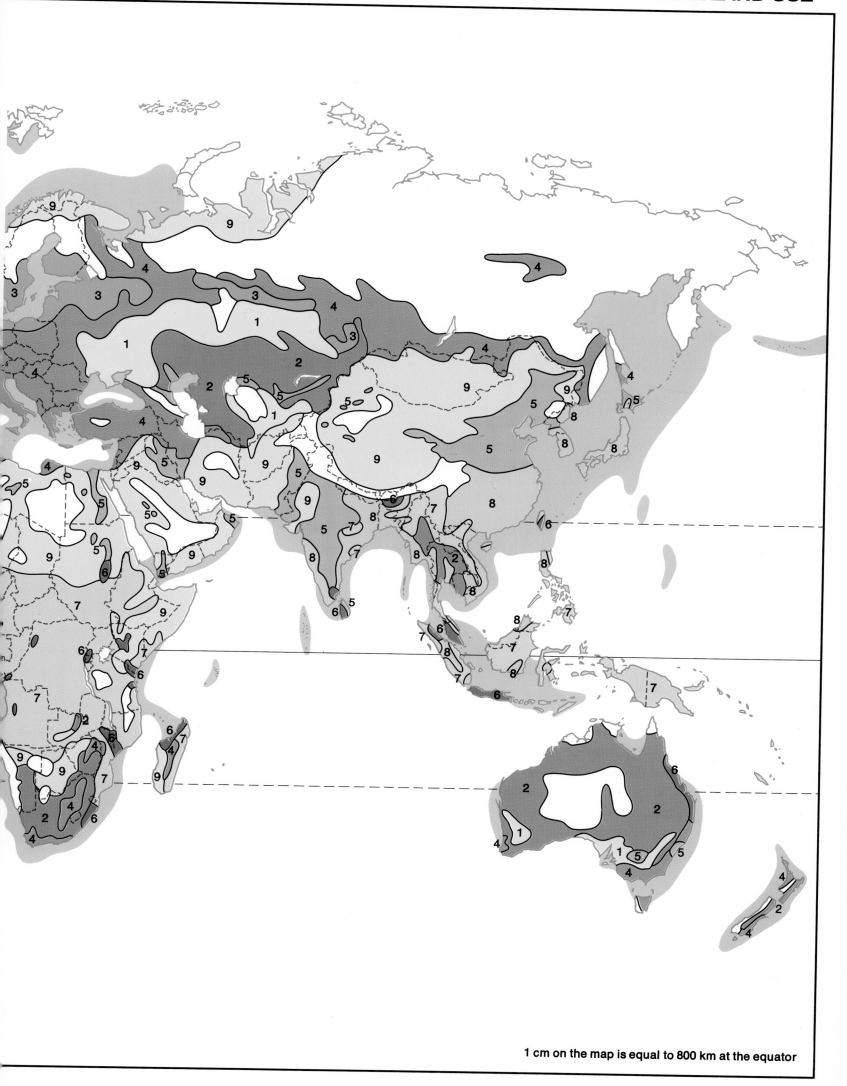

1 cm on the map is equal to 800 km at the equator

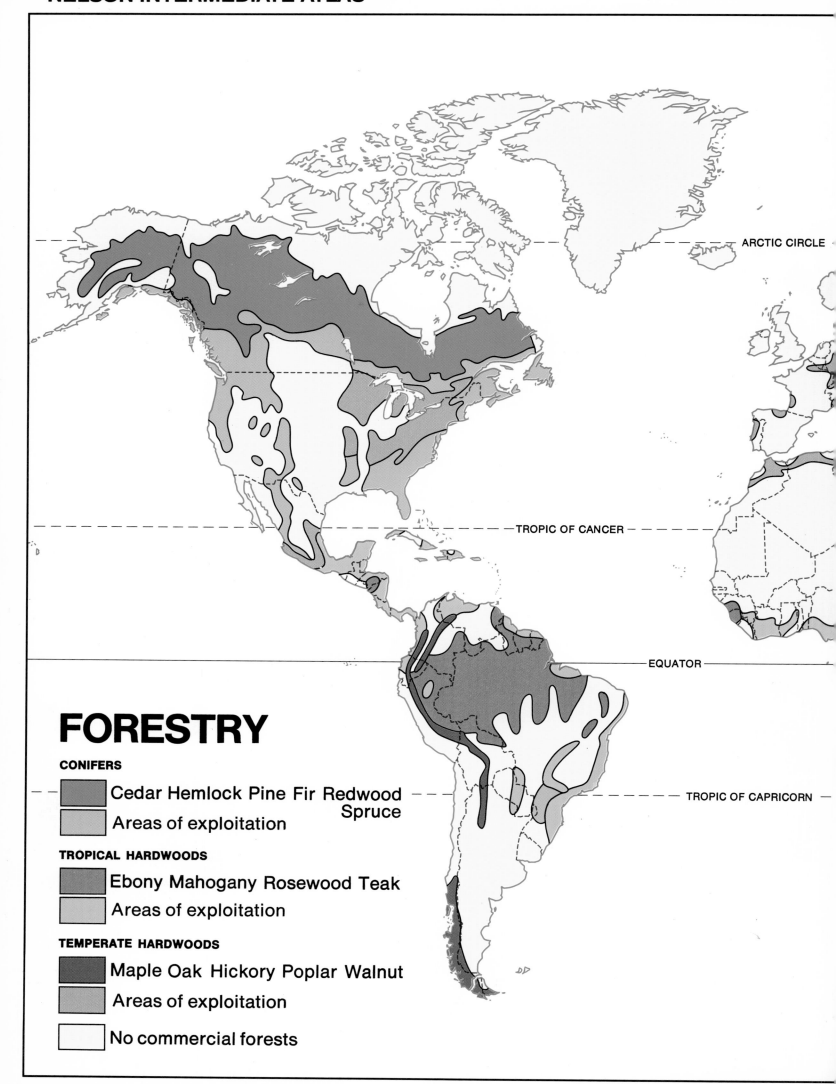

FORESTRY

CONIFERS

Cedar Hemlock Pine Fir Redwood
Spruce

Areas of exploitation

TROPICAL HARDWOODS

Ebony Mahogany Rosewood Teak

Areas of exploitation

TEMPERATE HARDWOODS

Maple Oak Hickory Poplar Walnut

Areas of exploitation

No commercial forests

ARCTIC CIRCLE

TROPIC OF CANCER

EQUATOR

TROPIC OF CAPRICORN

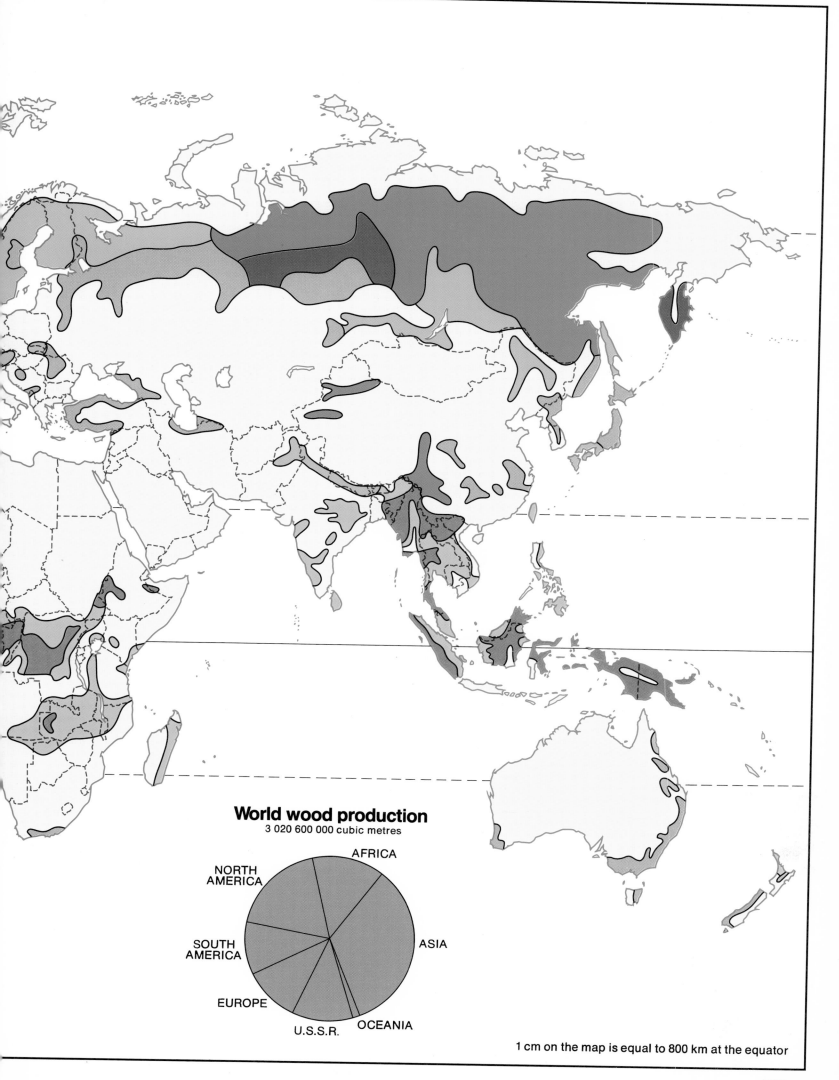

World wood production
3 020 600 000 cubic metres

AFRICA

NORTH
AMERICA

ASIA

SOUTH
AMERICA

EUROPE

U.S.S.R. OCEANIA

1 cm on the map is equal to 800 km at the equator

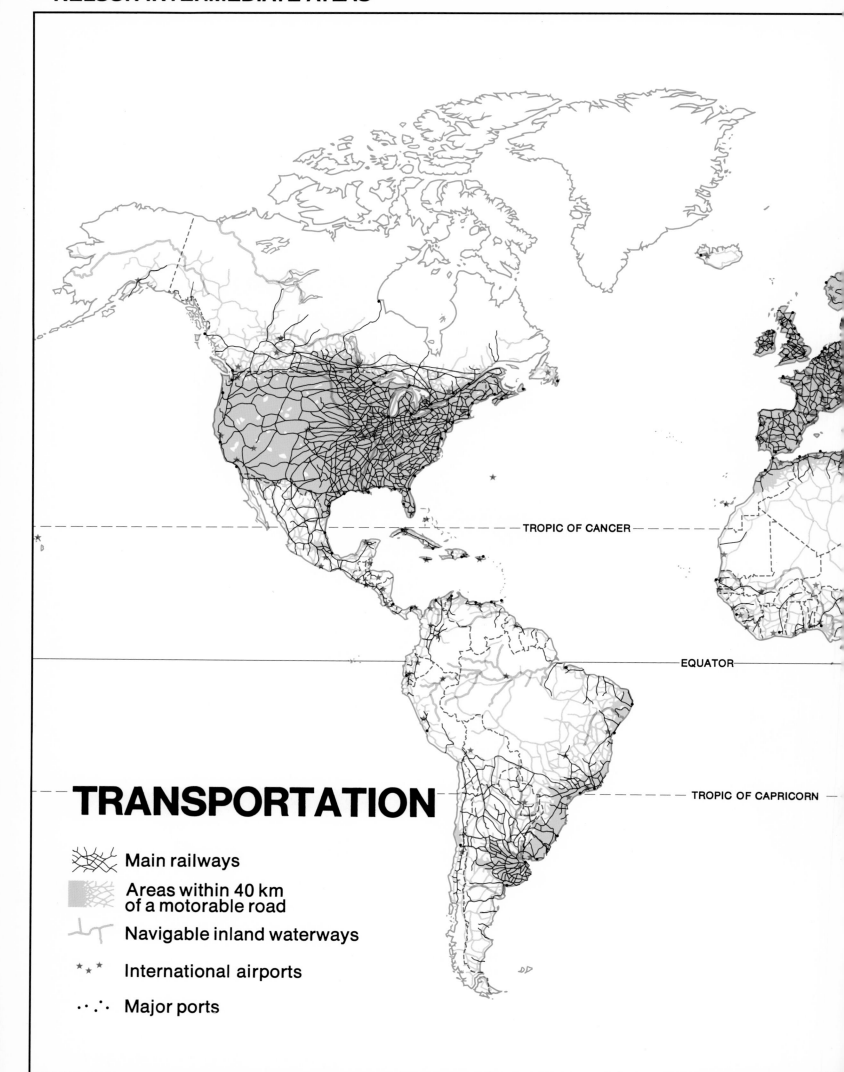

TROPIC OF CANCER

EQUATOR

TROPIC OF CAPRICORN

TRANSPORTATION

Main railways

Areas within 40 km
of a motorable road

Navigable inland waterways

International airports

Major ports

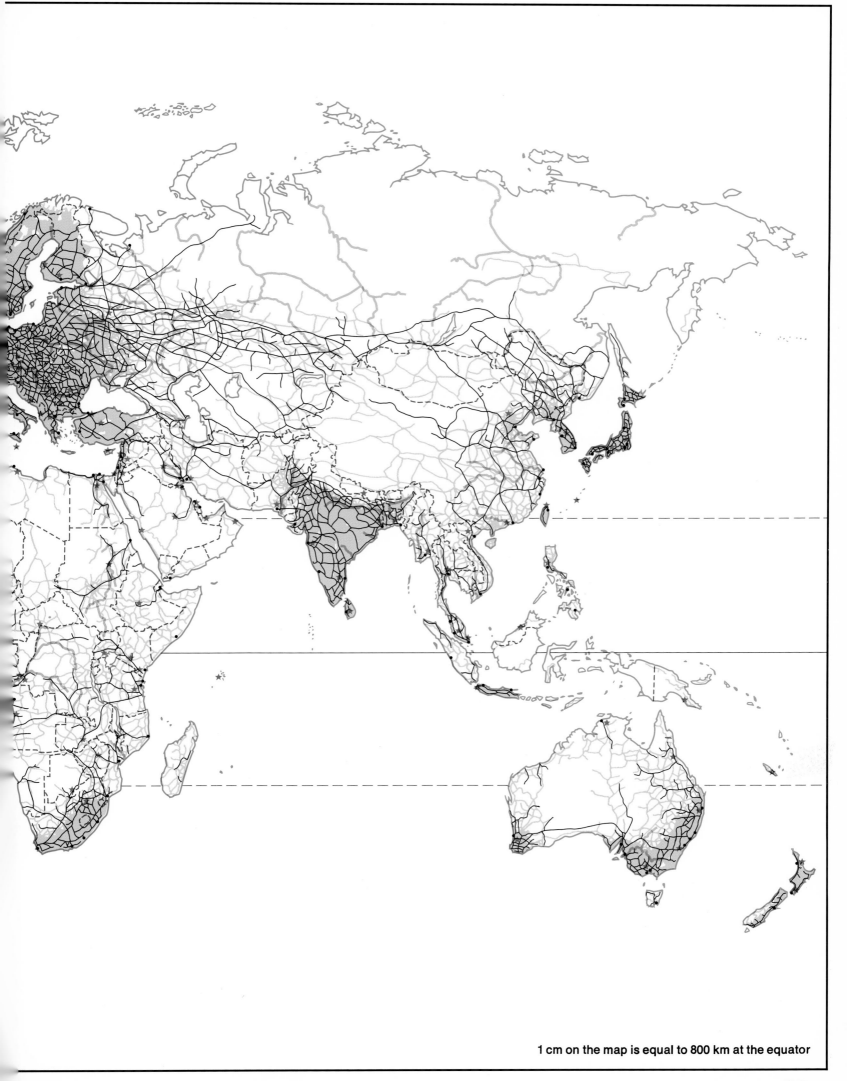

1 cm on the map is equal to 800 km at the equator

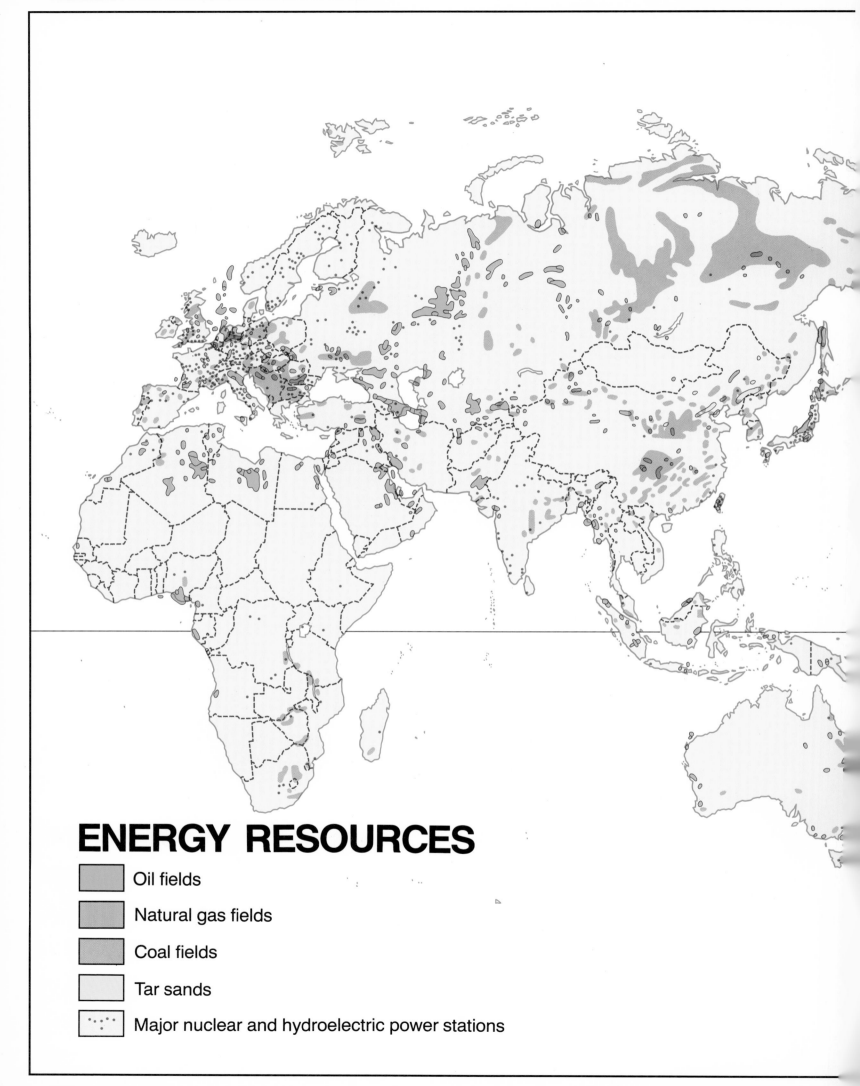

ENERGY RESOURCES

Oil fields

Natural gas fields

Coal fields

Tar sands

Major nuclear and hydroelectric power stations

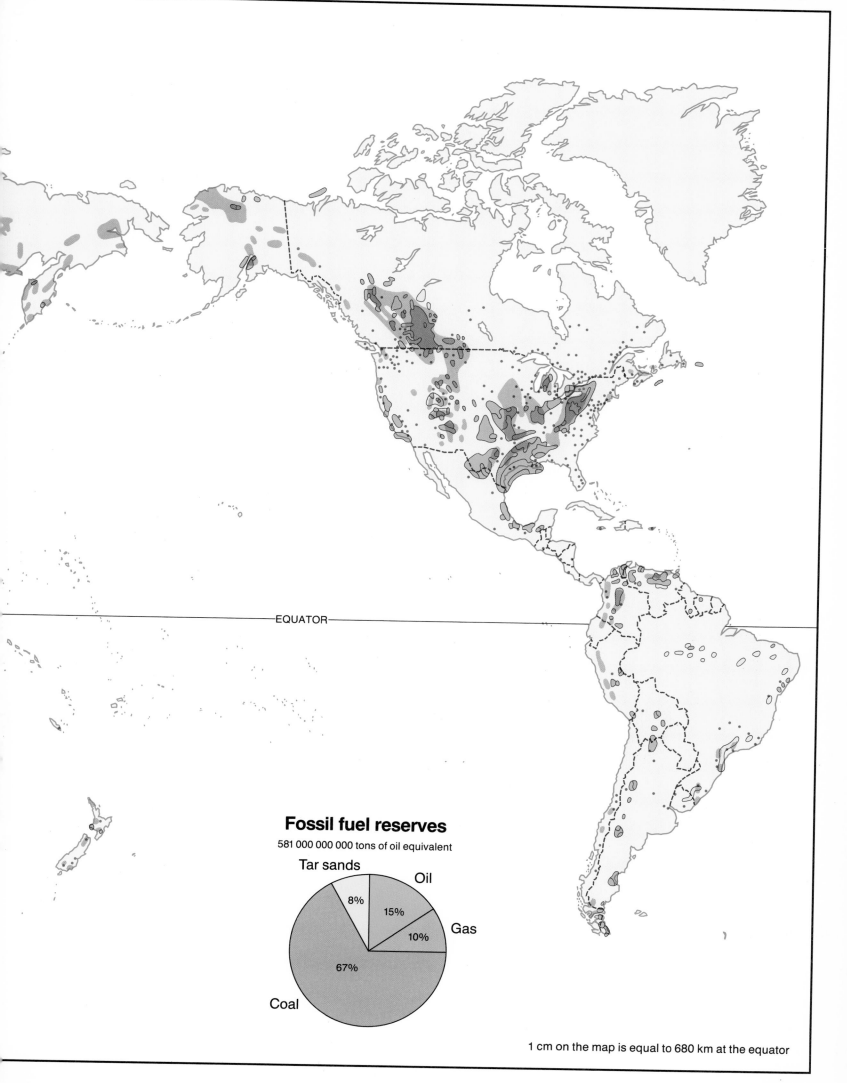

EQUATOR

Fossil fuel reserves

581 000 000 000 tons of oil equivalent

Tar sands

Oil

8%

15%

10%

Gas

67%

Coal

1 cm on the map is equal to 680 km at the equator

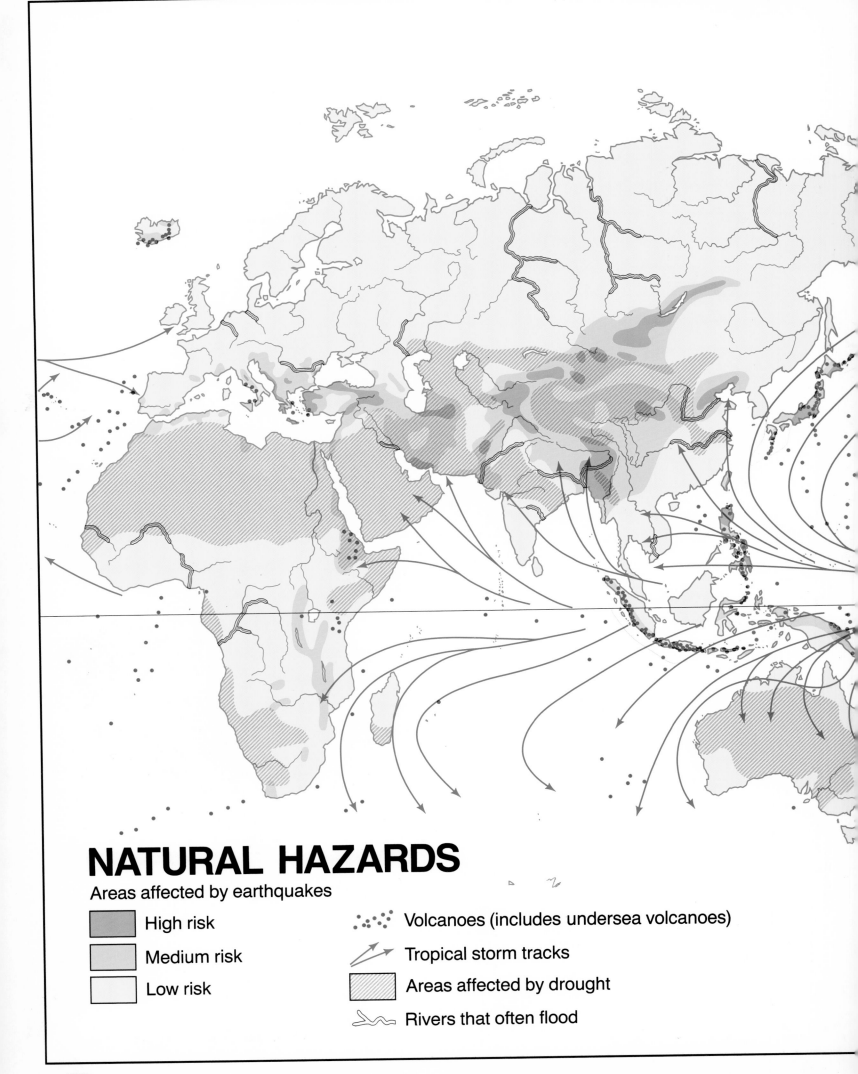

NATURAL HAZARDS

Areas affected by earthquakes

High risk	
Medium risk	
Low risk	

Volcanoes (includes undersea volcanoes)

Tropical storm tracks

Areas affected by drought

Rivers that often flood

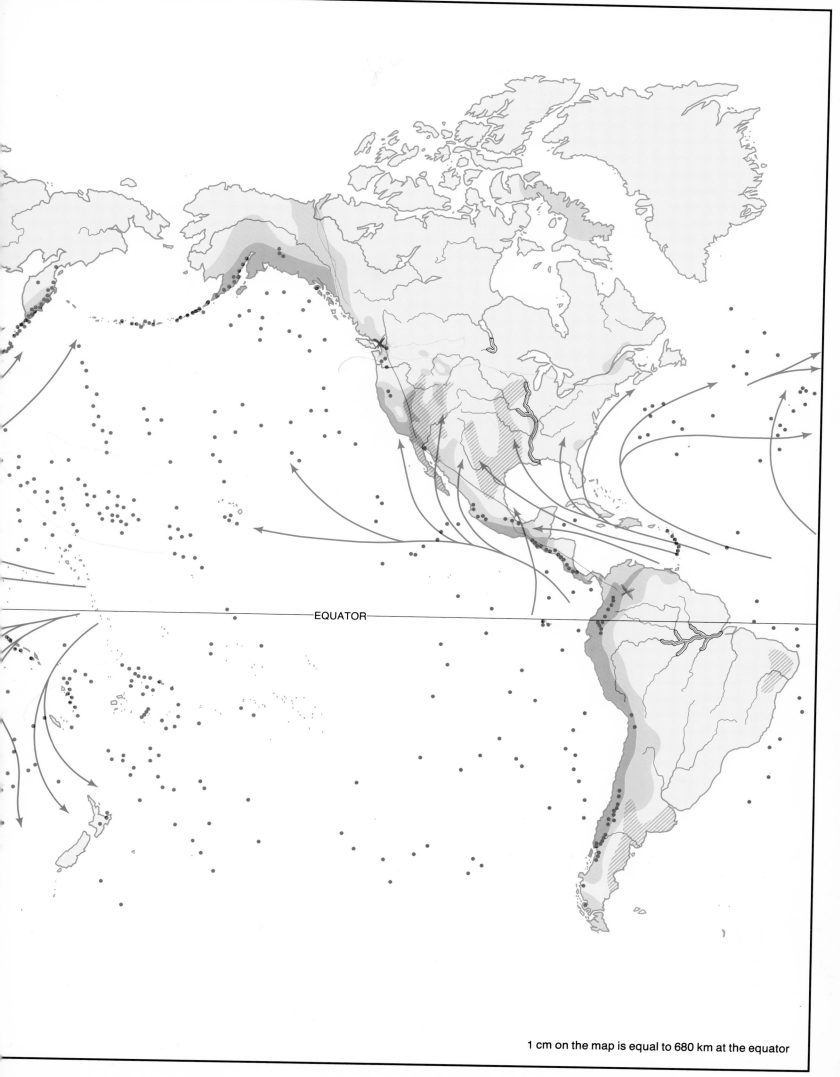

EQUATOR

1 cm on the map is equal to 680 km at the equator

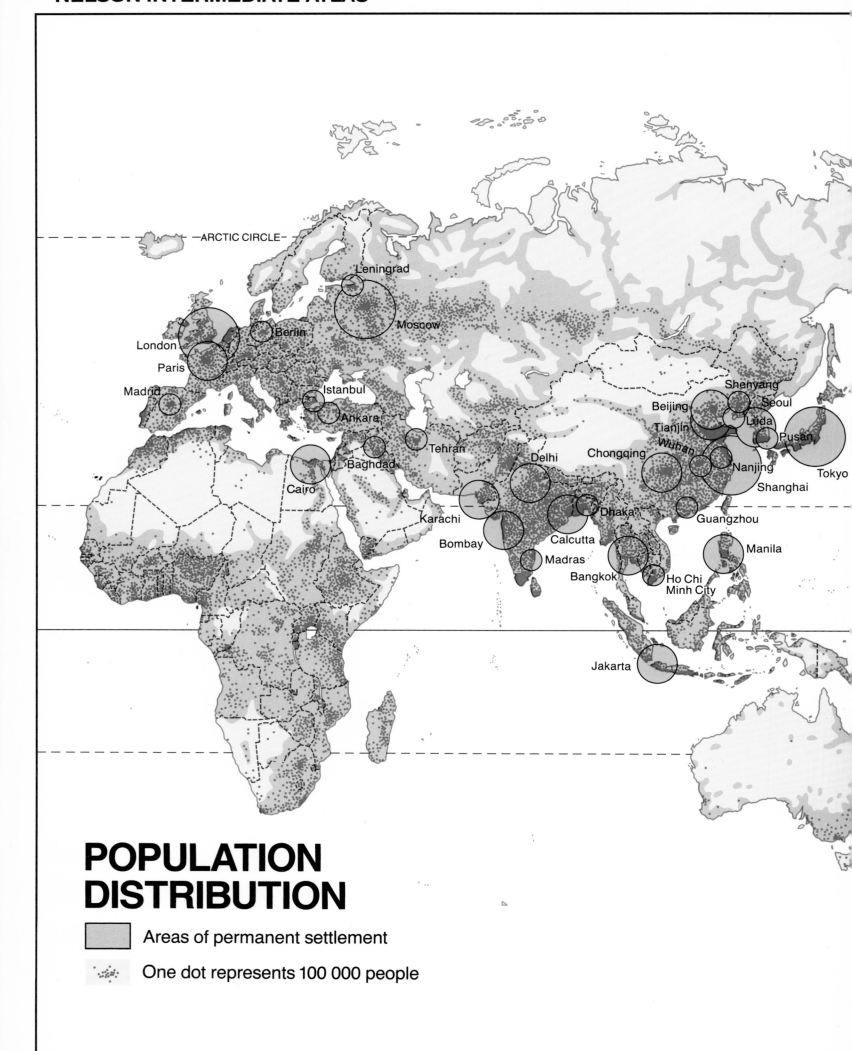

POPULATION DISTRIBUTION

Areas of permanent settlement

One dot represents 100 000 people

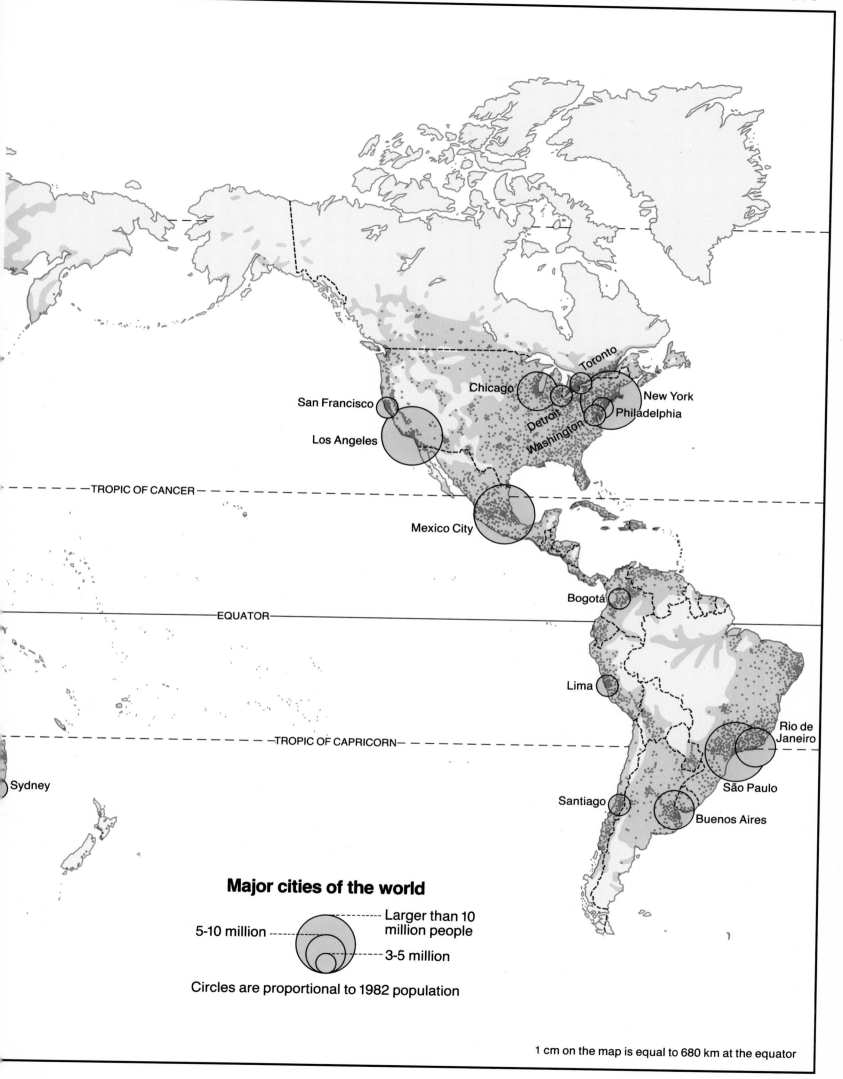

POPULATION DISTRIBUTION

Major cities of the world

5-10 million
Larger than 10 million people
3-5 million

Circles are proportional to 1982 population

1 cm on the map is equal to 680 km at the equator

81

ICELAND

GREENLAND SEA

PRIME MERIDIAN

0°

10°

30°

60°

40°

50°

50°

St. John's

SAINT-PIERRE AND MIQUELON (France)

NEWFOUNDLAND

Charlottetown P.E.I.

N.B.

Fredericton

NOVA SCOTIA

LABRADOR SEA

70°

KALAALLIT NUNAAT
(Denmark)

Nuuk

Québec

08°

QUÉBEC

ONTARIO

HUDSON BAY

NORTH POLE

Magnetic North Pole

ARCTIC CIRCLE

CANADA

NORTHWEST TERRITORIES

MANITOBA

Winnipeg

SASKATCHEWAN

Regina

ARCTIC

OCEAN

80°

Yellowknife

ALBERTA

Edmonton

MONT

BEAUFORT SEA

DATE LINE

YUKON TERRITORY

Whitehorse

BRITISH COLUMBIA

WASHINGTON

Olympia

Victoria

Sa

70°

ALASKA
(United States)

Juneau

N

U.S.S.R.

GULF OF ALASKA

170°

180°

60°

170°

160°

150°

50°

140°

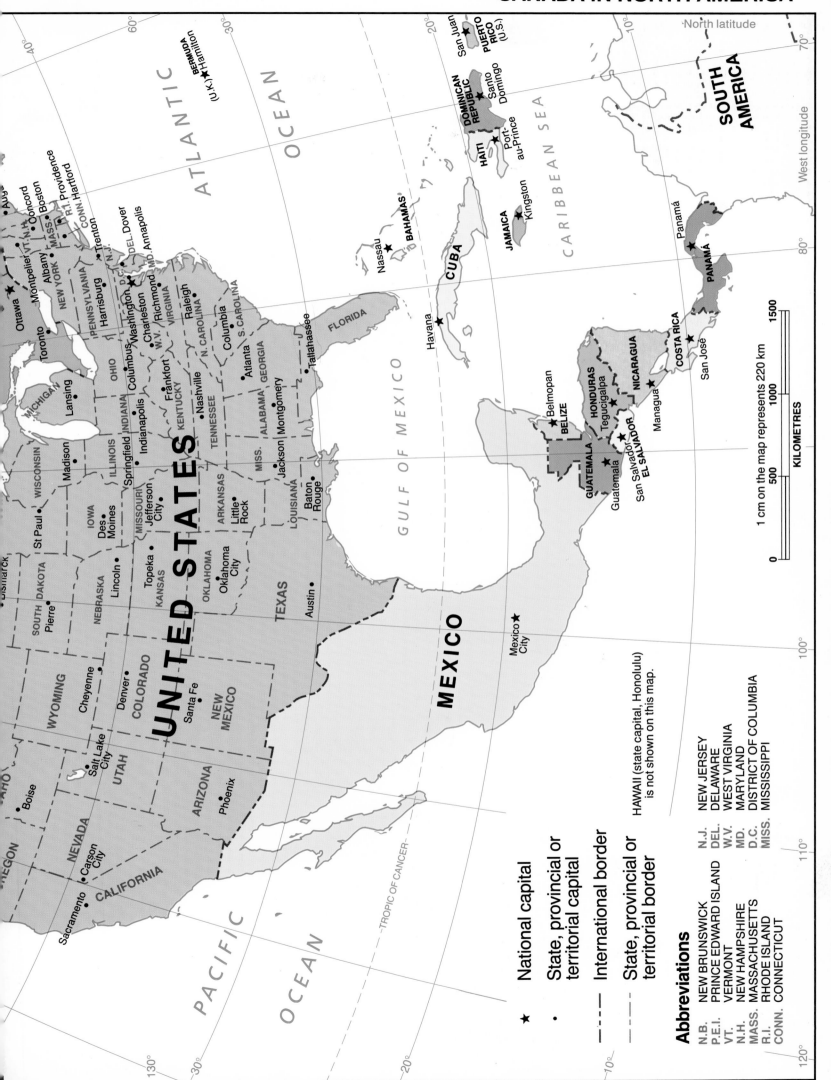

Abbreviations

N.B.	NEW BRUNSWICK	N.J.	NEW JERSEY
P.E.I.	PRINCE EDWARD ISLAND	DEL.	DELAWARE
VT.	VERMONT	W.V.	WEST VIRGINIA
N.H.	NEW HAMPSHIRE	MD.	MARYLAND
MASS.	MASSACHUSETTS	D.C.	DISTRICT OF COLUMBIA
R.I.	RHODE ISLAND	MISS.	MISSISSIPPI
CONN.	CONNECTICUT		

★ National capital

• State, provincial or territorial capital

— ⋅ — International border

— — — State, provincial or territorial border

HAWAII (state capital, Honolulu) is not shown on this map.

1 cm on the map represents 220 km

KILOMETRES

0   500   1000   1500

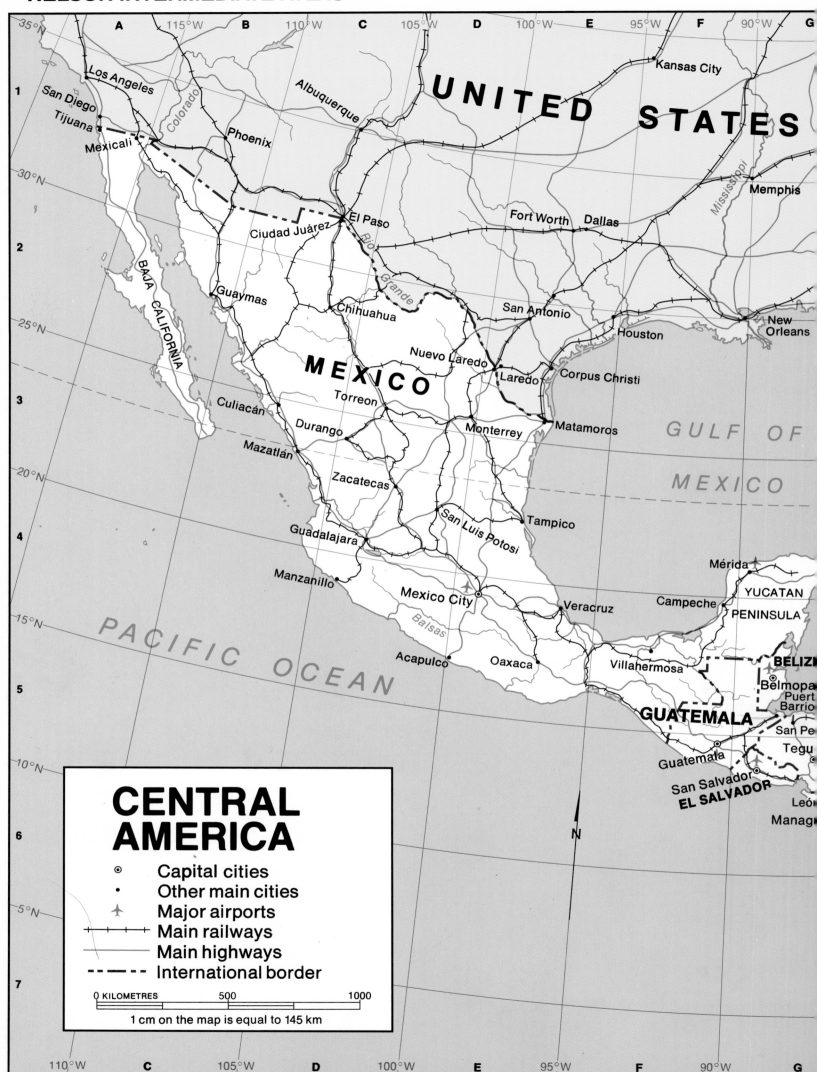

CENTRAL AMERICA

⊙ Capital cities
• Other main cities
✈ Major airports
┼┼┼ Main railways
── Main highways
▬ ▬ ▬ International border

0 KILOMETRES 500 1000

1 cm on the map is equal to 145 km

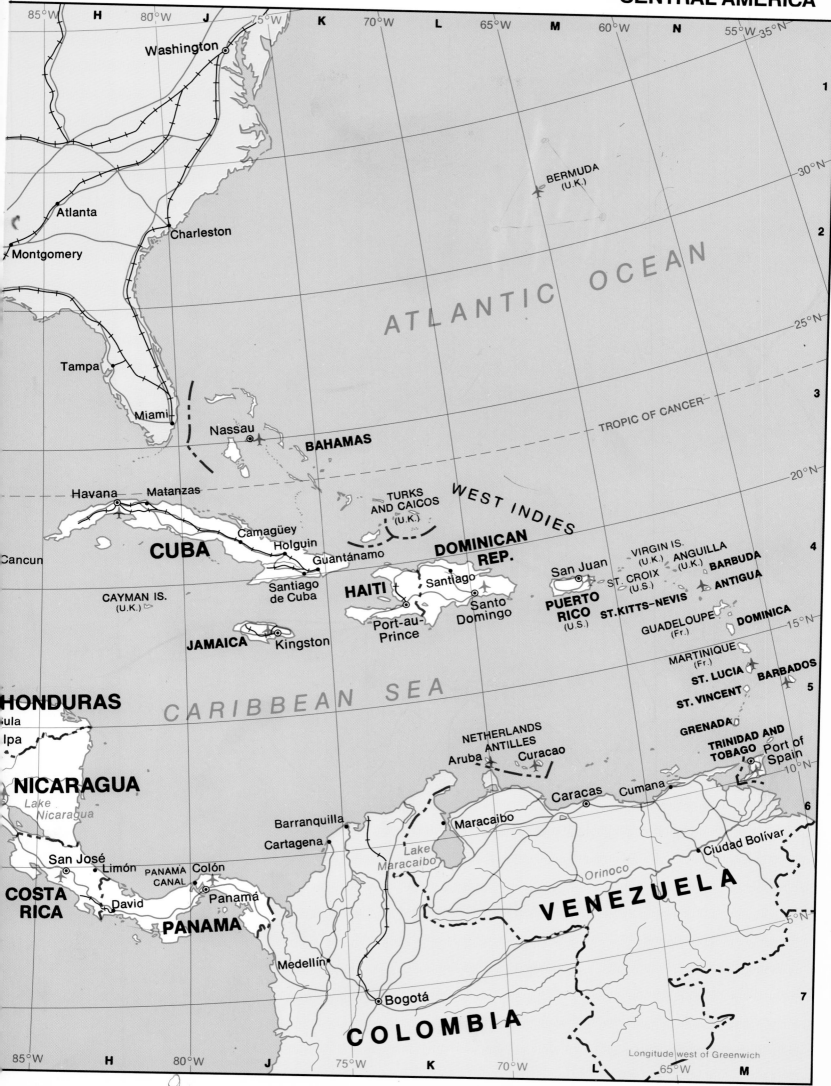

85

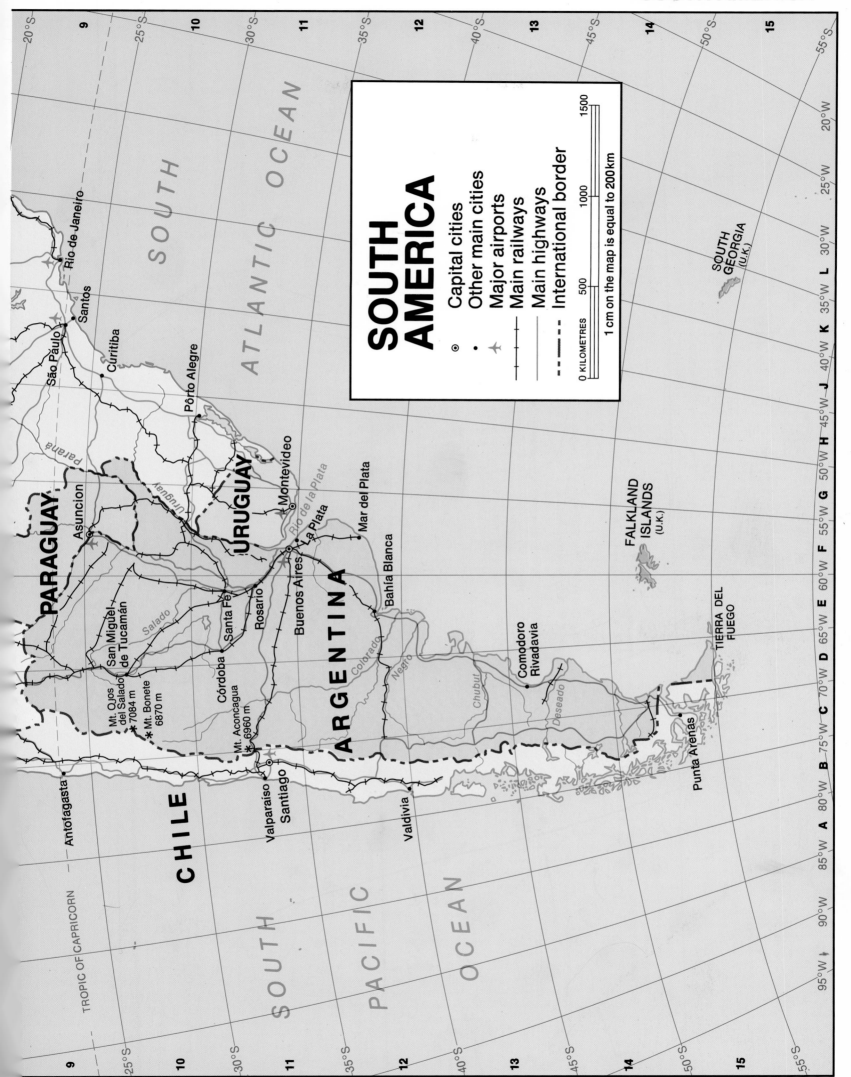

SOUTH AMERICA

- ◉ Capital cities
- • Other main cities
- ✈ Major airports
- ┼ Main railways
- ── Main highways
- ▬ ▬ International border

0 KILOMETRES   500   1000   1500

1 cm on the map is equal to 200km

SOUTH ATLANTIC OCEAN

SOUTH PACIFIC OCEAN

Rio de Janeiro

Santos

São Paulo

Curitiba

Pôrto Alegre

Paraná

Uruguay

PARAGUAY

Asuncion

URUGUAY

Montevideo

Río de la Plata

La Plata

Mar del Plata

Buenos Aires

Bahía Blanca

Salado

San Miguel de Tucamán

Santa Fe

Rosario

ARGENTINA

Córdoba

Mt. Ojos del Salado 7084 m

Mt. Bonete 6870 m

Mt. Aconcagua 6960 m

Colorado

Negro

Chubut

Deseado

Comodoro Rivadavia

FALKLAND ISLANDS (U.K.)

SOUTH GEORGIA (U.K.)

TIERRA DEL FUEGO

Punta Arenas

Antofagasta

CHILE

Valparaiso

Santiago

Valdivia

TROPIC OF CAPRICORN

20°S

25°S

30°S

35°S

40°S

45°S

50°S

55°S

95°W 90°W 85°W 80°W 75°W 70°W 65°W 60°W 55°W 50°W 45°W 40°W 35°W 30°W 25°W 20°W

A B C D E F G H J K L

9 10 11 12 13 14 15

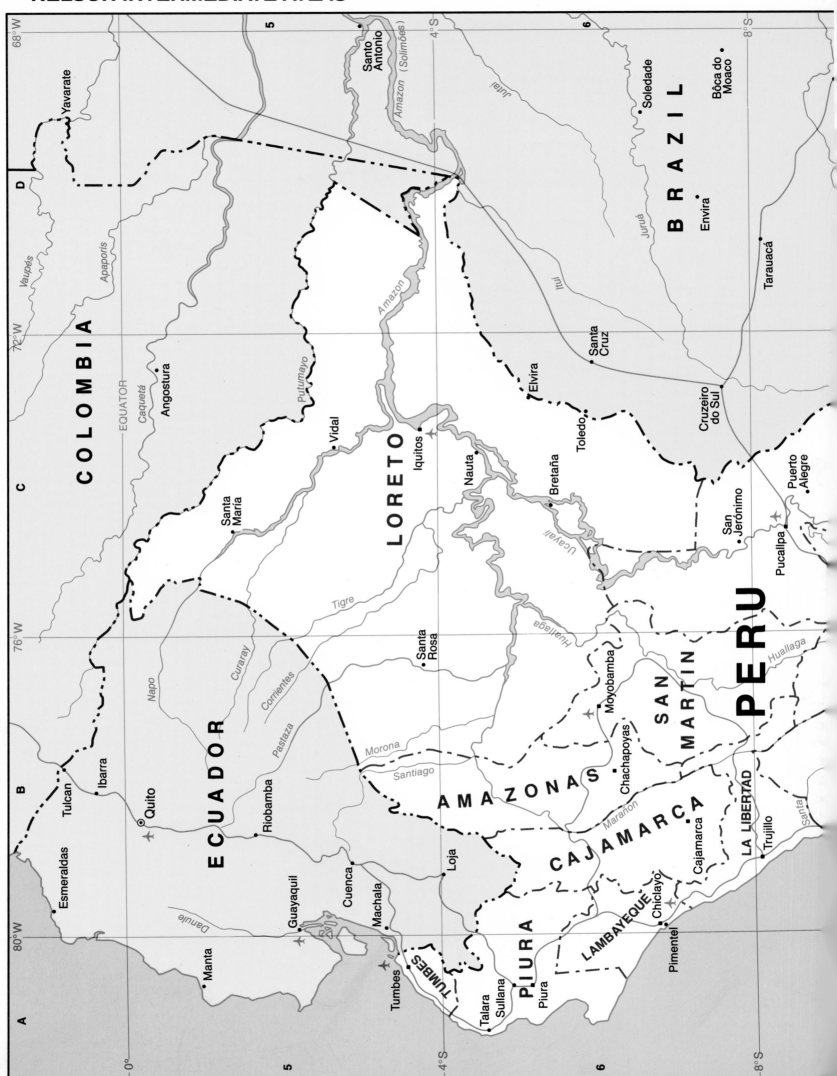

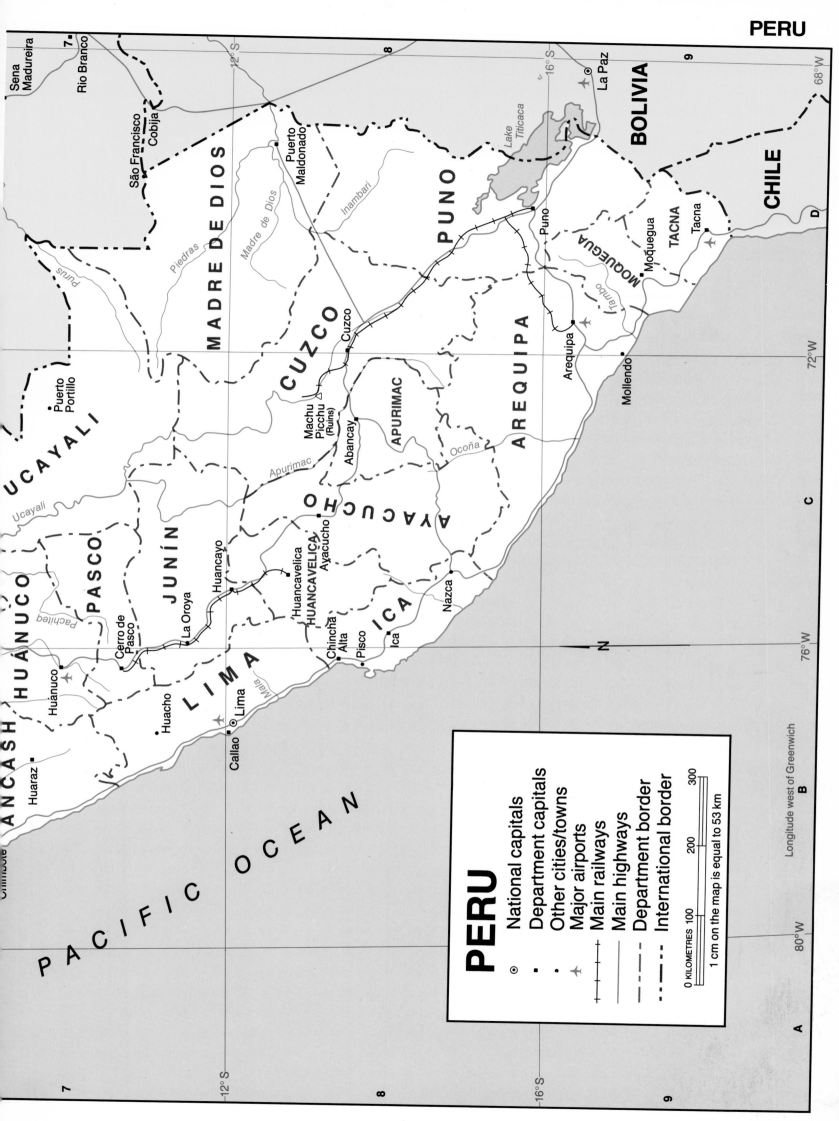

PERU

- National capitals
- Department capitals
- Other cities/towns
- Major airports
- Main railways
- Main highways
- Department border
- International border

0 KILOMETRES 100 200 300

1 cm on the map is equal to 53 km

PACIFIC OCEAN

BOLIVIA

CHILE

Lake Titicaca

La Paz

MADRE DE DIOS

PUNO

CUZCO

AREQUIPA

MOQUEGUA

TACNA

APURIMAC

AYACUCHO

UCAYALI

HUÁNUCO

PASCO

JUNÍN

HUANCAVELICA

LIMA

ICA

ANCASH

São Francisco
Cobija
Sena Madureira
Rio Branco

Puerto Maldonado

Puerto Portillo

Cuzco

Machu Picchu (Ruins)

Abancay

Puno

Moquegua

Tacna

Arequipa

Mollendo

Ayacucho

Huancavelica

Nazca

Ica

Pisco

Chincha Alta

Huancayo

La Oroya

Cerro de Pasco

Huánuco

Huaraz

Huacho

Callao

Lima

Chimbote

Inambari

Madre de Dios

Piedras

Purus

Ucayali

Pachitea

Apurímac

Ocoña

Tambo

Mala

Longitude west of Greenwich

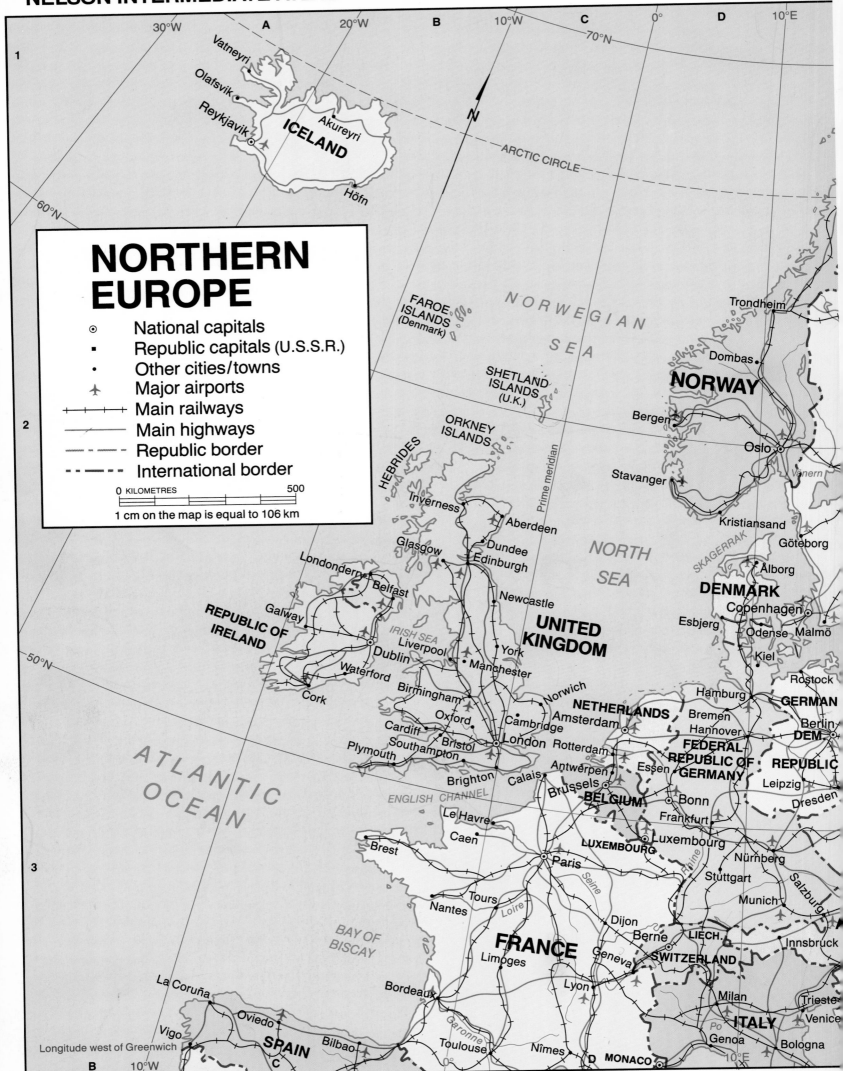

NORTHERN EUROPE

⊙ National capitals
▪ Republic capitals (U.S.S.R.)
• Other cities/towns
✈ Major airports
╫ Main railways
— Main highways
– · – Republic border
– ·· – International border

0 KILOMETRES 500

1 cm on the map is equal to 106 km

30°W   A   20°W   B   10°W   C   0°   D   10°E

70°N

1

Vatneyri
Olafsvik
Reykjavik ⊙
ICELAND
Akureyri
Höfn

ARCTIC CIRCLE

60°N

NORWEGIAN SEA

Trondheim
Dombas •
NORWAY
Bergen •

FAROE ISLANDS (Denmark)

2

SHETLAND ISLANDS (U.K.)

Oslo ⊙
Vänern
Stavanger •

ORKNEY ISLANDS

Kristiansand •
SKAGERRAK
Göteborg •
Ålborg •

HEBRIDES

NORTH SEA

DENMARK
Copenhagen ⊙
Esbjerg •
Odense • Malmö •
Kiel •

Prime meridian

Inverness •
Aberdeen •
Glasgow • Dundee •
Edinburgh ✈
Newcastle •

Rostock •
Hamburg •
GERMAN

Londonderry •
Belfast •
REPUBLIC OF IRELAND
Galway •
IRISH SEA
Liverpool •
York •
UNITED KINGDOM

Bremen •
Hannover •
Berlin
DEM.
REPUBLIC

50°N

Dublin ⊙
Waterford •
Cork •
Manchester •
Birmingham •
Norwich •
NETHERLANDS
Amsterdam ⊙
Essen •
FEDERAL REPUBLIC OF GERMANY
Leipzig •
Dresden •

Cardiff •
Oxford •
Cambridge •
Bristol •
Southampton •
London ⊙ ✈
Rotterdam •
Antwerpen •
Brussels ⊙
BELGIUM
Bonn •
Frankfurt •

Plymouth •
Brighton •
Calais •
ENGLISH CHANNEL
Le Havre •
LUXEMBOURG
Luxembourg ⊙
Rhine
Nürnberg •

ATLANTIC OCEAN

Caen •
Brest •
Paris ⊙
Seine
Stuttgart •
Munich •
Salzburg •

3

Tours •
Nantes •
Loire
Dijon •
Berne ⊙
LIECH.
Innsbruck •

BAY OF BISCAY

FRANCE
Limoges •
Geneva •
SWITZERLAND

La Coruña •
Oviedo •
Bordeaux •
Garonne
Lyon •
Milan •
Trieste •

Vigo •
Bilbao •
SPAIN
Toulouse •
Nîmes •
MONACO
Po
Genoa •
ITALY
Venice •
Bologna •

Longitude west of Greenwich

B   10°W   C   0°   D   10°E

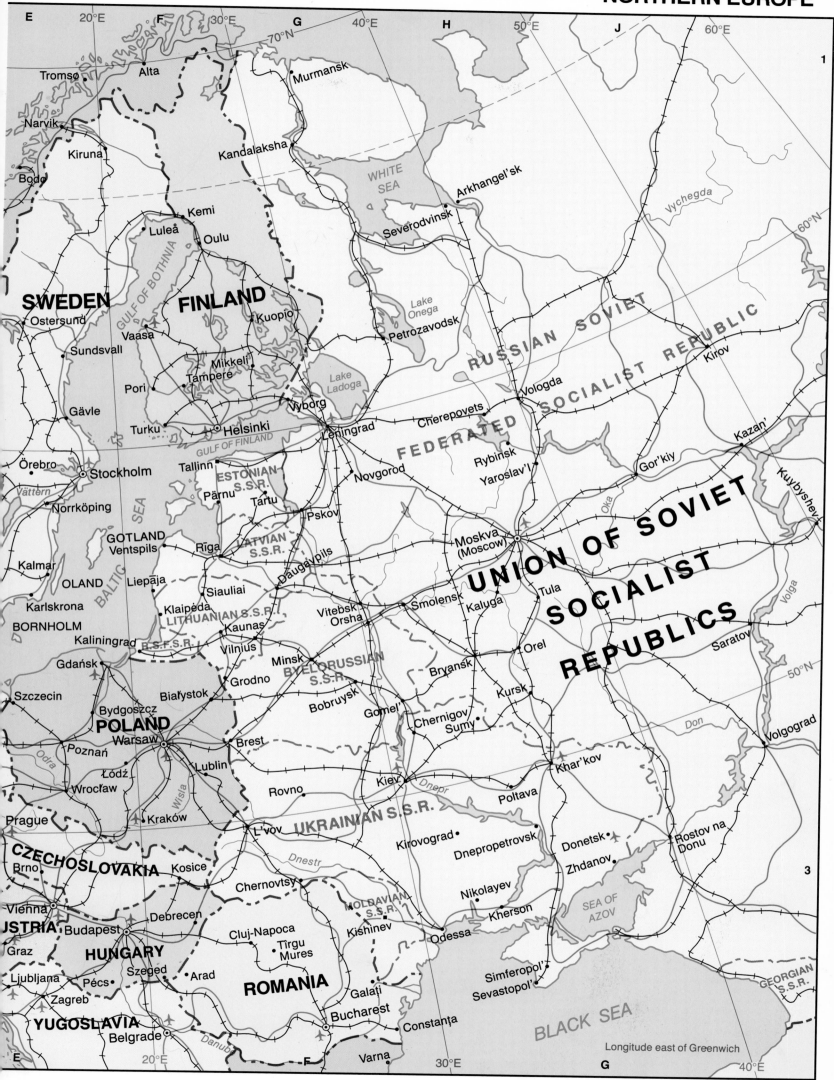

E   20°E   F   30°E   G   40°E   H   50°E   J   60°E

1

70°N

Tromsø
Alta
Narvik
Kiruna
Bodø
Murmansk
Kandalaksha
WHITE SEA
Arkhangel'sk
Severodvinsk
Vychegda
60°N

Kemi
Luleå
Oulu

SWEDEN
Östersund
Sundsvall
Gävle
Vaasa
FINLAND
Kuopio
Mikkeli
Tampere
Pori
Turku
Helsinki
GULF OF BOTHNIA
Lake Onega
Petrozavodsk
RUSSIAN SOVIET
SOCIALIST REPUBLIC
Kirov

Örebro
Stockholm
Norrköping
Vättern
GOTLAND
Ventspils
Kalmar
OLAND
Karlskrona
BORNHOLM
Kaliningrad
Gdańsk
Szczecin
Bydgoszcz
POLAND
Poznań
Warsaw
Łódź
Wrocław
Prague
Odra

Tallinn
ESTONIAN S.S.R.
Pärnu
Tartu
Pskov
Rīga
LATVIAN S.S.R.
Daugavpils
Siauliai
Klaipėda
LITHUANIAN S.S.R.
Kaunas
Vilnius
R.S.F.S.R.
Grodno
Białystok
Brest
Lublin
BALTIC SEA
GULF OF FINLAND
Vyborg
Leningrad
Novgorod

Lake Ladoga

Cherepovets
Vologda
FEDERATED

Rybinsk
Yaroslav'l
Moskva (Moscow)
UNION OF SOVIET
SOCIALIST
REPUBLICS
Gor'kiy
Kazan'
Kuybyshev
Oka
Volga

Vitebsk
Orsha
Minsk
BYELORUSSIAN S.S.R.
Bobruysk
Gomel'
Smolensk
Kaluga
Tula
Orel
Bryansk
Kursk
Chernigov
Sumy
Saratov
50°N

Kiev
Rovno
L'vov
UKRAINIAN S.S.R.
Dnepr
Poltava
Khar'kov
Volgograd
Don
Rostov na Donu

CZECHOSLOVAKIA
Brno
Vienna
AUSTRIA
Graz
Budapest
HUNGARY
Ljubljana
Pécs
Zagreb
YUGOSLAVIA
Belgrade
Košice
Chernovtsy
Debrecen
Szeged
Arad
Cluj-Napoca
Tîrgu Mures
ROMANIA
Galati
Bucharest
Danube
Varna
Dnestr
MOLDAVIAN S.S.R.
Kishinev
Kirovograd
Nikolayev
Odessa
Kherson
Dnepropetrovsk
Donetsk
Zhdanov
SEA OF AZOV
Simferopol'
Sevastopol'
BLACK SEA
GEORGIAN S.S.R.
3

Kraków

20°E   30°E   40°E

Longitude east of Greenwich

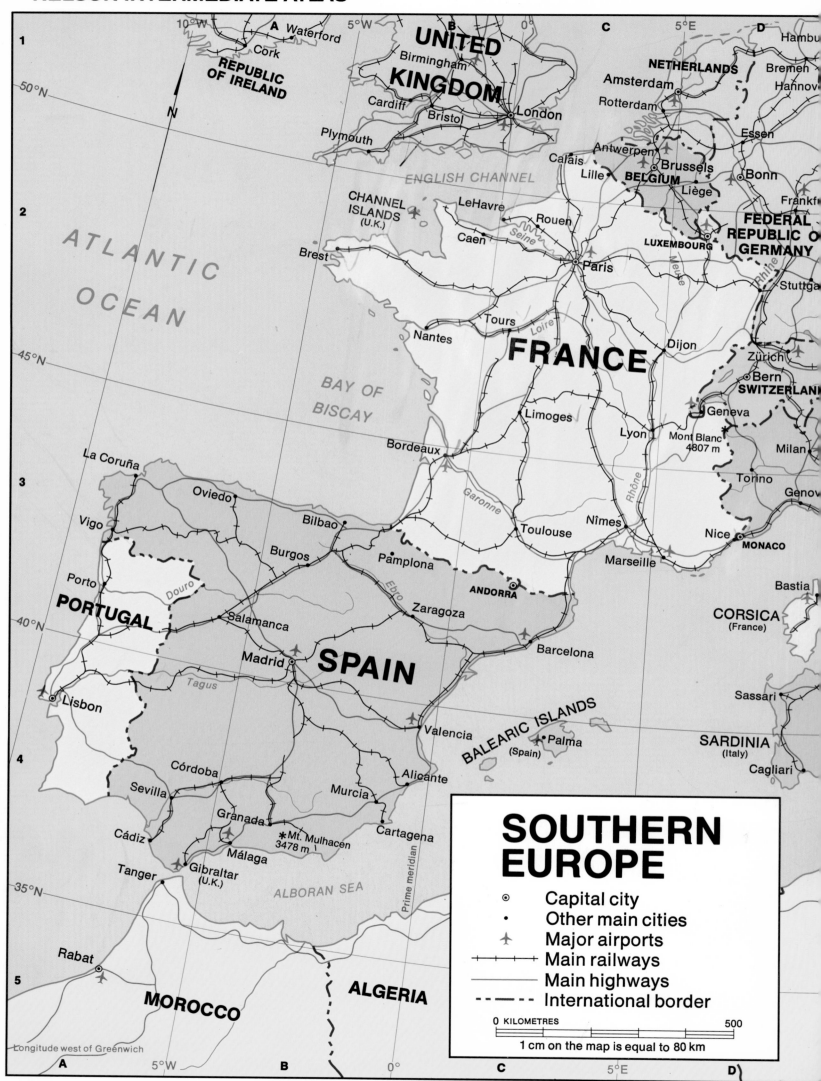

SOUTHERN EUROPE

- ⊙ Capital city
- • Other main cities
- ✈ Major airports
- ┼┼┼┼ Main railways
- ──── Main highways
- ─ ─ ─ International border

0 KILOMETRES 500

1 cm on the map is equal to 80 km

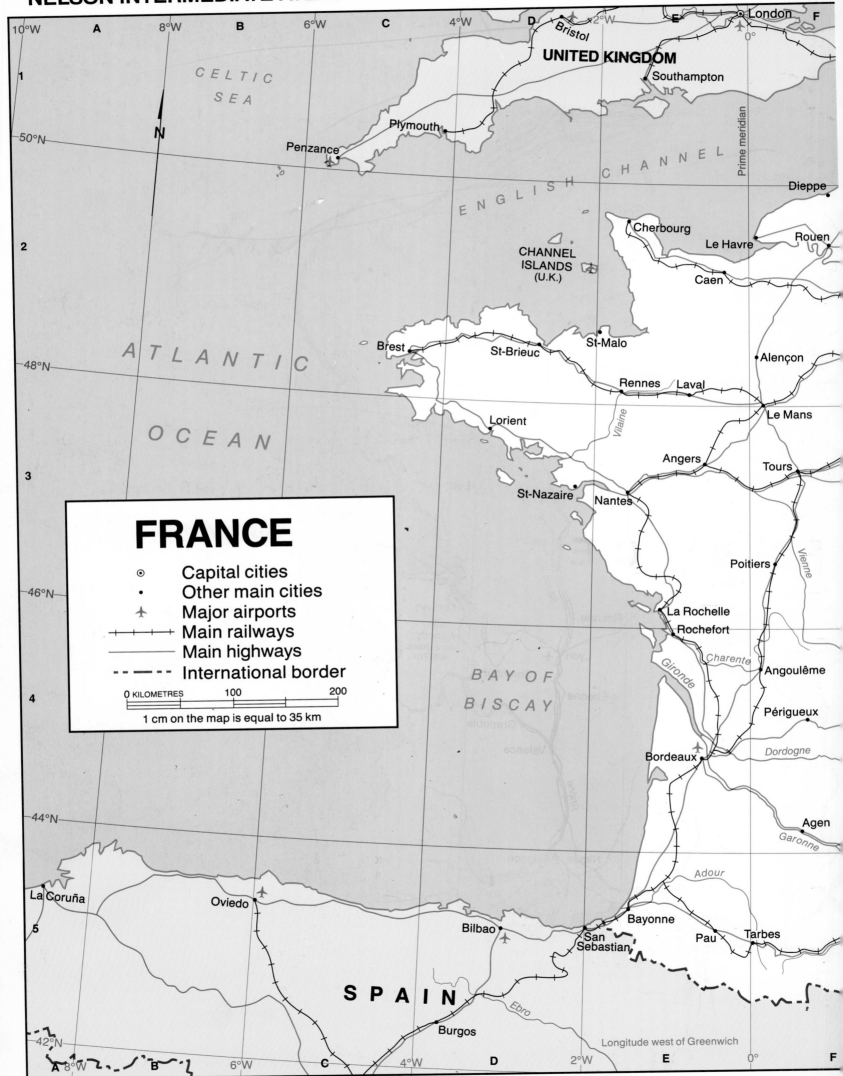

FRANCE

- ⊙ Capital cities
- • Other main cities
- ✈ Major airports
- ┼┼┼┼ Main railways
- —— Main highways
- - - - International border

0 KILOMETRES 100 200

1 cm on the map is equal to 35 km

GERMAN
DEMOCRATIC
REPUBLIC

BELGIUM

Dover
Calais
Oostende
Dunkerque
Boulogne
Lille
Lens
Arras
Douai
Amiens
Charleville-
Mézières
Brussels
Liège
Cologne
Bonn
Frankfurt

FEDERAL

REPUBLIC OF

GERMANY

LUXEMBOURG
Luxembourg
Metz
Nancy
Strasbourg
Nürnberg
Munich

Reims
Chalons
Paris
Chartres
Troyes
Épinal
Orléans
Auxerre
Mulhouse

Bourges
Nevers
Dijon
Besançon
Basle
Lac de
Neuchâtel
Berne

F R A N C E

Montluçon
Chalon
SWITZERLAND
Lac
Léman

Limoges
Clermont-
Ferrand
Roanne
Lyon
Chambéry
Geneva
Annecy
Mont Blanc
4807 m

St-Étienne
Grenoble
Valence
Turin
Po

Montauban
Nîmes
Avignon
Durance
Arles
Aix
MONACO
Nice
Monaco
Cannes
Genoa
GOLFO DI
GENOVA
Bologna

I T A L Y
Pisa

Toulouse
Montpellier
Béziers
Marseille
Toulon

Carcassonne
Narbonne
GOLFE DU
LION
M E D I T E R R A N E A N   S E A

ANDORRA Perpignan
Andorra

Longitude east of Greenwich

CORSICA
(France)
Ajaccio

CORSICA inset:
Rogliano
Calvi
Bastia
Corte
C O R S I C A
(France)
Ajaccio
Sartène
Bonifacio

0 KILOMETRES 25
1 cm on the map is equal to 9 km

Innsbruck
AUSTRIA
Verona

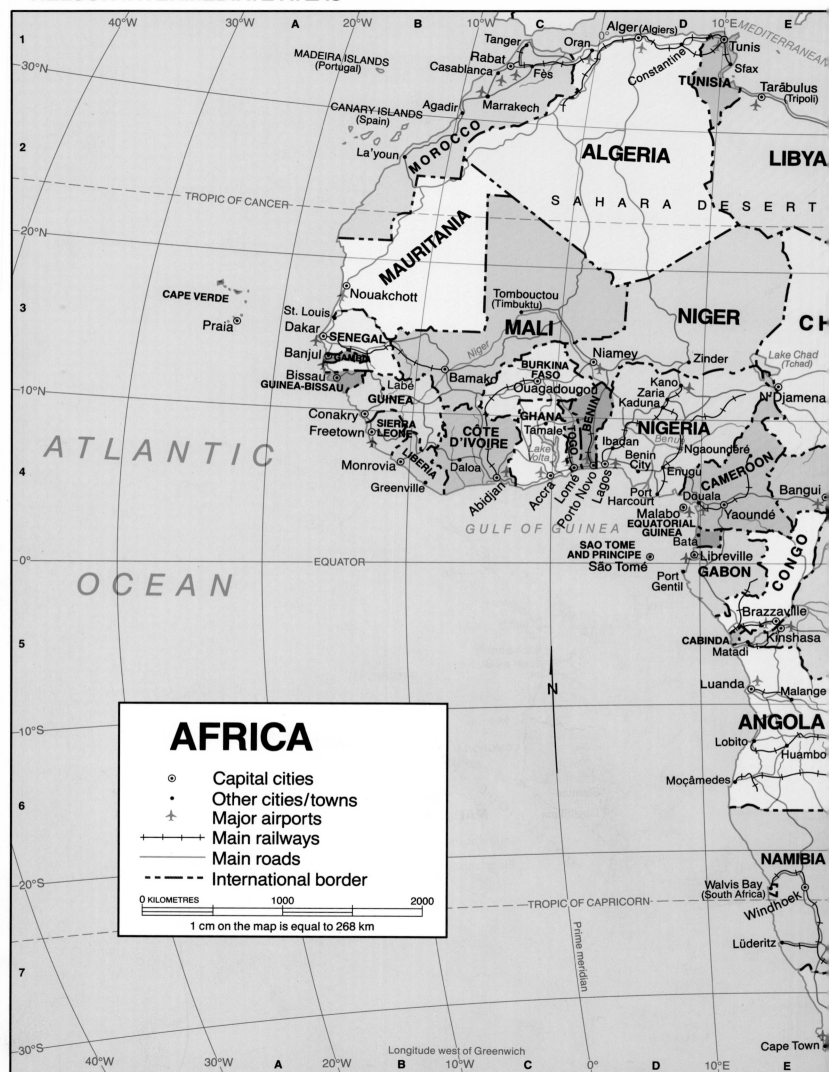

40°W   30°W   A   20°W   B   10°W   C   D   10°E   E

1

30°N

MADEIRA ISLANDS
(Portugal)

Tanger
Rabat
Casablanca
Fès
Oran
Alger (Algiers)
Tunis
Sfax

TUNISIA

Tarābulus
(Tripoli)

CANARY ISLANDS
(Spain)

Agadir
Marrakech

MOROCCO

ALGERIA

LIBYA

2

TROPIC OF CANCER

20°N

SAHARA DESERT

La'youn

MAURITANIA

CAPE VERDE

Nouakchott

Tombouctou
(Timbuktu)

NIGER

CH

3

Praia

St. Louis
Dakar
SENEGAL
Banjul GAMBIA
Bissau
GUINEA-BISSAU
Labé
GUINEA

Niger

MALI

Bamako

Niamey

Zinder

Lake Chad
(Tchad)

10°N

BURKINA
FASO

Ouagadougou

Kano
Zaria
Kaduna

N'Djamena

ATLANTIC

Conakry
Freetown
SIERRA
LEONE

CÔTE
D'IVOIRE

GHANA

Tamale

Lake
Volta

TOGO

BENIN

NIGERIA

Ibadan

Benin
City

Enugu

Ngaoundéré

CAMEROON

Bangui

4

Monrovia

LIBERIA

Daloa

Abidjan

Accra

Lomé
Porto Novo
Lagos

Port
Harcourt

Douala

Yaoundé

Greenville

Malabo
EQUATORIAL
GUINEA

Bata

CONGO

OCEAN

GULF OF GUINEA

SAO TOME
AND PRINCIPE
São Tomé

Libreville

0°   EQUATOR

Port
Gentil

GABON

N

Brazzaville

5

CABINDA

Kinshasa

Matadi

Luanda

Malange

10°S

ANGOLA

AFRICA

⊙ Capital cities
• Other cities/towns
✈ Major airports
╫╫ Main railways
── Main roads
╌ ╌ ╌ International border

Lobito

Huambo

6

Moçâmedes

0 KILOMETRES   1000   2000

1 cm on the map is equal to 268 km

NAMIBIA

20°S

Walvis Bay
(South Africa)

Windhoek

TROPIC OF CAPRICORN

Lüderitz

7

30°S

Cape Town

40°W   30°W   A   20°W   B   10°W   C   0°   D   10°E   E

Longitude west of Greenwich

Prime meridian

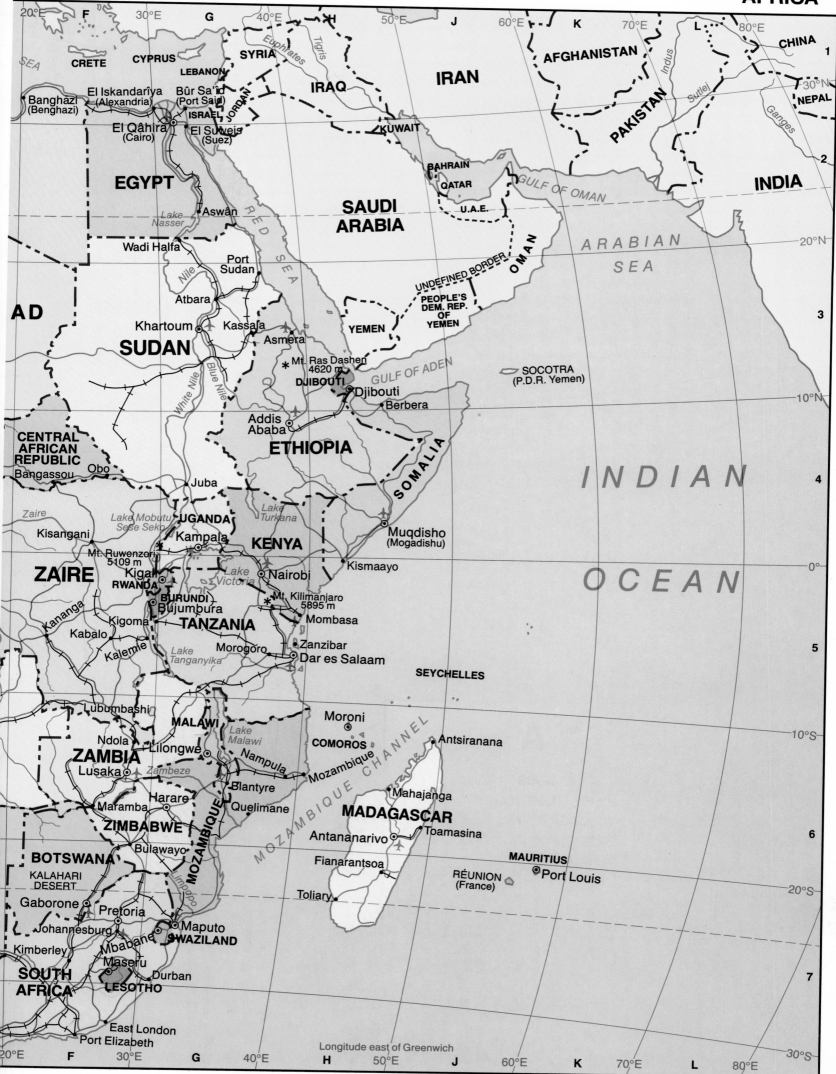

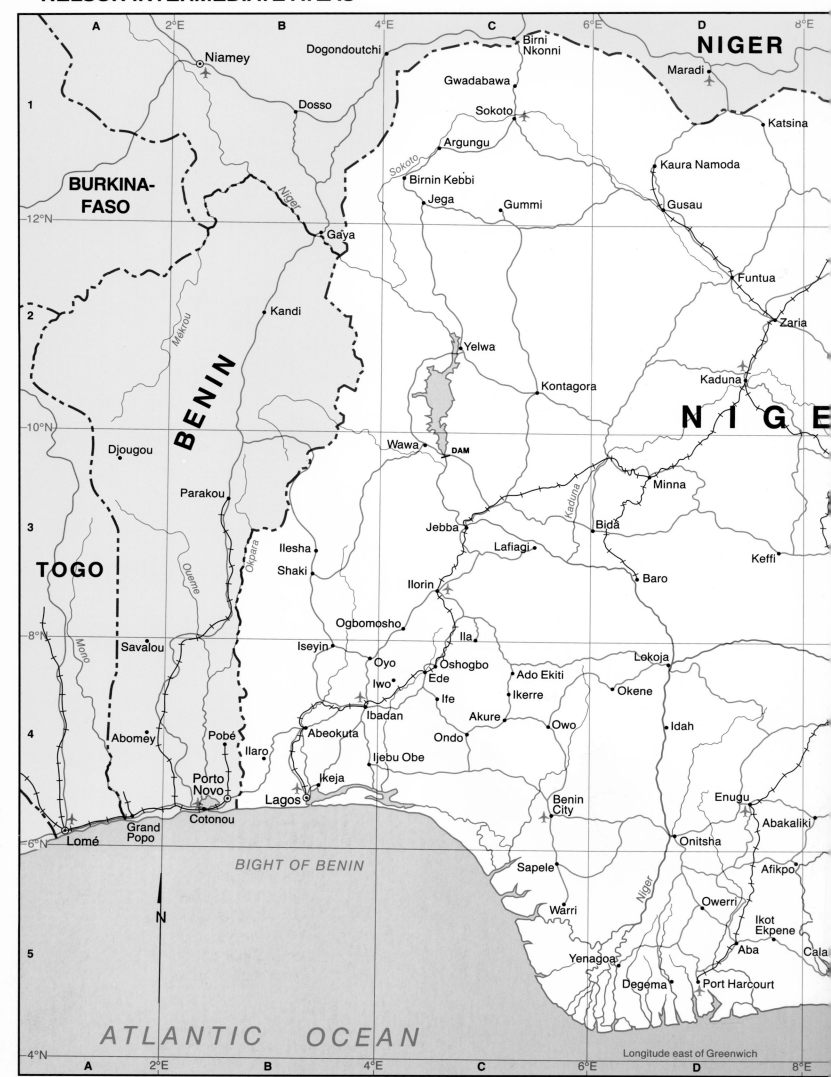

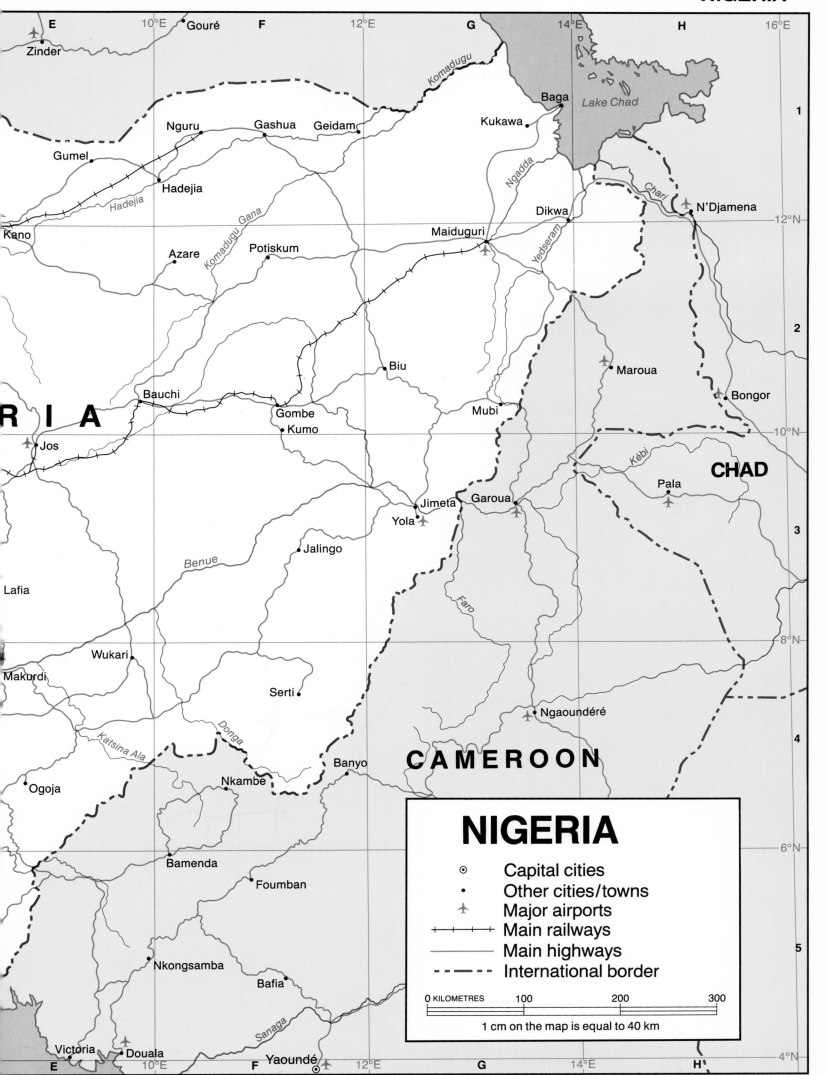

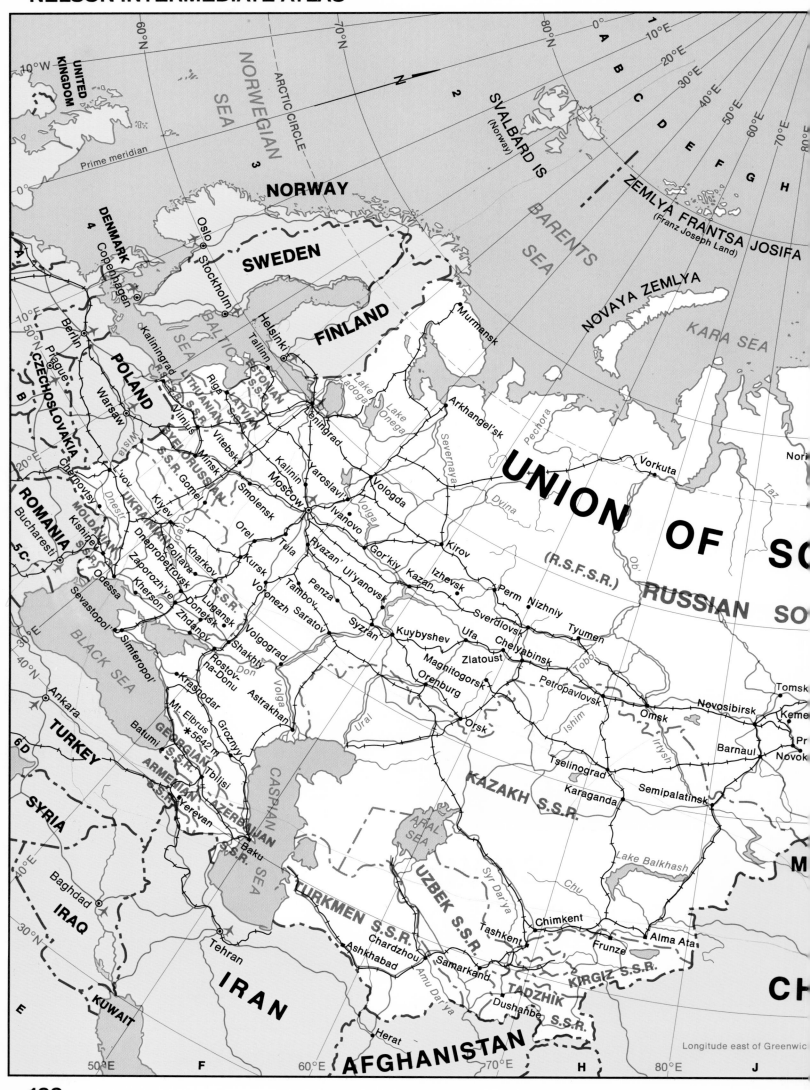

ARCTIC OCEAN

SEVERNAYA ZEMLYA (North Land)

NOVOSIBIRSKIYE OSTROVA (New Siberian Islands)

EAST SIBERIAN SEA

LAPTEV SEA

BERING SEA

ARCTIC CIRCLE

Omolon

Kolyma

Indigirka

Yana

Olenek

Kotuy

Lena

Magadan

Petropavlovsk -Kamchatskiy

SEA OF OKHOTSK

Yakutsk

Aldan

KURIL ISLANDS

SAKHALIN

Vitim

Nikolayevsk -na-Amure

Komsomol'sk

Yuzhno -Sakhalinsk

Lena

Amur

Yenisey

Krasnoyarsk

Bratsk

Lake Baykal

Khabarovsk

Blagoveshchensk

Chita

JAPAN

Sapporo

Ulan Ude

Irkutsk

Vladivostok

Niigata

Sendai

SOVIET SOCIALIST REPUBLICS

VIET FEDERATED SOCIALIST REPUBLIC

NGOLIA

NA

SOVIET UNION

◎	National capitals	+—+—+	Main railways
■	Republic capitals	——	Main highways and roads
•	Other cities/towns	—·—·—	Republic border
✈	Major airports	———	International border

KILOMETRES

0   500   1000   1500   2000

1 cm on the map is equal to 210 km

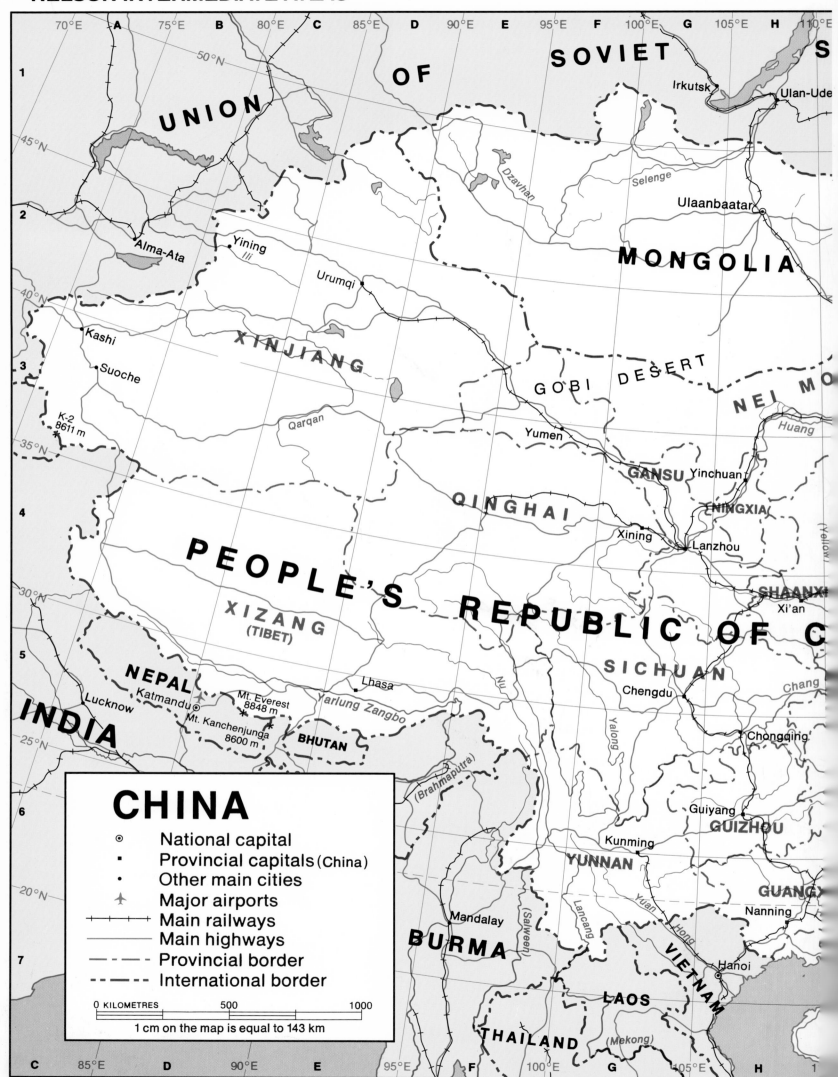

UNION OF SOVIET S

70°E A 75°E B 80°E C 85°E D 90°E E 95°E F 100°E G 105°E H 110°E

50°N
1

45°N

Irkutsk
Ulan-Ude

2
Alma-Ata
Yining
Ili

Dzavhan
Selenge

Ulaanbaatar

MONGOLIA

40°N
Urumqi

Kashi
XINJIANG

3
Suoche

GOBI DESERT

NEI MO

K-2
8611 m
Qarqan
Yumen
Huang

35°N
GANSU Yinchuan

QINGHAI
NINGXIA

4
Xining
Lanzhou

(Yellow)

30°N
PEOPLE'S REPUBLIC OF C

SHAANXI
Xi'an

XIZANG
(TIBET)

SICHUAN
Chang

5
NEPAL
Lhasa
Chengdu

Lucknow
Katmandu
Mt. Everest
8848 m
Yarlung Zangbo
Nu
Yalong

INDIA
Mt. Kanchenjunga
8600 m
BHUTAN

25°N
Chongqing

(Brahmaputra)

6
Guiyang
GUIZHOU

Kunming
YUNNAN

20°N
GUANG

Nanning

(Salween)
Mandalay
Lancang
Yuan
Hong

BURMA
VIETNAM

7
Hanoi

LAOS

THAILAND
(Mekong)

C 85°E D 90°E E 95°E F 100°E G 105°E H

CHINA

⊙ National capital
▪ Provincial capitals (China)
• Other main cities
✈ Major airports
�┼╼╼╼ Main railways
──── Main highways
─·─·─ Provincial border
─ ─ ─ International border

0 KILOMETRES   500   1000

1 cm on the map is equal to 143 km

J 115°E K 120°E L 125°E M 130°E N 135°E O 140°E P 145°E Q 150°E

OCIALIST

R E P U B L I C S

(Amur)

Heilong Jiang

50°N

1

SEA OF
OKHOTSK

45°N

SAKHALIN

Khabarovsk

HEILONGJIANG

Herlen

Qiqihar

Songhua

Harbin

HOKKAIDO

2

Sapporo

40°N

Changchun

JILIN

Jilin

Vladivostok

Shenyang

HONSHU

3

**DEMOCRATIC PEOPLE'S
REPUBLIC OF KOREA
(NORTH KOREA)**

Sendai

JAPAN

·Fushun

NGGOL

Jinzhou

·Anshan

LIAONING

Dandong

Niigata

35°N

Iohhot

Zhangjiakou

**BEIJING
SHI**

Tangshan

Lüda

P'yongyang

SEA OF JAPAN

Kanazawa

Tokyo

Beijing

Tianjin

**TIANJIN
SHI**

Soul
(Seoul)

Yokohama

Inch'on

Nagoya

aiyuan

Shijiazhuang

HEBEI

**REPUBLIC
OF KOREA
(SOUTH KOREA)**

Kyoto

Osaka

4

SHANXI

Jinan

SHANDONG

Qingdao

Pusan

Hiroshima

SHIKOKU

Zhengzhou

Da Yunhe

Xuzhou

YELLOW
SEA

Kitakyushu

Fukuoka

30°N

HENAN

Bengbu

JIANGSU

Nagasaki

KYUSHU

5

HINA

Nanjing

Heifei

Wuxi

Suzhou

Shanghai

**SHANGHAI
SHI**

HUBEI

Wuhan

ANHUI

Hangzhou

(Yangtze)

·Ningbo

25°N

ang

ZHEJIANG

Nanchang

Wenzhou

RYUKYU ISLANDS

hangsha

UNAN

JIANGXI

OKINAWA-JIMA
(Japan)

Hengyang

FUJIAN

Naha

6

Xiang

Fuzhou

TROPIC OF CANCER

Taipei

P A C I F I C   O C E A N

Xiamen

TAIWAN

20°N

GUANGDONG

T'ainan

Guangzhou

·Shantou

Kaohsiung

T'AIWAN

hui

P

HONG KONG

MACAU
(Portugal)

(U.K.)

7

Zhanjiang

aikou

SOUTH CHINA SEA

Longitude east of Greenwich

HAINANDAO

PHILIPPINES

LUZON

J 115°E K 120°E L 125°E M 130°E N 135°E O

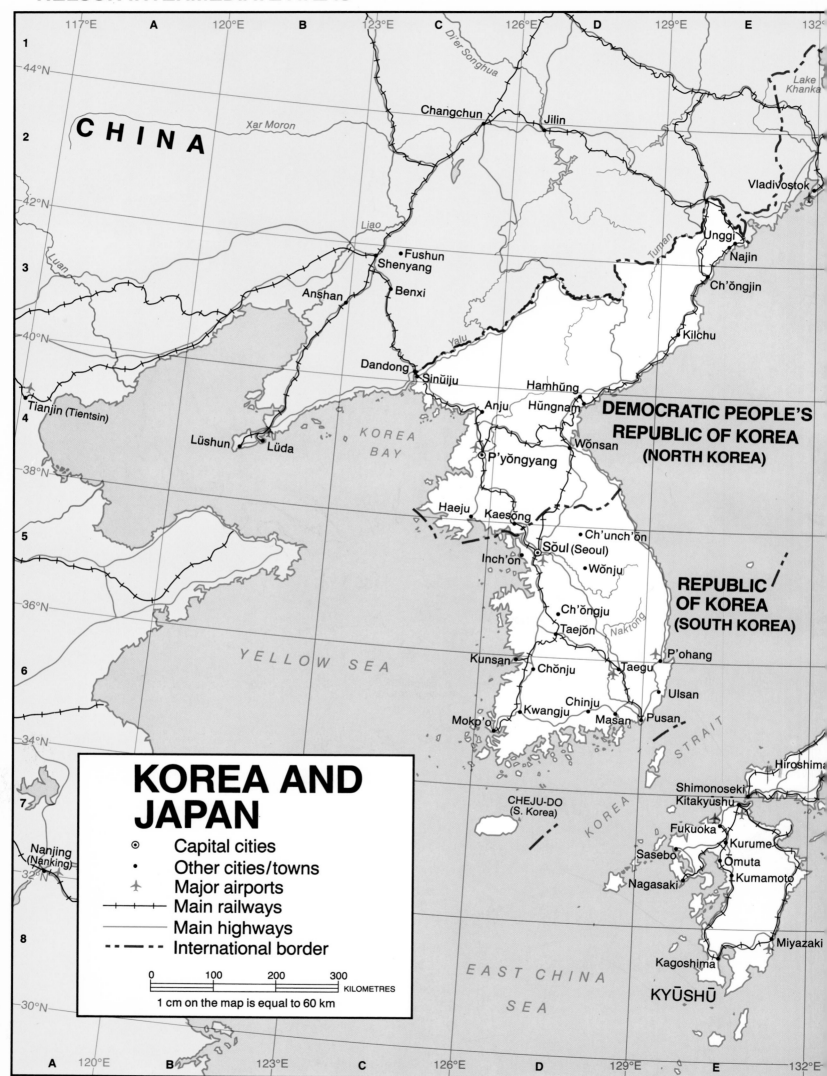

KOREA AND JAPAN

⊙ Capital cities

• Other cities/towns

✈ Major airports

├─┼─┼─┤ Main railways

──── Main highways

– · – · – International border

```
0      100    200    300
                           KILOMETRES
```
1 cm on the map is equal to 60 km

CHINA

Xar Moron

Di'er Songhua

Changchun

Jilin

Luan

Liao

Lake Khanka

Vladivostok

•Fushun
Shenyang

Anshan

•Benxi

Tuman

Unggi

•Najin

Ch'ŏngjin

Yalu

•Kilchu

Dandong

Sinŭiju

Hamhŭng

Tianjin (Tientsin)

Anju

Hŭngnam

**DEMOCRATIC PEOPLE'S
REPUBLIC OF KOREA
(NORTH KOREA)**

Lüshun

Lüda

KOREA
BAY

Wŏnsan

P'yŏngyang

Haeju

Kaesŏng

•Ch'unch'ŏn

Sŏul (Seoul)

Inch'ŏn

•Wŏnju

**REPUBLIC
OF KOREA
(SOUTH KOREA)**

Naktong

YELLOW SEA

•Ch'ŏngju

Taejŏn

Kunsan

•Chŏnju

✈ P'ohang

Taegu

•Chinju

•Ulsan

Kwangju

Masan

Pusan

Mokp'o

KOREA
STRAIT

CHEJU-DO
(S. Korea)

Hiroshima

Shimonoseki
Kitakyūshū

Fukuoka

•Kurume

Sasebo

•Ōmuta

•Kumamoto

Nagasaki

Nanjing
(Nanking)

EAST CHINA
SEA

Miyazaki

KYŪSHŪ

Kagoshima

BULGARIA

BLACK SEA

Istanbul

Ankara

Izmir

Kayseri

TURKEY

Adana

Nicosia

CYPRUS

MEDITERRANEAN SEA

LEBANON
Beirut

Aleppo

SYRIA

Damascus

ISRAEL
Jerusalem

Amman

JORDAN

Cairo

SUEZ CANAL

EGYPT

Nile

Aswan

Medina

Jiddah • Mecca

Port Sudan

SUDAN

Asmera

RED SEA

DJIBOUTI

Djibouti

ETHIOPIA

Addis Ababa

Astrakhan

Tbilisi

Yerevan

Baku

CASPIAN SEA

ARAL SEA

SOVIET UNI

Amu Darya

Krasnovodsk

Ashkhabad

Tabriz

Mashad

Euphrates

Tigris

Mosul

Baghdad

IRAQ

Al Basrah

KUWAIT

Kuwait

Tehran

Esfahan

Abadan

IRAN

Shiraz

Kerman

Herat

AFGHAN

Kandahar

SAUDI

ARABIA

Riyadh

Dhahran

BAHRAIN

Doha

QATAR

Abu Dhabi

PERSIAN GULF

UNITED ARAB EMIRATES

Muscat

GULF OF OMAN

Kara

TROPIC OF CANCER

OMAN

UNDEFINED BORDER

YEMEN

Sana

PEOPLE'S DEMOCRATIC REPUBLIC OF YEMEN

Aden

ARABIAN

N

GULF OF ADEN

SOCOTRA
(P.D.R. Yemen)

INDIAN O

SOMALIA

Longitude east of Greenwich

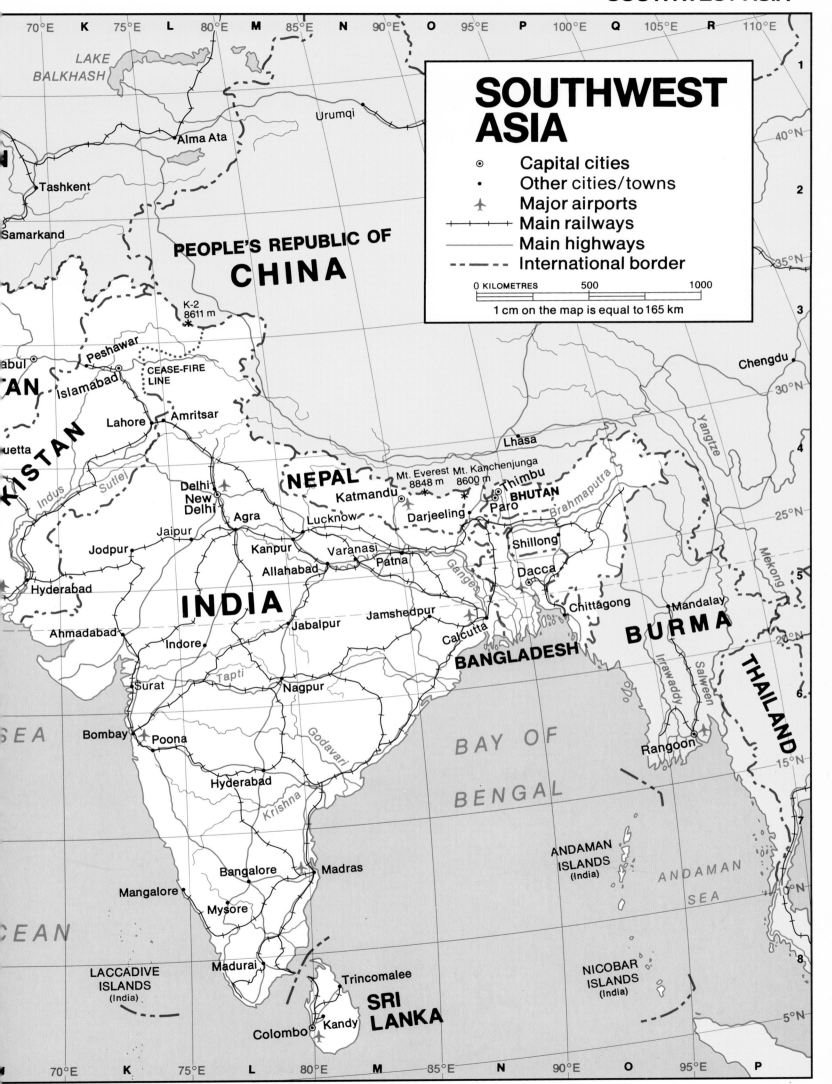

SOUTHWEST ASIA

- ⊙ Capital cities
- • Other cities/towns
- ✈ Major airports
- ┼┼┼ Main railways
- ─── Main highways
- ─ ∙ ─ International border

0 KILOMETRES   500   1000

1 cm on the map is equal to 165 km

LAKE BALKHASH

Urumqi

•Alma Ata

•Tashkent

Samarkand

PEOPLE'S REPUBLIC OF
CHINA

K-2
8611 m
✱

Chengdu

abul⊙
•Peshawar
CEASE-FIRE
LINE

Islamabad

•Quetta

Lahore• •Amritsar

Indus   *Sutlej*

Delhi✈
New
Delhi

Agra•

•Jaipur

•Jodpur

•Hyderabad

INDIA

Kanpur•

Lucknow•

NEPAL

Katmandu✈

Mt. Everest Mt. Kanchenjunga
8848 m   8600 m
✱   ✱

Darjeeling•

Lhasa•

Thimbu⊙
BHUTAN
Paro

Brahmaputra

Varanasi•
Allahabad• Patna•

Shillong•

Dacca⊙

Chittagong•

Ganges

•Mandalay

BURMA

Yangtze

Mekong

Jamshedpur•

Calcutta⊙

BANGLADESH

Irrawaddy   *Salween*

THAILAND

•Ahmadabad

•Indore

Tapti

•Nagpur

Jabalpur•

Surat•

Bombay✈
•Poona

•Hyderabad

Godavari

Krishna

**BAY OF
BENGAL**

Rangoon✈

Mangalore•

•Bangalore
•Madras

Mysore•

ANDAMAN
ISLANDS
(India)

*ANDAMAN
SEA*

Madurai•

LACCADIVE
ISLANDS
(India)

OCEAN

SEA

Trincomalee•

Colombo⊙ •Kandy
✈

**SRI
LANKA**

NICOBAR
ISLANDS
(India)

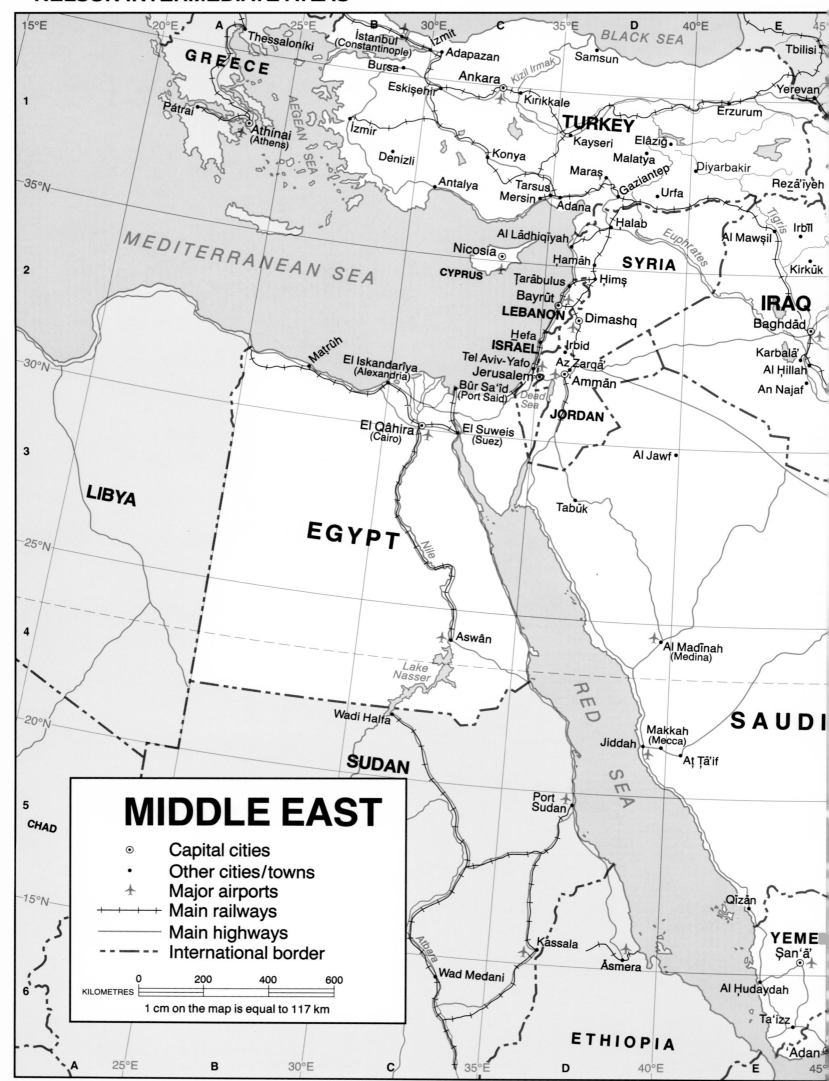

MIDDLE EAST

⊙	Capital cities
•	Other cities/towns
✈	Major airports
┼┼┼┼	Main railways
——	Main highways
–·–·–	International border

KILOMETRES

0   200   400   600

1 cm on the map is equal to 117 km

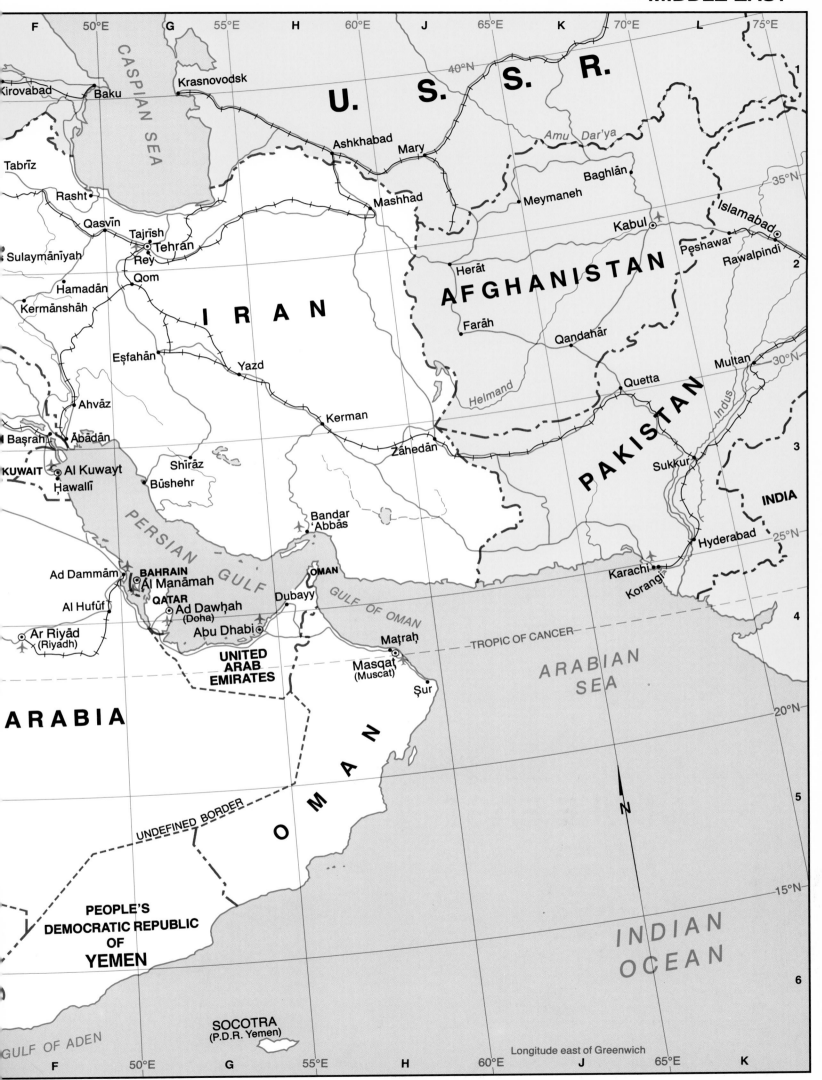

F 50°E G 55°E H 60°E J 65°E K 70°E L 75°E

Kirovabad • Baku • Krasnovodsk

CASPIAN SEA

U. S. S. R.

40°N

Amu Dar'ya

Ashkhabad Mary

35°N

Tabrīz

Rasht •

Mashhad

Baghlān

Qasvīn Tajrīsh

Meymaneh

Kabul ⊙

Islamabad ⊙

Sulaymānīyah

Tehrān

Rey

Peshawar

Rawalpindi

2

Hamadān

Qom

I R A N

Herāt

A F G H A N I S T A N

Kermānshāh

Esfahān

Yazd

Farāh

Qandahār

Multan

30°N

Ahvāz

Kerman

Helmand

Quetta

Indus

Basrah • Ābādān

Zāhedān

P A K I S T A N

3

KUWAIT ⊙ Al Kuwayt

Shīrāz

Sukkur

INDIA

Hawallī

Būshehr

Bandar 'Abbās

Korangi

Hyderabad

25°N

Ad Dammām

BAHRAIN

OMAN

Karachi

Al Manāmah

Korangi

Al Hufūf

QATAR

Dubayy

GULF OF OMAN

4

Ar Riyād (Riyadh)

Ad Dawḥah (Doha)

Abu Dhabi

Matraḥ

TROPIC OF CANCER

ARABIAN SEA

UNITED ARAB EMIRATES

Masqaṭ (Muscat)

Şur

A R A B I A

20°N

O M A N

N

5

UNDEFINED BORDER

15°N

PEOPLE'S DEMOCRATIC REPUBLIC OF YEMEN

INDIAN OCEAN

6

GULF OF ADEN

SOCOTRA (P.D.R. Yemen)

Longitude east of Greenwich

F 50°E G 55°E H 60°E J 65°E K

INDIA

Myitkyina

PEOPLE'S REPUBLIC OF
CHINA

Taipei

TAIWAN

Mandalay

Kunming

Kengtung

Lao Cai

Guangzhou

Kaohsiung

BURMA

Sittwe

Hanoi

Haiphong

Zhanjiang

HONG KONG
(U.K.)

LUZON STRAIT

20°N

Luang
Prabang

Chiang
Mai

Vientiane

LAOS

HAINAN

Aparri

Rangoon

Moulmein

THAILAND

Ubon
Ratchathani

Hue

Da Nang

LUZON

2

Red

Hong

Black Da

Salween

Mekong

Krung Thep
(Bangkok)

VIETNAM

SOUTH

Manila

MINDORO

ANDAMAN
ISLANDS
(India)

Mergui

KAMPUCHEA

CHINA

PANAY

ANDAMAN

Phnom
Penh

Nha Trang

SEA

Iloilo

Cel

10°N

SEA

GULF OF
THAILAND

Ho Chi Minh City
(Saigon)

PALAWAN

NEGROS

NICOBAR
ISLANDS
(India)

Surat Thani

SULU
SEA

Zamboanga

3

Banda Aceh

Pinang

Kota Baharu

MALAYSIA

BRUNEI
Bandar Seri
Begawan

Sandakan

CELEBES

Medan

MALAYA

Kuala
Lumpur

SARAWAK

SEA

STRAIT OF MALACCA

SINGAPORE

Paloh

Kuching

Manad

0°

EQUATOR

Pontianak

Kapuas

BORNEO

MAKASSAR STRAIT

Padang

SUMATRA

Samarinda

BANGKA

Barito

SULAWESI

Palembang

Banjarmasin

4

Telukbetung

Jakarta

Surabaya

I N D O N E S I A

Ujung
Padang

Bandung

JAVA

BALI LOMBOK

Raba

FLORES

Larantu

Yogyakarta

Denpasar

Mataram

SUMBAWA

Ruteng

INDIAN

Memboro

Baing

SUMBA

Kupang

10°S

OCEAN

TIMO

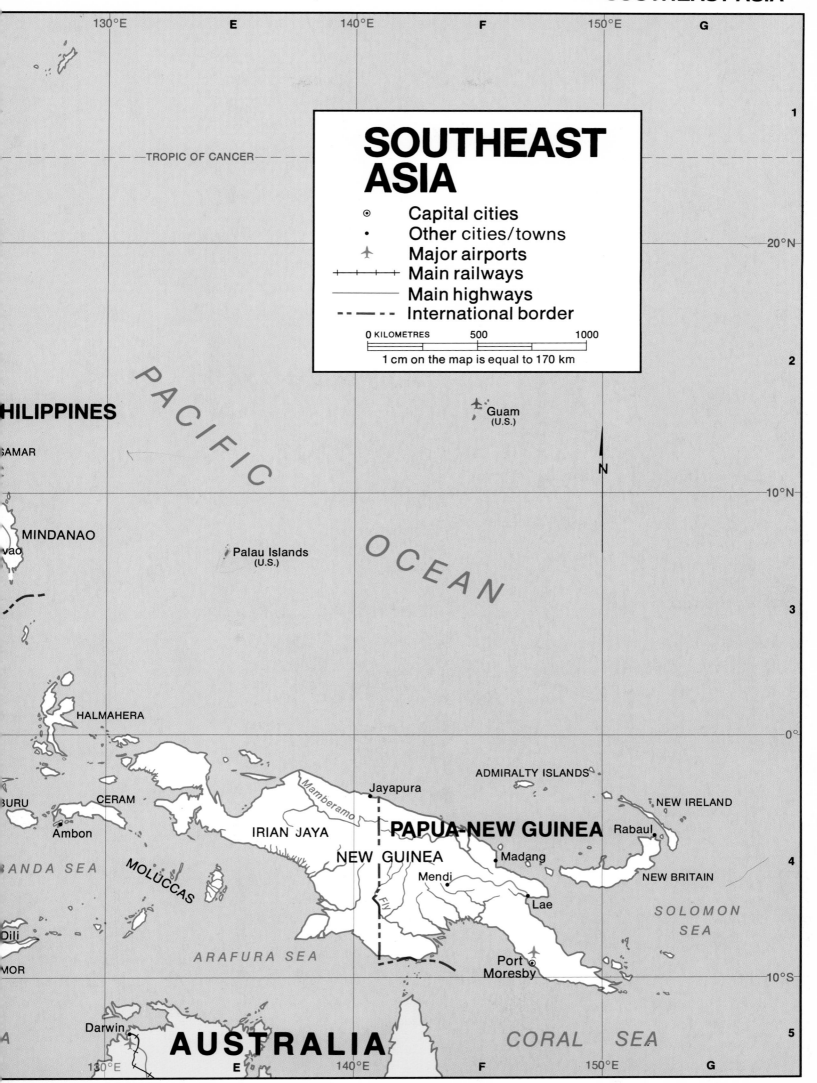

1

SOUTHEAST ASIA

⊙ Capital cities
· Other cities/towns
✈ Major airports
┼┼┼┼ Main railways
──── Main highways
▬ ▬ ▬ International border

0 KILOMETRES   500   1000

1 cm on the map is equal to 170 km

TROPIC OF CANCER

20°N

2

PACIFIC

✈ Guam
(U.S.)

N

PHILIPPINES

SAMAR

10°N

OCEAN

MINDANAO

vao

Palau Islands
(U.S.)

3

HALMAHERA

0°

BURU   CERAM

ADMIRALTY ISLANDS

NEW IRELAND

Ambon

Mamberamo

Jayapura

IRIAN JAYA

PAPUA-NEW GUINEA

Rabaul

BANDA SEA

MOLUCCAS

NEW GUINEA

Madang

NEW BRITAIN

Mendi

Lae

SOLOMON
SEA

4

Dili

Fly

ARAFURA SEA

Port
Moresby ✈

10°S

MOR

Darwin

AUSTRALIA

CORAL   SEA

5

AUSTRALIA AND NEW ZEALAND

⊙ National capitals	┼┼┼┼ Main railways
▪ State capitals	──── Main roads
• Other cities/towns	──·──· State borders
✈ Major airports	──·──·· International borders

0 KILOMETRES   500   1000   1500

1 cm on the map is equal to 152 km

	H	150°W	J	155°W	K	160°W	L	165°W	M	170°W	N
145°W											

PAPUA - NEW GUINEA

GUADALCANAL

SOLOMON ISLANDS

SAN CRISTOBAL

SANTA CRUZ ISLANDS (U.K.)

10°S

1

CORAL SEA

areeba
Cairns
Innisfail

ESPIRITU SANTO

MALEKULA

15°S

VANUATU

GREAT BARRIER REEF

Townsville

Vila
EFATE

2

Bowen

Mackay

NEW CALEDONIA (France)

QUEENSLAND

20°S

Longreach

Rockhampton

Nouméa

TROPIC OF CAPRICORN

3

Charleville

Bundaberg

PACIFIC

25°S

Toowoomba

Brisbane
Gold Coast

NORFOLK ISLAND (Aust.)

4

OCEAN

Narrabri

LORD HOWE ISLAND (Aust.)

30°S

NEW SOUTH

Tamworth

Dubbo

Orange
Maitland
Newcastle

WALES

Sydney
Wollongong

5

Wagga Wagga
Canberra
AUSTRALIAN CAPITAL TERRITORY

ndigo
Albury
* Mt. Kosciusko 2227 m

35°S

VICTORIA
Melbourne

TASMAN SEA

Auckland

NORTH ISLAND

Geelong

NEW

6

BASS STRAIT FLINDERS I.

ZEALAND

Cook Strait

Launceston

Napier

TASMANIA

40°S

Hobart

Wellington

SOUTH ISLAND

7

N

Christchurch

Mt. Cook 3764 m

CHATHAM I. (N.Z.)

Dunedin

Longitude west of Greenwich

STEWART I.

45°S

145°W	H	150°W	J	155°W	K	160°W	L	165°W	M	170°W	N	175°W	O	180°	8

West longitude   180°   East longitude

150°W   160°W   170°W   170°E   160°E   150°E

140°W

130°W

120°W

110°W

100°W

90°W

80°W

70°W

60°W

50°W

40°W

30°W

20°W

140°E

130°E

120°E

110°E

100°E

90°E

80°E

70°E

60°E

50°E

40°E

30°E

20°E

60°N

70°N

80°N

PACIFIC OCEAN

BERING SEA

SEA OF OKHOTSK

Okhotsk

Anchorage
*Mt. McKinley
6194 m

Nome

ALASKA
(United States)

Fairbanks

UNION OF SOVIET

SOCIALIST REPUBLICS

Fort Norman

Inuvik

ARCTIC OCEAN

CANADA

Resolute

PERMANENT PACK ICE

THE ARCTIC

· NORTH POLE

Noril'sk ·

BAFFIN BAY

Frobisher Bay

GREENLAND
(Denmark)

BARENTS SEA

Godthåb

Murmansk

Arkhangel'sk

Tromso

NORWEGIAN

Narvik

NORWAY

FINLAND

ARCTIC CIRCLE

Reykjavik ⊙ **ICELAND**

SEA

SWEDEN

Helsinki

Leningrad

Moscow

ATLANTIC OCEAN

Bergen

Oslo

Stockholm

UNITED KINGDOM

DENMARK

POLAND

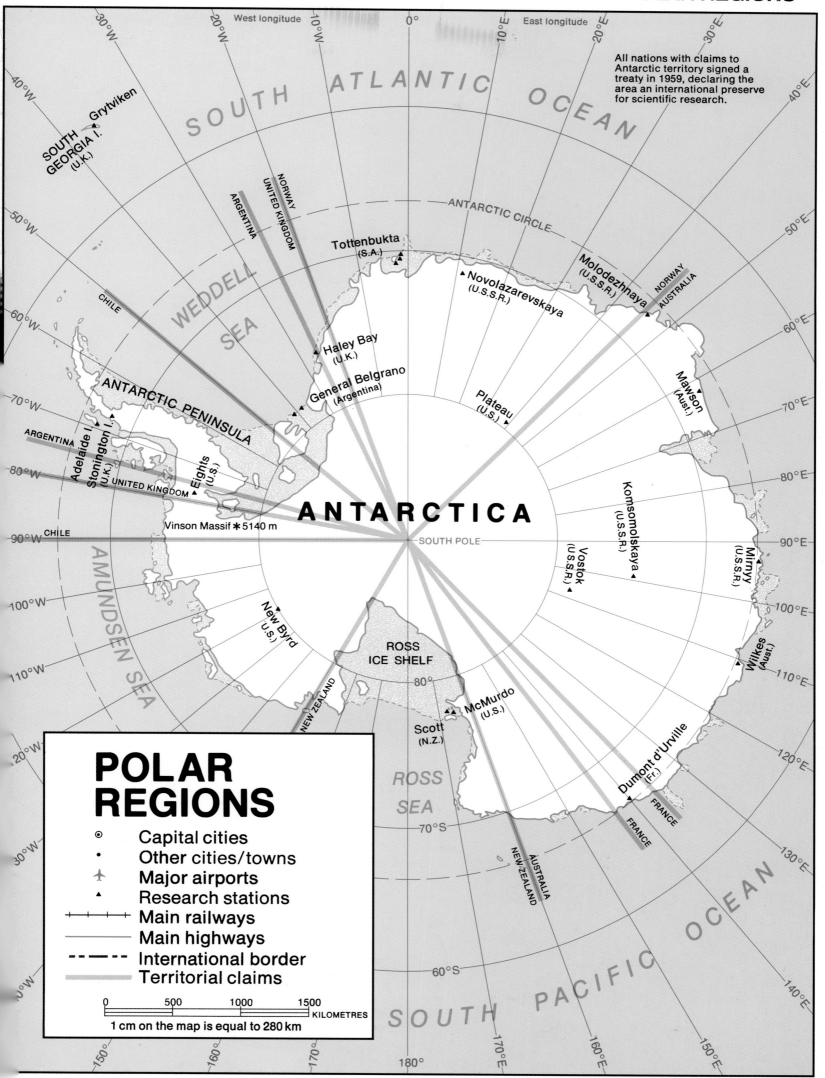

West longitude · East longitude

SOUTH ATLANTIC OCEAN

All nations with claims to Antarctic territory signed a treaty in 1959, declaring the area an international preserve for scientific research.

ANTARCTIC CIRCLE

SOUTH GEORGIA I. (U.K.) · Grytviken

NORWAY · UNITED KINGDOM · ARGENTINA

WEDDELL SEA

CHILE

Tottenbukta (S.A.)

Novolazarevskaya (U.S.S.R.)

Molodezhnaya (U.S.S.R.) · NORWAY · AUSTRALIA

Haley Bay (U.K.)

General Belgrano (Argentina)

ANTARCTIC PENINSULA

Plateau (U.S.)

Mawson (Aust.)

Adelaide I. · Stonington I. (U.K.) · ARGENTINA · UNITED KINGDOM · Eights (U.S.)

ANTARCTICA

Komsomolskaya (U.S.S.R.)

Mirny (U.S.S.R.)

CHILE · Vinson Massif ✳ 5140 m

SOUTH POLE

Vostok (U.S.S.R.)

AMUNDSEN SEA

New Byrd (U.S.)

ROSS ICE SHELF

Wilkes (Aust.)

NEW ZEALAND

McMurdo (U.S.)

Scott (N.Z.)

Dumont d'Urville (Fr.) · FRANCE

ROSS SEA

FRANCE

AUSTRALIA · NEW ZEALAND

SOUTH PACIFIC OCEAN

POLAR REGIONS

⊙ Capital cities
• Other cities/towns
✈ Major airports
▲ Research stations
+++++ Main railways
——— Main highways
– – – International border
▬▬▬ Territorial claims

0 — 500 — 1000 — 1500
KILOMETRES

1 cm on the map is equal to 280 km

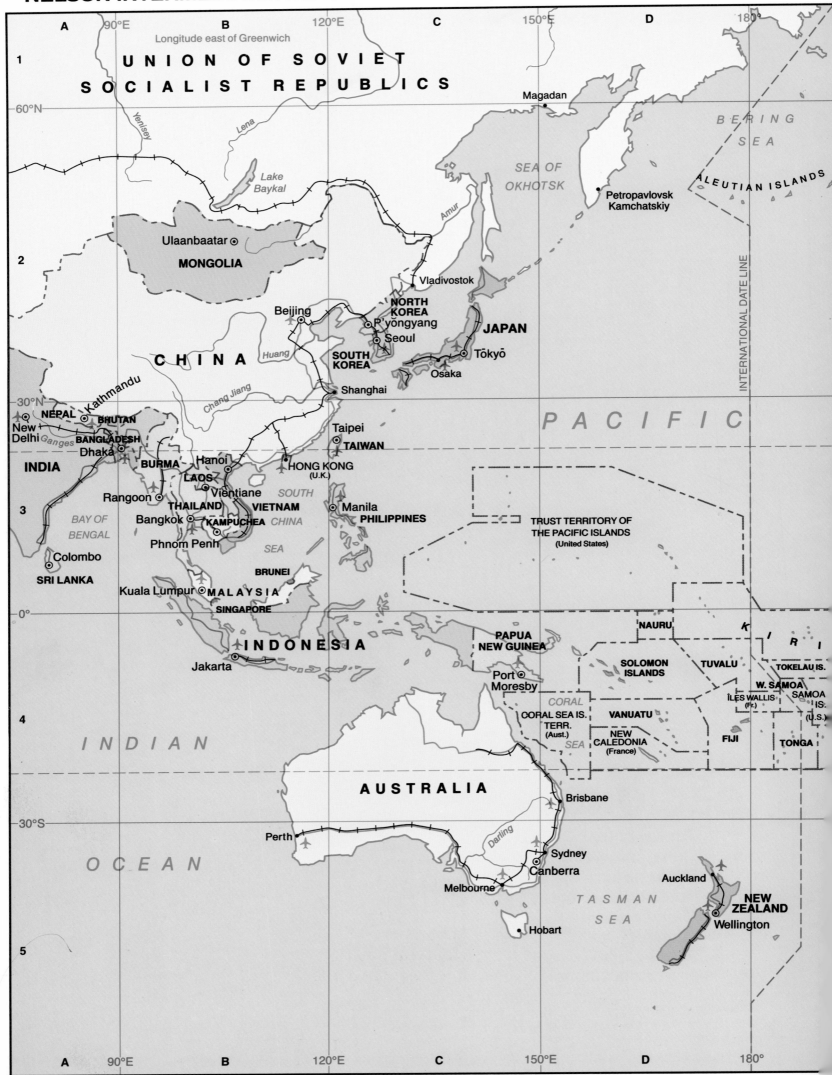

A 90°E B 120°E C 150°E D 180°

Longitude east of Greenwich

1

UNION OF SOVIET
SOCIALIST REPUBLICS

60°N

Magadan

BERING
SEA

SEA OF
OKHOTSK

Petropavlovsk
Kamchatskiy

ALEUTIAN ISLANDS

Yenisey

Lena

Lake
Baykal

Amur

2

Ulaanbaatar ⊙

MONGOLIA

Vladivostok

Beijing

NORTH
KOREA
P'yŏngyang
Seoul

JAPAN

Tōkyō

CHINA

SOUTH
KOREA

Osaka

Huang

Chang Jiang

Shanghai

30°N

Kathmandu

NEPAL

BHUTAN

New
Delhi

Ganges

BANGLADESH

Dhaka

INDIA

BURMA

Hanoi

LAOS

Taipei

TAIWAN

PACIFIC

3

Rangoon

Vientiane

THAILAND

VIETNAM

HONG KONG
(U.K.)

Bangkok

KAMPUCHEA

CHINA

Manila

PHILIPPINES

TRUST TERRITORY OF
THE PACIFIC ISLANDS
(United States)

BAY OF
BENGAL

Phnom Penh

SOUTH

SEA

Colombo

SRI LANKA

BRUNEI

Kuala Lumpur ⊙ MALAYSIA

SINGAPORE

0°

INDONESIA

NAURU

K
I
R
I

Jakarta

PAPUA
NEW GUINEA

SOLOMON
ISLANDS

TUVALU

TOKELAU IS.

W. SAMOA

Port ⊙
Moresby

ÎLES WALLIS
(Fr.)

SAMOA
IS.
(U.S.)

CORAL

4

INDIAN

CORAL SEA IS.
TERR.
(Aust.)

SEA

VANUATU

NEW
CALEDONIA
(France)

FIJI

TONGA

AUSTRALIA

Brisbane

30°S

OCEAN

Perth

Darling

Sydney

Canberra

Auckland

Melbourne

TASMAN

NEW
ZEALAND

SEA

Wellington

Hobart

5

A 90°E B 120°E C 150°E D 180°

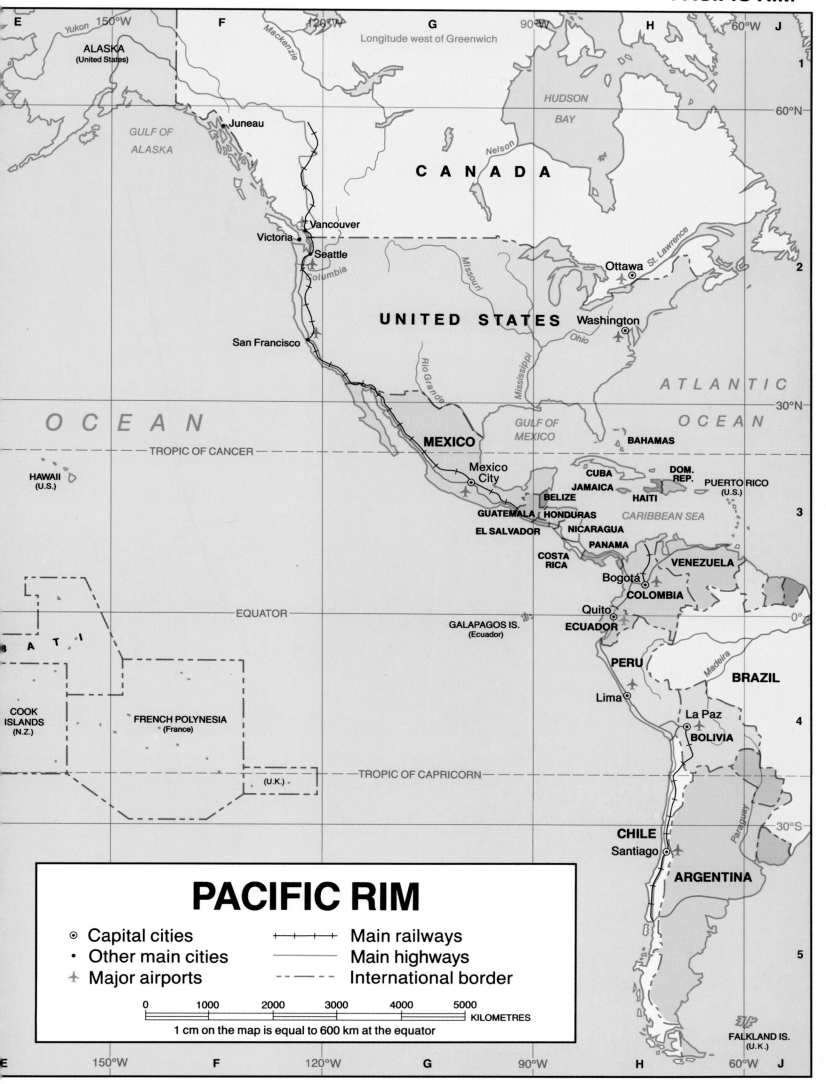

PACIFIC RIM

⊙ Capital cities	┼┼┼┼ Main railways
• Other main cities	———— Main highways
✈ Major airports	– – – – International border

0 1000 2000 3000 4000 5000 KILOMETRES

1 cm on the map is equal to 600 km at the equator

E 150°W **F** 120°W **G** 90°W **H** 60°W **J**

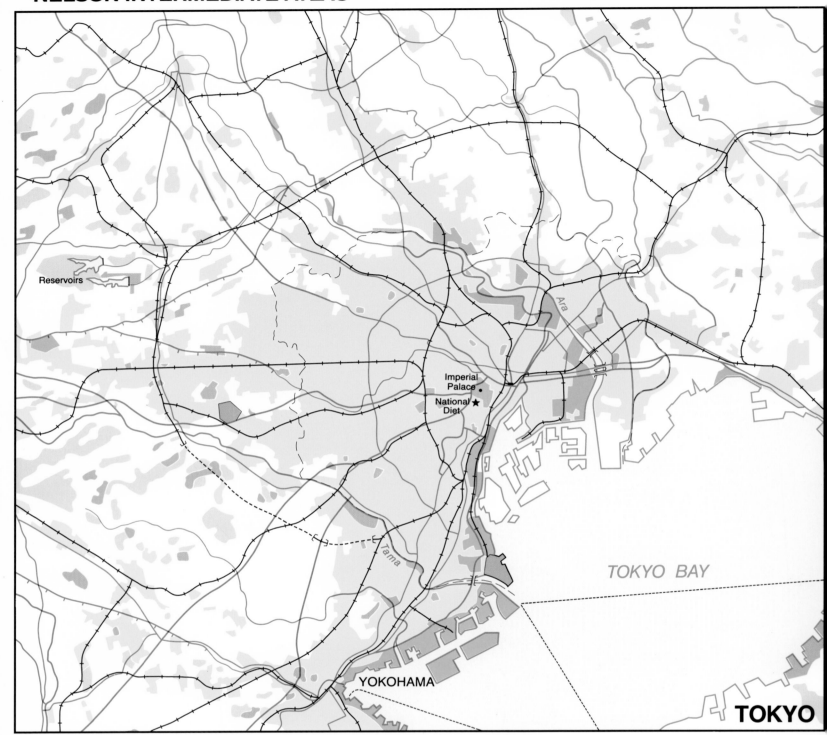

Reservoirs

Imperial
Palace
National
Diet ★

Ara

Tama

TOKYO BAY

YOKOHAMA

TOKYO

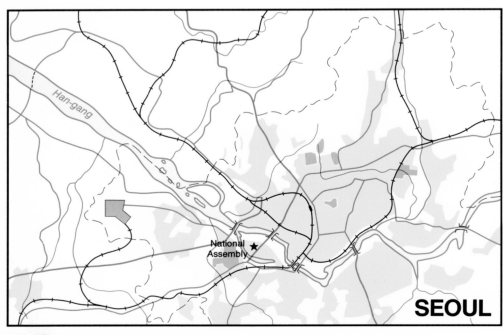

Han-gang

National
Assembly ★

SEOUL

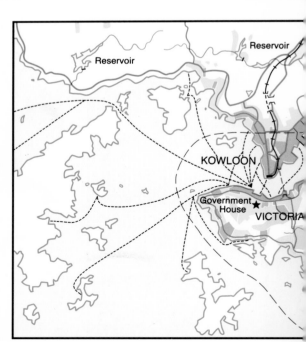

Reservoir

Reservoir

KOWLOON

Government
House ★
VICTORIA

PACIFIC RIM CITIES

Residential areas

Industrial and business

Major airports

Parks

Wooded areas

Main railways and stations

Main highways and roads

Tunnel

Bridge

Canals

Dams

Ferry routes

City boundaries

KILOMETRES

0   5   10   15

1 cm on the map is equal to 3 km

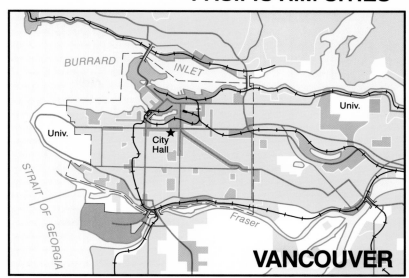

VANCOUVER

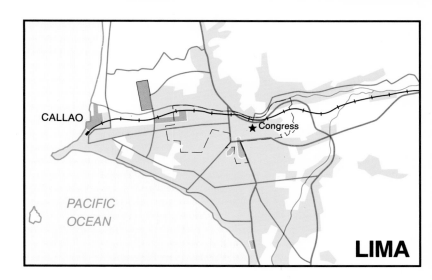

LIMA

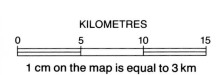

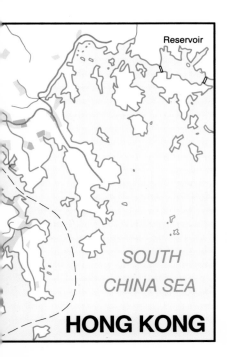

HONG KONG

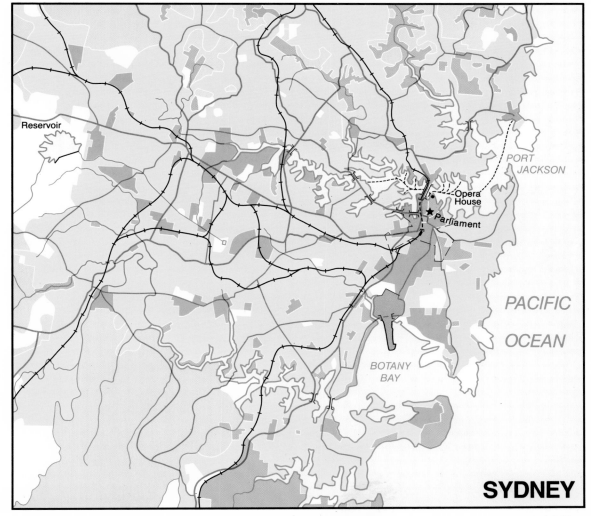

SYDNEY

119

● VANCOUVER

● HONG KONG

● TOKYO

SYDNEY

SEOUL

LIMA

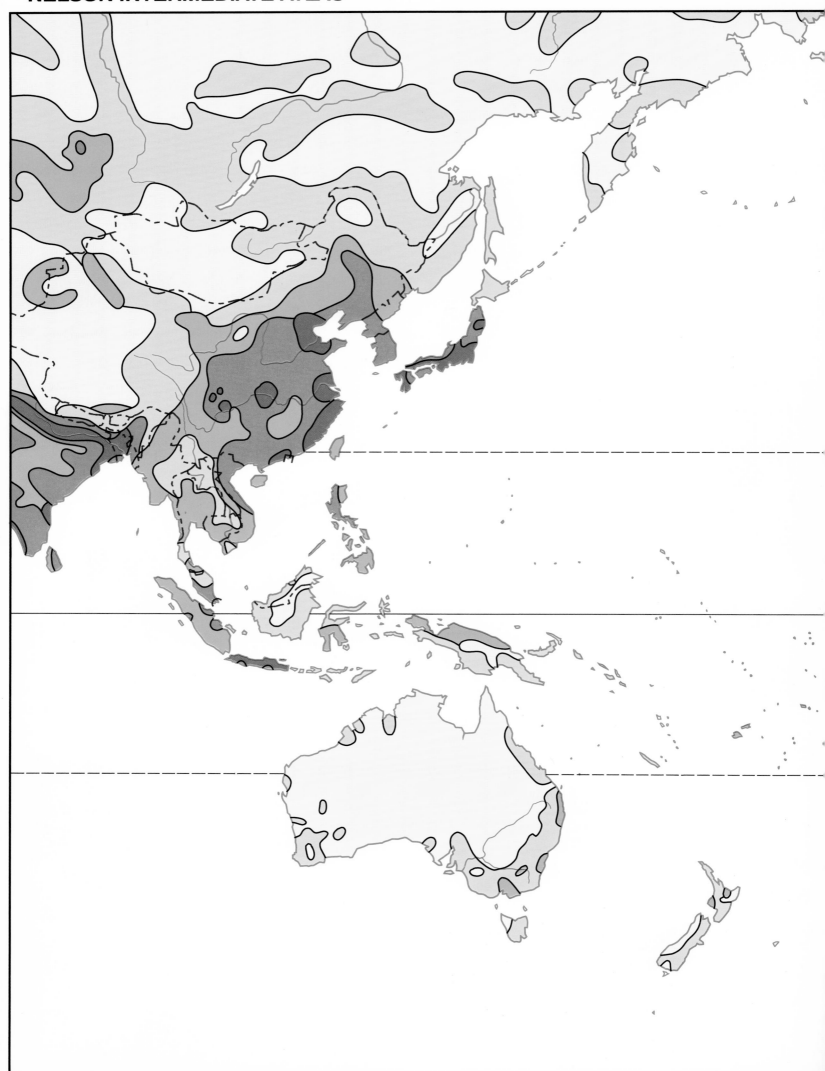

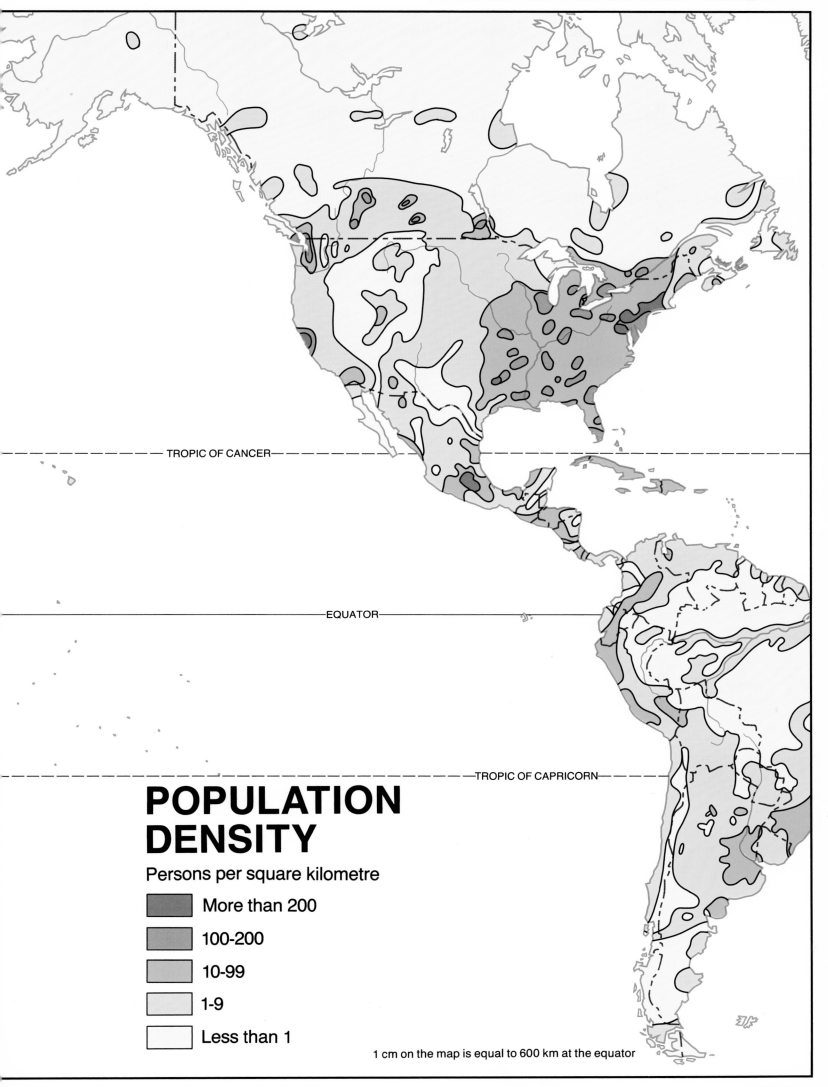

POPULATION DENSITY

Persons per square kilometre

More than 200

100-200

10-99

1-9

Less than 1

TROPIC OF CANCER

EQUATOR

TROPIC OF CAPRICORN

1 cm on the map is equal to 600 km at the equator

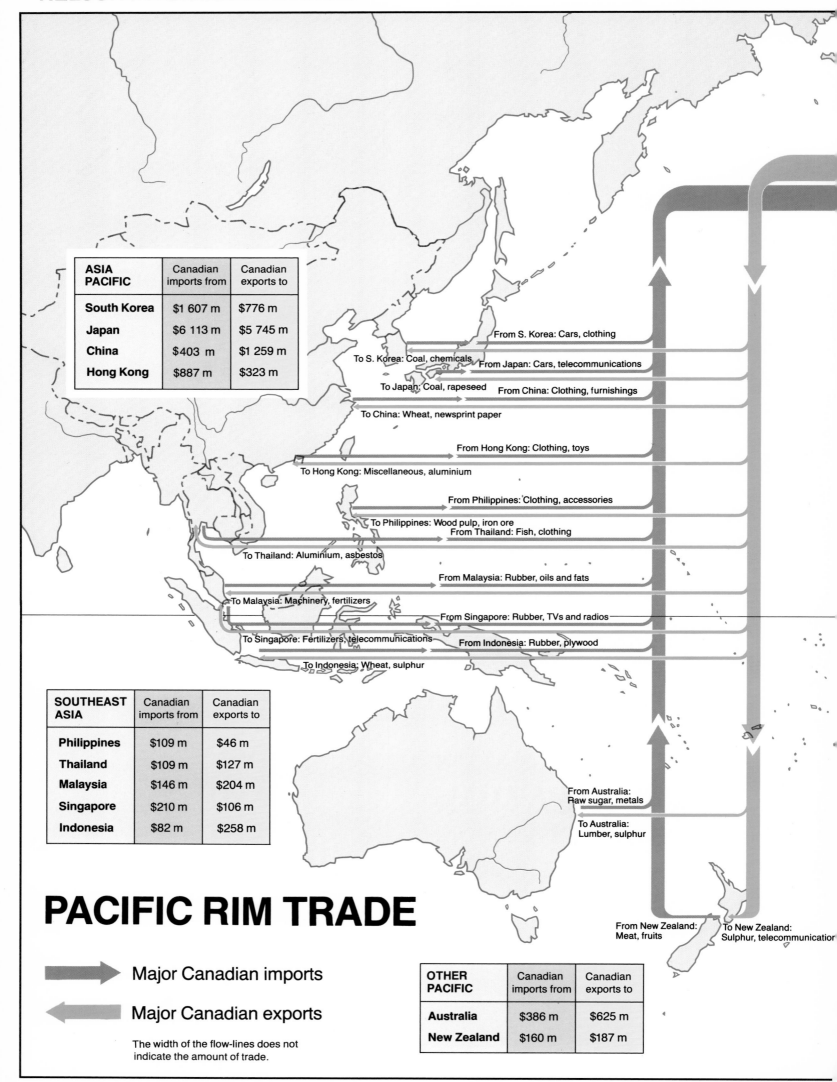

ASIA PACIFIC	Canadian imports from	Canadian exports to
South Korea	$1 607 m	$776 m
Japan	$6 113 m	$5 745 m
China	$403 m	$1 259 m
Hong Kong	$887 m	$323 m

From S. Korea: Cars, clothing
To S. Korea: Coal, chemicals
From Japan: Cars, telecommunications
To Japan: Coal, rapeseed
From China: Clothing, furnishings
To China: Wheat, newsprint paper
From Hong Kong: Clothing, toys
To Hong Kong: Miscellaneous, aluminium
From Philippines: Clothing, accessories
To Philippines: Wood pulp, iron ore
From Thailand: Fish, clothing
To Thailand: Aluminium, asbestos
From Malaysia: Rubber, oils and fats
To Malaysia: Machinery, fertilizers
From Singapore: Rubber, TVs and radios
To Singapore: Fertilizers, telecommunications
From Indonesia: Rubber, plywood
To Indonesia: Wheat, sulphur

SOUTHEAST ASIA	Canadian imports from	Canadian exports to
Philippines	$109 m	$46 m
Thailand	$109 m	$127 m
Malaysia	$146 m	$204 m
Singapore	$210 m	$106 m
Indonesia	$82 m	$258 m

From Australia: Raw sugar, metals
To Australia: Lumber, sulphur

PACIFIC RIM TRADE

From New Zealand: Meat, fruits
To New Zealand: Sulphur, telecommunication

Major Canadian imports

Major Canadian exports

The width of the flow-lines does not indicate the amount of trade.

OTHER PACIFIC	Canadian imports from	Canadian exports to
Australia	$386 m	$625 m
New Zealand	$160 m	$187 m

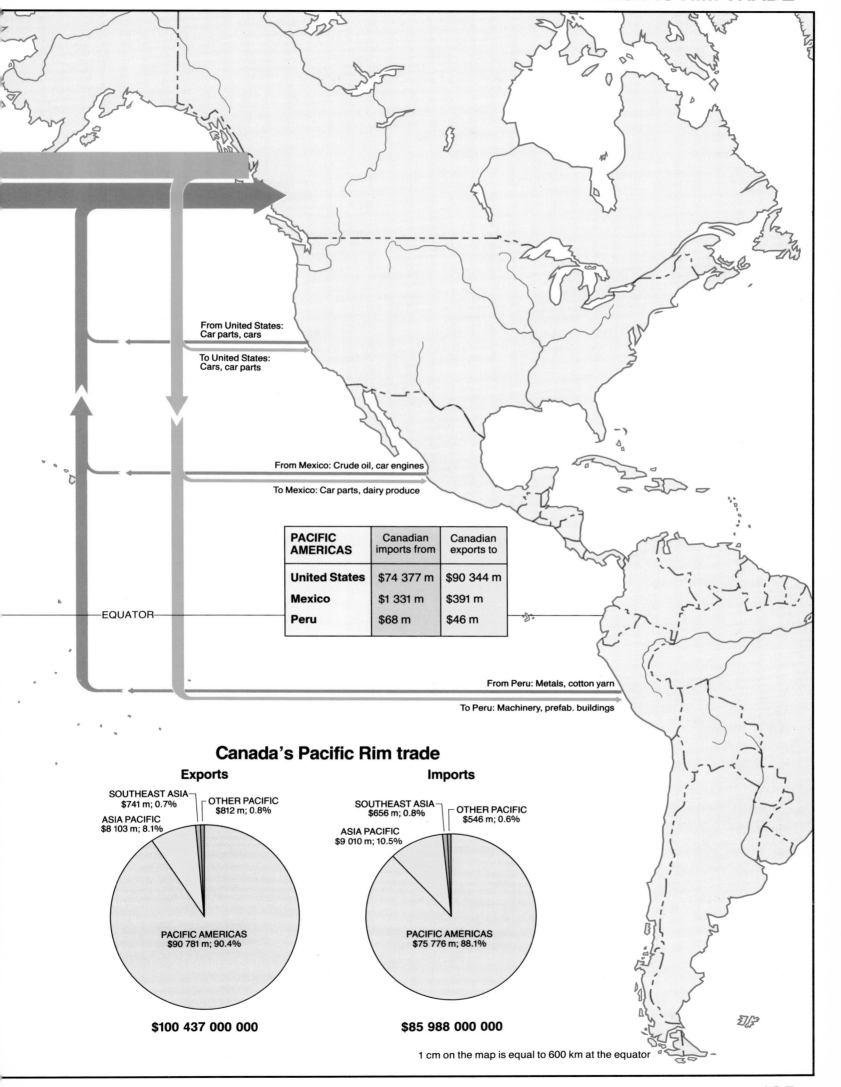

From United States:
Car parts, cars

To United States:
Cars, car parts

From Mexico: Crude oil, car engines

To Mexico: Car parts, dairy produce

PACIFIC AMERICAS	Canadian imports from	Canadian exports to
United States	$74 377 m	$90 344 m
Mexico	$1 331 m	$391 m
Peru	$68 m	$46 m

EQUATOR

From Peru: Metals, cotton yarn

To Peru: Machinery, prefab. buildings

Canada's Pacific Rim trade

Exports

SOUTHEAST ASIA
$741 m; 0.7%

OTHER PACIFIC
$812 m; 0.8%

ASIA PACIFIC
$8 103 m; 8.1%

PACIFIC AMERICAS
$90 781 m; 90.4%

$100 437 000 000

Imports

SOUTHEAST ASIA
$656 m; 0.8%

OTHER PACIFIC
$546 m; 0.6%

ASIA PACIFIC
$9 010 m; 10.5%

PACIFIC AMERICAS
$75 776 m; 88.1%

$85 988 000 000

1 cm on the map is equal to 600 km at the equator

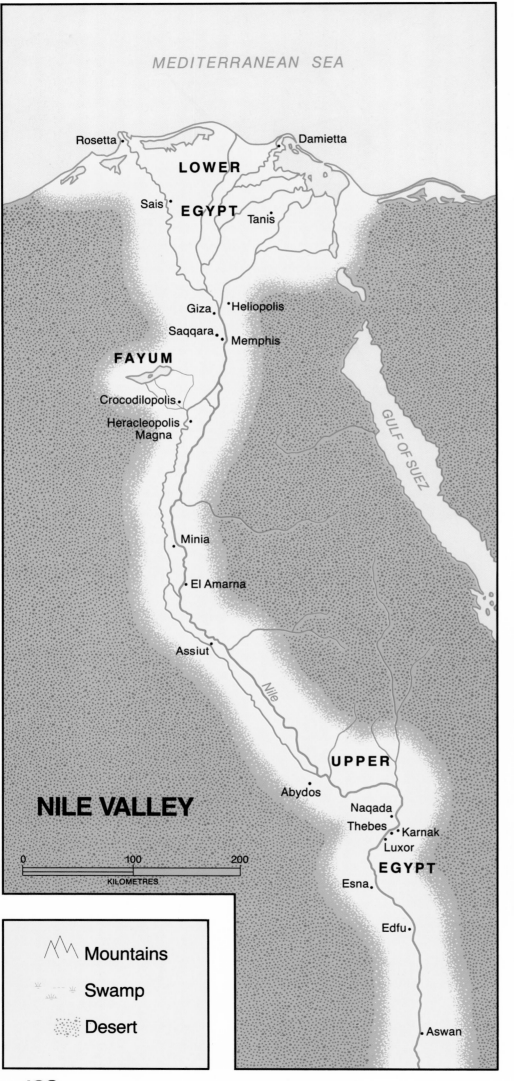

MEDITERRANEAN SEA

Rosetta •
Damietta •

LOWER

Sais •

EGYPT

Tanis •

Giza • • Heliopolis
Saqqara • • Memphis

FAYUM

Crocodilopolis •
Heracleopolis •
Magna

Nile

GULF OF SUEZ

Minia •

El Amarna •

Assiut •

NILE VALLEY

UPPER

Abydos •

Naqada •
Thebes • • Karnak
Luxor •

EGYPT

Esna •

Edfu •

| 0 | 100 | 200 |

KILOMETRES

Aswan •

⋀ Mountains

⋓ Swamp

Desert

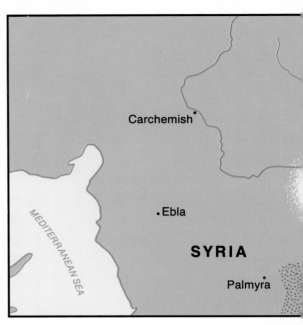

Carchemish •

MEDITERRANEAN SEA

Ebla •

SYRIA

Palmyra •

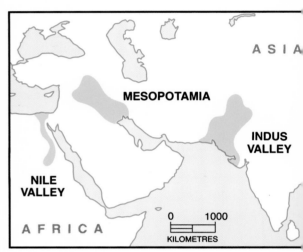

A S I A

MESOPOTAMIA

INDUS VALLEY

NILE VALLEY

A F R I C A

| 0 | 1000 |

KILOMETRES

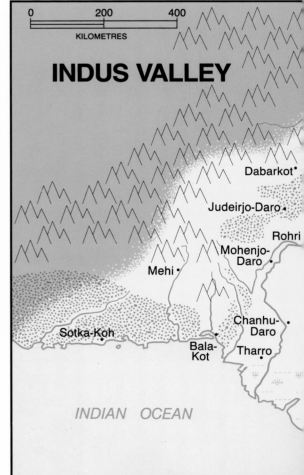

| 0 | 200 | 400 |

KILOMETRES

INDUS VALLEY

Dabarkot •

Judeirjo-Daro •

Rohri •

Mohenjo-
Daro •

Mehi •

Chanhu-
Daro •

Sotka-Koh •

Bala-
Kot •

Tharro •

INDIAN OCEAN

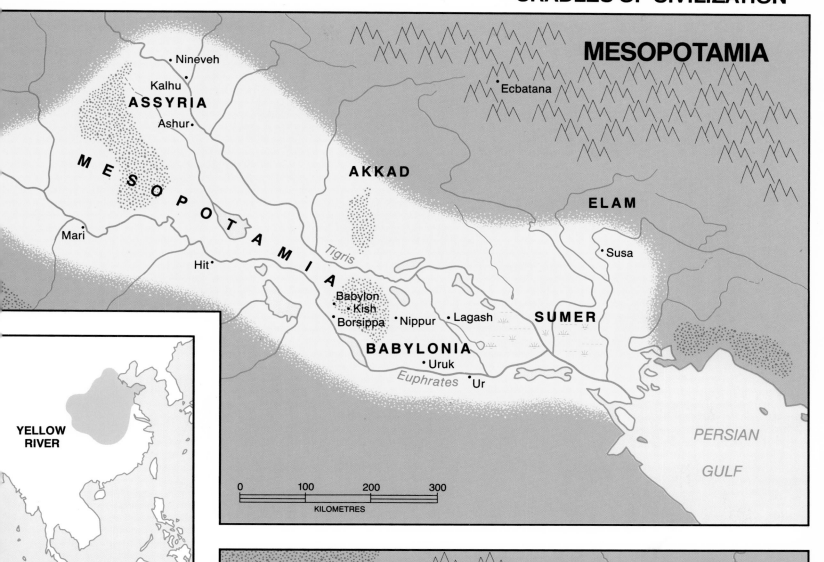

MESOPOTAMIA

- Nineveh
- Kalhu
- **ASSYRIA**
- Ashur
- **M E S O P O T A M I A**
- Mari
- Hit
- **AKKAD**
- Ecbatana
- **ELAM**
- Susa
- Babylon
- Kish
- Borsippa
- Nippur
- Lagash
- **SUMER**
- **BABYLONIA**
- Uruk
- Ur
- *Tigris*
- *Euphrates*

PERSIAN GULF

YELLOW RIVER

0	100	200	300

KILOMETRES

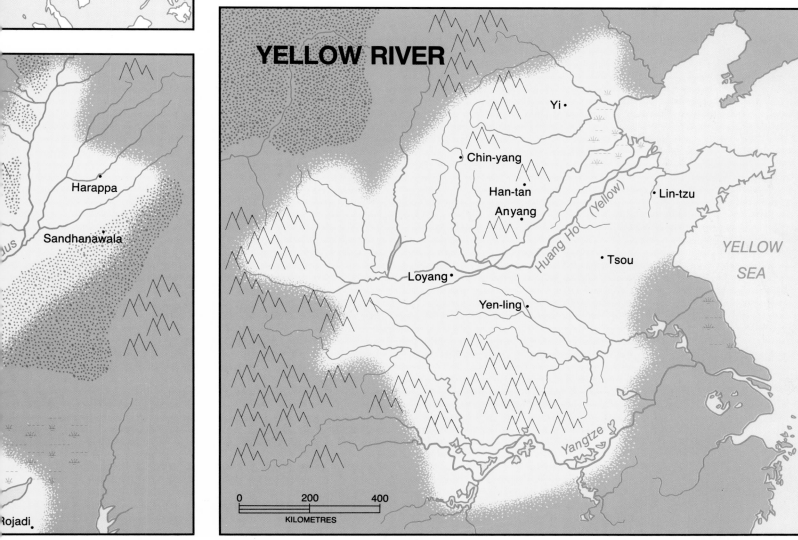

YELLOW RIVER

- Harappa
- Sandhanawala
- Rojadi
- Yi
- Chin-yang
- Han-tan
- Anyang
- Lin-tzu
- Tsou
- Loyang
- Yen-ling
- *Huang Ho (Yellow)*
- *Yangtze*

YELLOW SEA

0	200	400

KILOMETRES

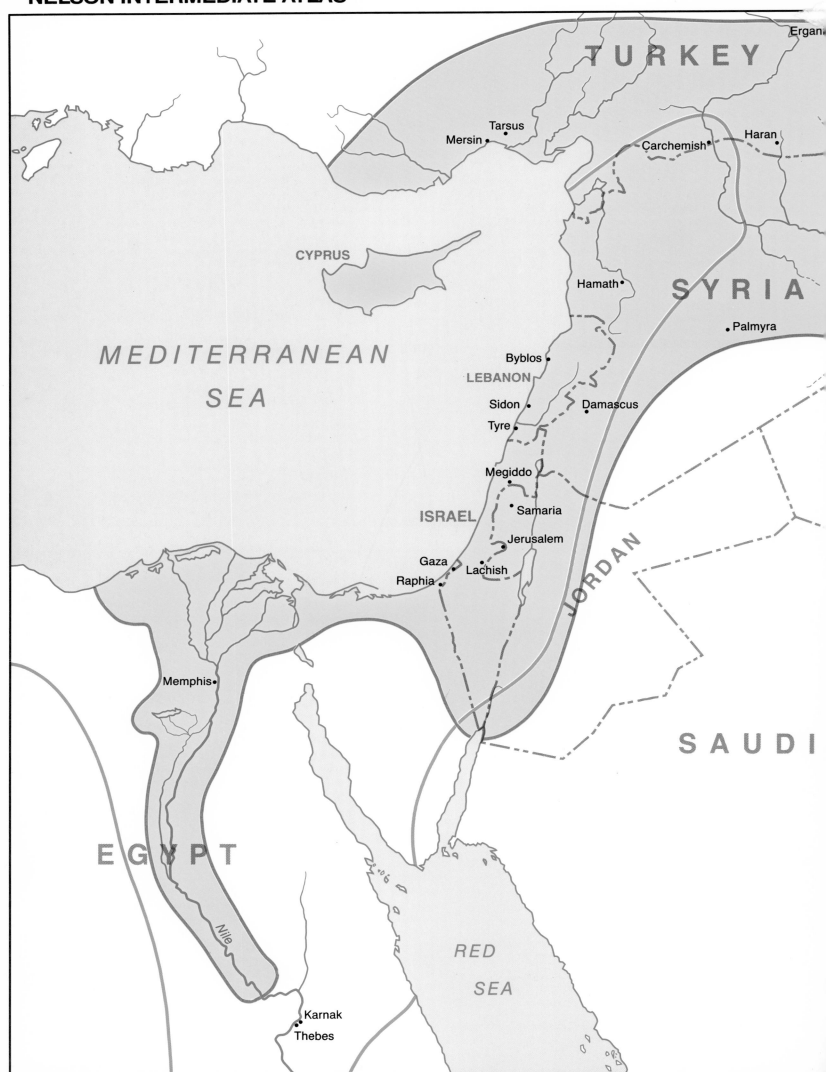

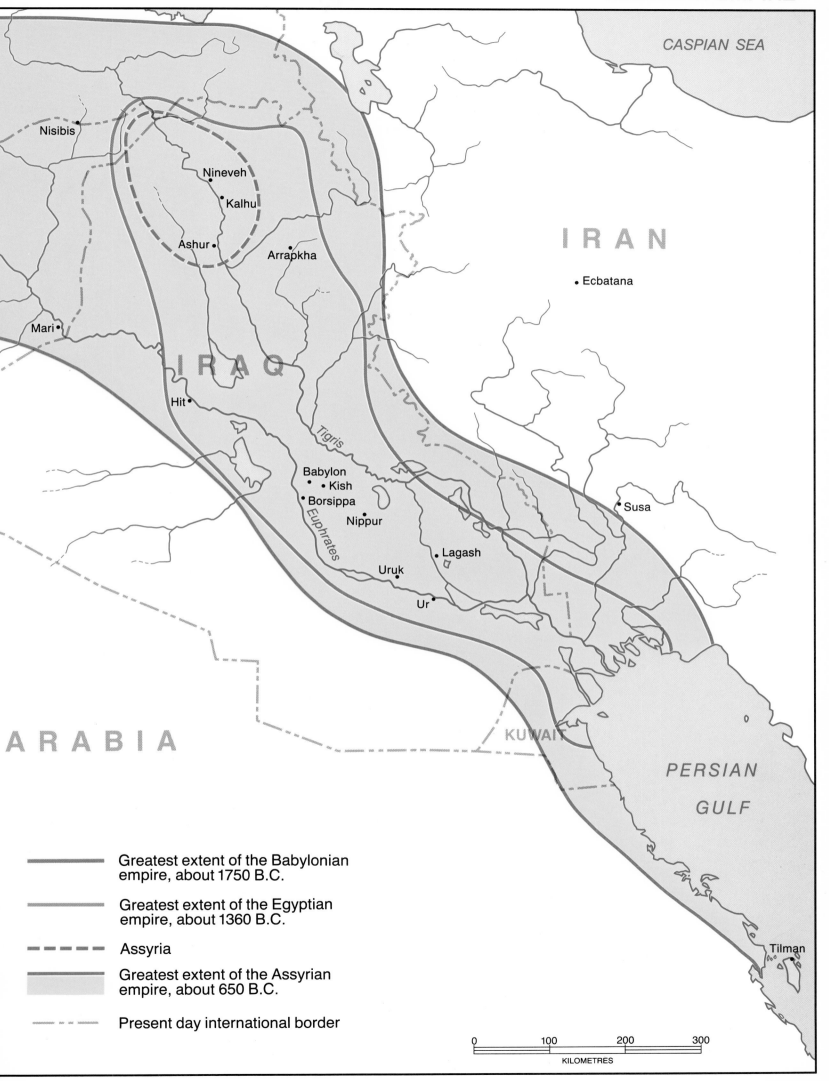

CASPIAN SEA

Nisibis

Nineveh

Kalhu

Ashur

Arrapkha

I R A N

• Ecbatana

Mari •

I R A Q

Hit •

Tigris

Babylon
• Kish
• Borsippa

Nippur

Euphrates

Susa

Lagash

Uruk

Ur •

A R A B I A

KUWAIT

PERSIAN

GULF

Tilman

Greatest extent of the Babylonian
empire, about 1750 B.C.

Greatest extent of the Egyptian
empire, about 1360 B.C.

Assyria

Greatest extent of the Assyrian
empire, about 650 B.C.

Present day international border

0   100   200   300

KILOMETRES

129

NELSON INTERMEDIATE ATLAS

BLACK SEA

Mount Olympus

Delphi
Troy
Thebes
Miletus
Mycenae
Athens
Sparta
Knossos

MEDITERRANEAN SEA

CRETE

MYCENAEAN WORLD, 1300 BC

0   500 km

HIBERNIA

Eboracum
(York)

BRITANNIA

Aquae Sulis
(Bath)

Londinium
(London)

GERMANIA
INFERIOR

Augusta
Treverorum
(Trier)

Colonia
Agrippinensis
(Cologne)

GERMANIA

O C E A N U S

A T L A N T I C U S

LUGDUNENSIS

BELGICA

Lutetia
(Paris)

GERMANIA
SUPERIOR

Vindobona
(Vienna)

RHAETIA

NORICUM

SUPERIOR

Aquincu
(Budapest)

AQUITANIA

Lugdunum
(Lyon)

ALPES
POENINAE

PANNONIA

INFERIOR

Brigantium
(La Coruña)

Burdigala
(Bordeaux)

NARBONENSIS

ALPES
COTTIAE

Mediolanum
(Milan)

ILLYRICUM

TARRACONENSIS

ALPES
MARITIMAE

Genua

Ravenna

MARE ADRIATICUM

Massalia
(Marseille)

ITALIA

LUSITANIA

CORSICA

Roma
(Rome)

Olisipo
(Lisbon)

Tarraco
(Tarragona)

Neapolis
(Naples)

Valentia
(Valencia)

SARDINIA

BAETICA

BALEARES

MARE
TYRRHENUM

Gades
(Cádiz)

Carthago Nova
(Cartagena)

SICILIA

Abdera
(Adra)

Caesarea
(Cherchell)

Syracuse
(Siracusa)

Tingis
(Tangier)

Utica

Sala
(Rabat)

Siga

Carthago
(Carthage)

MA

MAURITANIA

NUMIDIA

MARE   IN

Leptis
Magna

Berenice
(Benghazi)

AFRICA

Greatest extent of the Roman Empire, AD 115

– – – Provincial border

——— Roman roads

• Towns

G A R A M A N T E S

C

1 cm on the map represents 129 km

0   200   400   600   800   1000

KILOMETRES

130

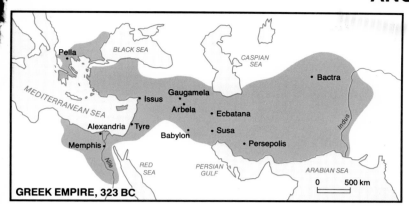

GREEK EMPIRE, 323 BC

Pella

BLACK SEA

CASPIAN SEA

Bactra

Issus · Gaugamela

Arbela · Ecbatana

MEDITERRANEAN SEA

Alexandria · Tyre

Babylon · Susa

Memphis · Persepolis

Indus

RED SEA

PERSIAN GULF

ARABIAN SEA

0 500 km

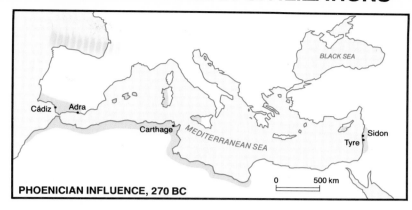

PHOENICIAN INFLUENCE, 270 BC

BLACK SEA

Cádiz · Adra

Carthage

MEDITERRANEAN SEA

Sidon

Tyre

0 500 km

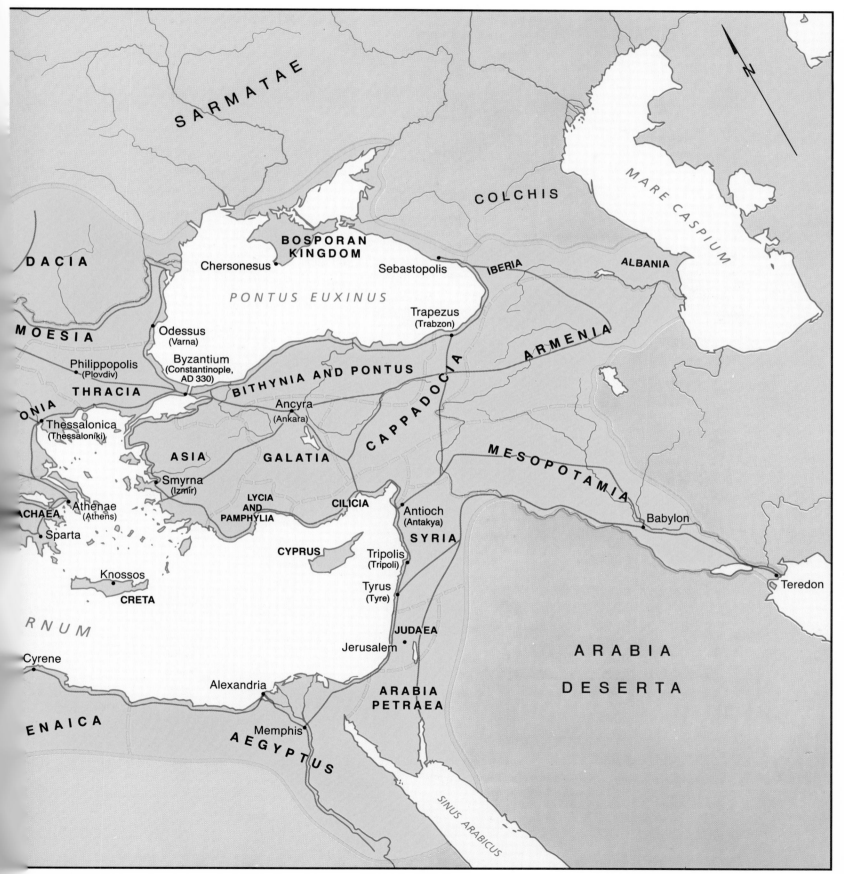

SARMATAE

COLCHIS

MARE CASPIUM

BOSPORAN KINGDOM

DACIA

Chersonesus

Sebastopolis

IBERIA

ALBANIA

PONTUS EUXINUS

MOESIA

Odessus
(Varna)

Trapezus
(Trabzon)

ARMENIA

Philippopolis
(Plovdiv)

Byzantium
(Constantinople,
AD 330)

BITHYNIA AND PONTUS

CAPPADOCIA

THRACIA

Ancyra
(Ankara)

MESOPOTAMIA

ONIA

ASIA

GALATIA

Thessalonica
(Thessaloníki)

Smyrna
(Izmír)

Babylon

ACHAEA

Athenae
(Athens)

LYCIA
AND
PAMPHYLIA

CILICIA

Antioch
(Antakya)

Sparta

SYRIA

CYPRUS

Tripolis
(Tripoli)

Teredon

Knossos

Tyrus
(Tyre)

CRETA

JUDAEA

RNUM

Jerusalem

A R A B I A

Cyrene

D E S E R T A

Alexandria

ARABIA
PETRAEA

ENAICA

Memphis

A E G Y P T U S

SINUS ARABICUS

N

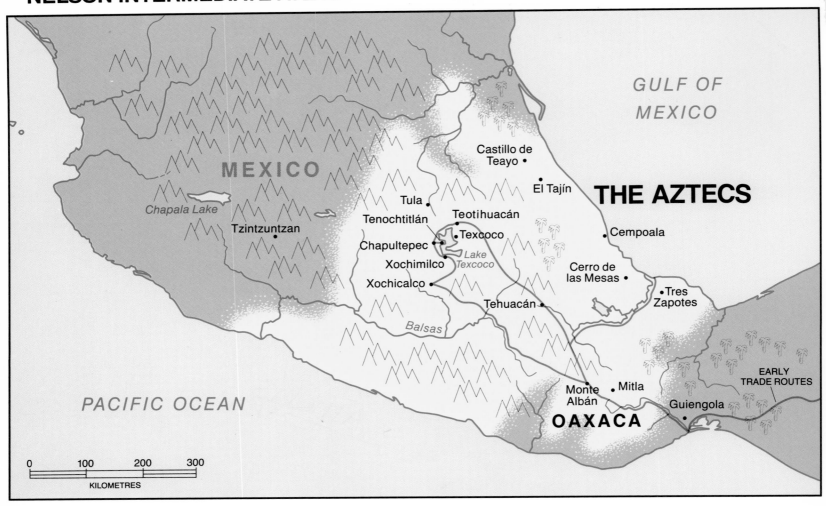

GULF OF
MEXICO

MEXICO

Chapala Lake

Tzintzuntzan

Castillo de
Teayo

El Tajín

THE AZTECS

Tula

Tenochtitlán
Teotihuacán

Chapultepec
Texcoco

Cempoala

Xochimilco

Lake Texcoco

Cerro de
las Mesas

Xochicalco

Tehuacán

Tres
Zapotes

Balsas

EARLY
TRADE ROUTES

PACIFIC OCEAN

Monte
Albán

Mitla

Guiengola

OAXACA

0	100	200	300

KILOMETRES

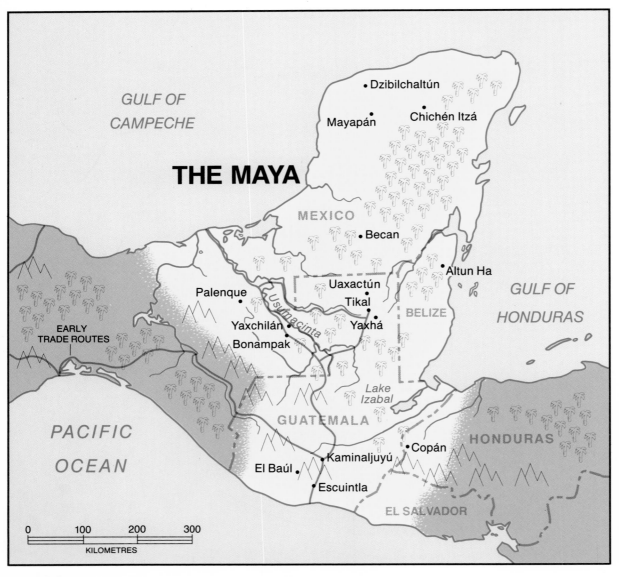

GULF OF
CAMPECHE

Dzibilchaltún

Mayapán

Chichén Itzá

THE MAYA

MEXICO

Becan

Altun Ha

Palenque

Uaxactún

Usumacinta

Tikal

BELIZE

GULF OF
HONDURAS

Yaxchilán

Yaxhá

Bonampak

EARLY
TRADE ROUTES

Lake Izabal

GUATEMALA

HONDURAS

PACIFIC
OCEAN

Copán

Kaminaljuyú

El Baúl

Escuintla

EL SALVADOR

0	100	200	300

KILOMETRES

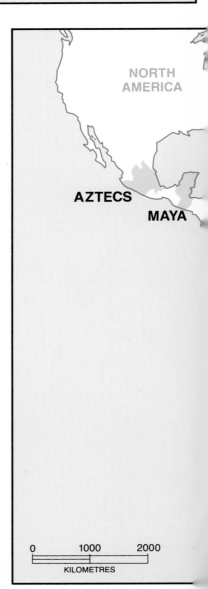

NORTH
AMERICA

AZTECS

MAYA

0	1000	2000

KILOMETRES

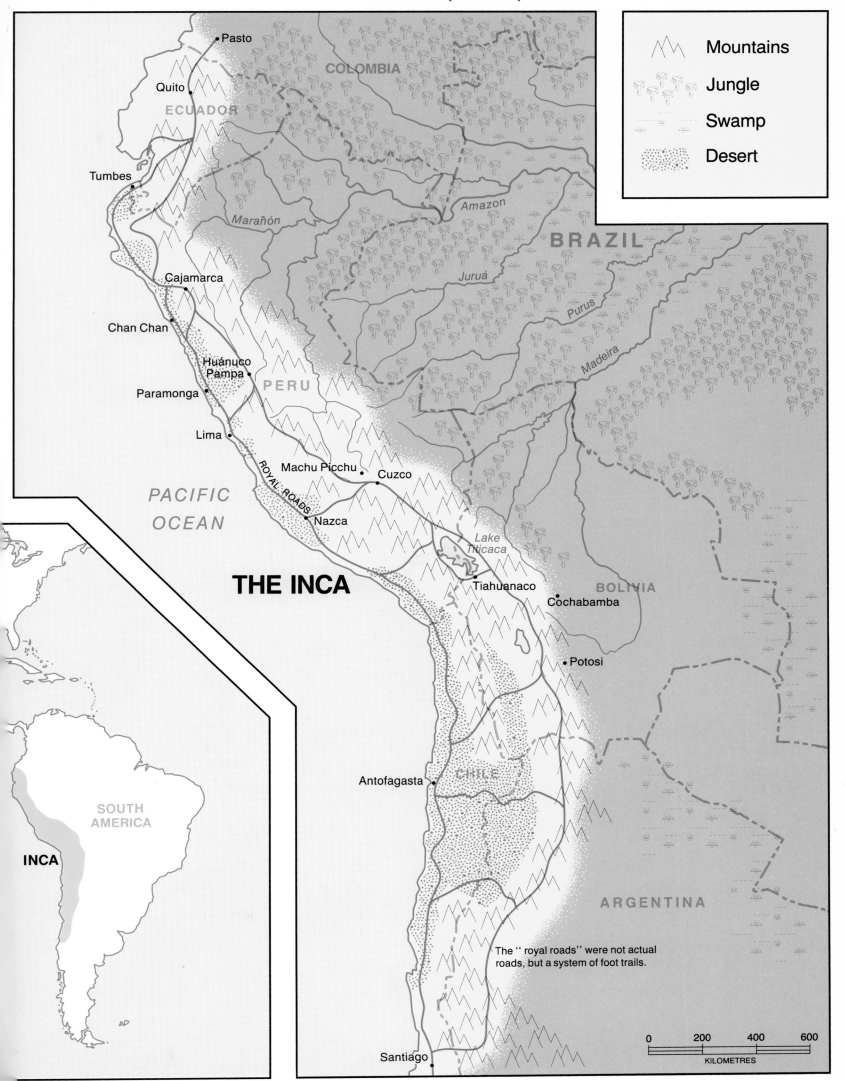

Mountains

Jungle

Swamp

Desert

Pasto

COLOMBIA

Quito

ECUADOR

Tumbes

Marañón

Amazon

BRAZIL

Cajamarca

Juruá

Chan Chan

Purus

Huánuco
Pampa

PERU

Madeira

Paramonga

Lima

Machu Picchu

Cuzco

ROYAL ROADS

Nazca

THE INCA

*Lake
Titicaca*

Tiahuanaco

BOLIVIA

Cochabamba

PACIFIC
OCEAN

Potosi

SOUTH
AMERICA

INCA

Antofagasta

CHILE

ARGENTINA

The "royal roads" were not actual
roads, but a system of foot trails.

| 0 | 200 | 400 | 600 |

KILOMETRES

Santiago

altitude: a height above sea level, usually given in metres on a map.

archipelago: a group of islands.

Arctic Circle: the line of latitude 66.5° north of the Equator.

badlands: dry land where the rocks have been worn away into strange shapes, as in southwest Saskatchewan and southeast Alberta.

bank: land at the edge of a lake, river, etc.

basin: a low area in the surface of the land or on the ocean floor.

bay: a part of a lake, sea, or ocean that stretches into the land.

bight: a very large open bay.

bog: land that is soft, wet, and spongy.

boreal: referring to an area of the north where there are many coniferous (evergreen) forests.

canal: a narrow channel of water, dug for irrigation or transportation.

canyon: a valley that has steep, high sides, and a stream at the bottom.

cape: a piece of land that extends out into the water.

channel: an area of water joining two larger bodies of water.

climate: the conditions of temperature, rainfall, humidity, and wind that a place has over a long period of time.

coral reef: a mass of coral and limestone rock made of the skeletons of millions of tiny sea animals.

cordillera: an area containing many different mountain ranges.

cyclone: a storm with very high winds and heavy rain. The winds rotate around a moving area of low air pressure. In the southern hemisphere these winds rotate clockwise, and in the northern hemisphere they rotate counterclockwise.

dam: a strong barrier built to hold back and store the water of a river.

degree: a measurement of distance on the earth. One degree (1°) of latitude equals approximately 110 km.

delta: a triangle-shaped deposit of sediment that forms at the mouth of some rivers.

deposit: something that has been laid down by natural forces.

desert: an area of land where there is very little precipitation. Desert plants and animals must adapt to the dry conditions.

drainage basin: an area of land drained by a river and its tributaries.

drought: a period of dry weather when crops are damaged or killed by the lack of rainfall.

earthquake: a trembling or shaking of the earth's crust.

elevation: the height of land above or below sea level, usually measured in metres.

Equator: the 0° line of latitude that circles the globe halfway between the North and South Poles.

erosion: the wearing away of land by natural forces, such as wind or water.

estuary: the wide mouth of a river, where the flow of the river water is affected by the ocean tides.

fault: a crack in the earth's crust, where the land on either side of the crack has risen up or dropped down.

field: land that has a large amount of some kind of natural product, for example a gas field or an oil field.

fiord: a long narrow bay with steep rocky sides eroded by a glacier.

geyser: a hot spring that shoots water and steam into the air at certain times.

glacier: a huge mass of ice that moves slowly down the side of a mountain or along a valley. The ice is formed from snow that is pressed down by its own weight. A glacier can also spread outward on a land surface.

gorge: a river valley that is narrow and deep, with steep sides.

gulf: a large bay; a part of the ocean that extends into the land.

hemisphere: a half of the earth. The earth can be divided into the Northern and Southern Hemispheres, or the Eastern and Western Hemispheres.

highland: land that is higher and more hilly than the surrounding area.

hurricane: the name of a tropical cyclone that forms over the Atlantic Ocean.

igneous rocks: rocks formed when hot molten material, such as lava from a volcano, cools and hardens.

International Date Line: the line of latitude that is both 180° east and west of the Prime Meridian (0°). Places west of the date line are one day ahead of places east of the date line.

island: an area of land completely surrounded by water.

isthmus: a narrow strip of land, with water on each side, connecting two large land areas.

lagoon: a small lake or pond cut off from a larger body of water by sand bars.

lake: a body of fresh water completely surrounded by land.

latitude: imaginary lines running east-west around the earth, used to measure the distance north and south of the Equator. The distance between these lines is measured in degrees (°).

legend: a list of the signs and symbols used on a map, with their meanings.

log boom: a large raft of logs made to float together on the water so they can be towed.

longitude: imaginary lines running north-south around the earth, with each line passing through the North and South Poles. The distance between these lines is measured in degrees (°). Longitude is measured east and west from the Prime Meridian.

meander: a wide curve or a loop in the course of a river.

meridian: another name for a line of longitude.

metamorphic rocks: igneous or sedimentary rocks that have changed form because of pressure or heat.

montane: referring to the mountain slopes below the timberline. These areas have moist, cool climates, and many large evergreen trees.

mountain: a part of the land that is higher than a hill.

natural resource: material found in nature and used by people. One example is water.

ocean: one of the five great areas of salt water surrounding the continents. These areas are named the Antarctic, Arctic, Atlantic, Indian, and Pacific Oceans.

pampas: a vast prairie in South America.

parallel: another name for a line of latitude.

pass: a narrow gap through the mountains.

peninsula: a piece of land surrounded on three sides by water.

permafrost: ground that does not completely thaw in the summer.

plain: a large area of flat land.

plateau: an elevated area of flat land.

prairie: a large area of grassy land that is flat or gently rolling and has few or no trees.

precipitation: the rain, snow, hail, etc. that falls on an area. Precipitation is measured in centimetres of water.

Prime Meridian: the 0° line of longitude that runs through Greenwich (England).

range: a long chain of mountains and plateaus.

relief: the differences in height of the land surface of an area.

reservoir: a place where water is collected and stored.

ridge: an area of land that is long and narrow, and is higher than the surrounding land.

river: a large stream of water that flows across the land and into another stream, a lake, or an ocean.

savannah: a tropical or sub-tropical grassland with scattered trees.

scale: the relationship between distance measured on a map and the real distance on the earth's surface.

sea: a large area of salt water that is smaller than an ocean.

sea level: the level of the surface of the sea, usually at the level halfway between high tide and low tide.

sediment: soil, stones, or other material that sinks to the bottom in water, or is deposited on the ground by wind or ice.

sedimentary rocks: rocks made from layers of sediment that have stuck together and hardened.

sierra: a mountain range that has a jagged outline like the teeth of a saw.

sound: a long narrow area of water between an island and the mainland, or joining two larger areas of water.

statistics: a collection of facts about people and places.

steppe: a large treeless plain in southeastern Europe or Asia.

strait: a narrow passage of water connecting two larger bodies of water.

swamp: land that is spongy and very wet, sometimes with parts completely covered by water.

tar sands: an area of sand mixed with a sticky, tar-like material. A special process can get the oil and petroleum out of the tar sands. Tar sands are found in northern Alberta.

tidal wave: a huge ocean wave caused by an earthquake. Tsunami is another name for a tidal wave.

time zone: an area where all the places use the same standard of time. The International Date Line is at the beginning and ending of the 24 time zones of the world.

tributary: a creek or river that flows into a larger river.

Tropic of Cancer: the line of latitude 23.5° north of the Equator.

Tropic of Capricorn: the line of latitude 23.5° south of the Equator.

tundra: a large treeless plain in the arctic area.

typhoon: the name of a tropical cyclone that forms over the Pacific Ocean.

valley: a long low area of land between hills or mountains. Also, an area of land drained by one large river system.

volcano: a mountain formed by lava (molten rock) and ash forced out of the earth through a crack in the earth's crust. Volcanoes may be active (able to erupt again) or extinct.

This index is a list of the place names on the regional maps. Beside each place name is the country or Canadian province, page number, and grid square. When a feature crosses over a political boundary or is in more than one grid square, the listing shows the location where it is easiest to find the feature. Water features are listed in italic type, and capital cities are in bold type in this index.

Abbreviations

Bermuda (U.K.) **85** 1M
Bern, Switzerland **92** 2D
Besancon, France **95** 3J
Betsiamites, PQ **47** 3F
Béziers, France **95** 5G
Bhutan **107** 4N
Bialystok, Poland **91** 2F
Bida, Nigeria **98** 3D
Big Sand Lake, Man. **40** 2B
Big Trout Lake, Ont. **42** 2C
Big Trout Lake, Ont. **42** 2C
Biggar, Sask. **39** 5B
Bight of Benin **98** 5B
Bilbao, Spain **92** 3B
Birmingham, U.K. **90** 2C
Birnin Kebbi, Nigeria **98** 1C
Biscay, Bay of, **92** 2B
Bishop's Falls, Nfld. **51** 2D
Bissau, Guinea-Bissau **96** 3B
Bissett, Man. **41** 5D
Bistcho Lake, Alta. **36** 2B
Biu, Nigeria **99** 2G
Black Da River, Asia **110** 1B
Black Lake, Sask. **38** 2D
Black Sea, **91** 3G
Blagoveshchensk, U.S.S.R. **101** 4N
Blanc, Mt., France-Italy **95** 4J
Blantyre, Malawi **97** 6G
Blind River, Ont. **44** 1B
Bloodvein River, Man. **41** 5C
Blue Nile River, Africa **97** 3G
Bobcaygeon, Ont. **45** 2D
Bobruysk, U.S.S.R. **91** 2F
Bodø, Norway **90** 1E
Bogotá, Colombia **86** 4C
Boissevain, Man. **41** 6A
Bolivia **86** 8D
Bologna, Italy **93** 3E
Bombay, India **107** 6K
Bonavista Bay, Nfld. **51** 2E
Bonavista, Nfld. **51** 2E
Bonete, Mt., Argentina **87** 10D
Bonifacio, Corsica **95** 7N
Bonn, F.R.G. **92** 1D
Boothia Peninsula, NWT **33** 3H
Boothia, Gulf of, NWT **33** 3H
Bordeaux, France **94** 4E
Borden, PEI **49** 2D
Borneo, Indonesia **110** 3C
Bornholm, Denmark **91** 2E
Bothnia, Gulf of, **91** 1F
Botswana **97** 7F
Boulogne, France **95** 1F
Bourges, France **95** 3G
Bow River, Alta. **37** 6E
Bowen, Australia **113** 3H
Bracebridge, Ont. **44** 2D
Bradford, Ont. **44** 2D
Brahmaputra River, India **107** 4O
Brampton, Ont. **44** 3D
Branco River, S. America **86** 4H
Brandon, Man. **41** 6B
Brantford, Ont. **44** 3C
Bras d'Or Lake, NS **49** 3E
Brasília, Brazil **86** 8H
Bratsk, U.S.S.R. **101** 4L
Brazil 86-87
Brazzaville, Congo **96** 5E
Bremen, F.R.G. **90** 2D
Brest, France **94** 2C
Brest, U.S.S.R. **91** 2F
Bretaña, Peru **88** 6C
Bridgetown, NS **48** 3C
Bridgetown, Barbados **86** 2F
Bridgewater, NS **48** 3C
Brighton, Ont. **45** 2E
Brighton, U.K. **90** 2C
Brisbane, Australia **113** 4J
Bristol, U.K. **90** 2C
Brno, Czechoslovakia **93** 2F
Brochet, Man. **40** 2A
Brockville, Ont. **45** 2F
Broken Hill, Australia **112** 5G
Brooks, Alta. **37** 6F
Broome, Australia **112** 2C
Brunei **110** 3C
Brussels, Belgium **92** 1C
Bryansk, U.S.S.R. **91** 2G
Bucaramanga, Colombia **86** 3C
Buchans, Nfld. **50** 2C
Bucharest, Romania **93** 3H
Buckingham, PQ **46** 5C
Buctouche, NB **48** 2C
Budapest, Hungary **93** 2F
Buenaventura, Colombia **86** 3B
Buenos Aires, Argentina **87** 11F
Bujumbura, Burundi **97** 5F

Bulawayo, Zimbabwe **97** 7F
Bulgaria **93** 3G
Bunbury, Australia **112** 5B
Bundaberg, Australia **113** 3J
Bûr Sa'îd (Port Said), Egypt **108** 2C
Burgeo, Nfld. **50** 3C
Burgos, Spain **92** 3B
Burin, Nfld. **51** 3D
Burkina Faso **96** 3C
Burlington, Ont. **44** 3D
Burma **110** 1A
Burns Lake, B.C. **35** 2D
Bursa, Turkey **108** 1B
Buru, Indonesia **111** 4D
Burundi **97** 5G
Büshehr, Iran **109** 3G
Bydgoszcz, Poland **91** 2E
Byelorussian S.S.R. **100** 4C
Bylot Island, NWT **33** 3K

C

Cabano, PQ **47** 4F
Cabinda **96** 5E
Cabonga Reservoir, PQ **46** 4B
Cabot Strait, NS/Nfld. **49** 2F
Cache Creek, B.C. **35** 3E
Cádiz, Spain **92** 4A
Caen, France **94** 2E
Cagliari, Italy **92** 4D
Cairns, Australia **113** 2H
Cairo (El Qahira), Egypt **108** 2C
Cajamarca (department), Peru **88** 6B
Cajamarca, Peru **88** 6B
Calabar, Nigeria **98** 5E
Calais, France **95** 1F
Calcutta, India **107** 5N
Calgary, Alta. **37** 6D
Cali, Colombia **86** 4B
Callao, Peru **89** 8B
Calvi, Corsica **95** 6M
Camagüey, Cuba **85** 3J
Cambodia (Kampuchea) **110** 2B
Cambridge Bay, NWT **32** 4G
Cambridge, Ont. **44** 3C
Cambridge, U.K. **90** 2D
Cameroon **96** 4E
Campbell River, B.C. **35** 3D
Campbellton, NB **48** 2B
Campeche, Mexico **84** 4F
Campobello Island, NB **48** 3B
Camrose, Alta. **37** 5E
Canaan River, NB **48** 3C
Canary Islands (Spain) **96** 2B
Canberra, Australia **113** 6H
Cancun, Mexico **84** 3G
Caniapiscau Lake, PQ **52** 3D
Caniapiscau River, PQ **52** 3D
Cannes, France **95** 5J
Canso, NS **49** 3E
Cap-Chat, PQ **47** 3G
Cap-aux-Meules, PQ **49** 2E
Cape Breton Island, NS **49** 3E
Cape Dorset, NWT **33** 5K
Cape Town, South Africa **96** 8E
Cape Verde Islands **96** 3A
Cape York Peninsula, Australia **112** 1G
Capreol, Ont. **43** 4E
Caracas, Venezuela **86** 2D
Caraquet, NB **48** 2C
Carbonear, Nfld. **51** 3E
Carcassonne, France **95** 5G
Cardiff, U.K. **90** 2C
Cardinal, Ont. **45** 2F
Cardston, Alta. **37** 7E
Caribbean Sea, **85** 4J
Caribou River, Man. **40** 1D
Carleton Place, Ont. **45** 2E
Carlyle, Sask. **39** 7E
Carman, Man. **41** 6B
Carmanville, Nfld. **51** 2D
Carnarvon, Australia **112** 3A
Carpentaria, Gulf of, Australia **112** 1F
Carrot River, Sask. **39** 5E
Cartagena, Colombia **86** 2B
Cartagena, Spain **92** 4B
Cartier, Ont. **43** 4E
Cartwright, Nfld. **53** 3G
Casablanca, Morocco **96** 1C
Caspian Sea, **106** 1F
Cassiar, B.C. **34** 1C
Castlegar, B.C. **35** 3F
Catalina, Nfld. **51** 2E
Causapscal, PQ **47** 3G
Cayenne, French Guiana **86** 4G
Cayman Islands (U.K.) **85** 4H
Cebu, Philippines **110** 2D

Cedar Lake, Man. **41** 4B
Celebes Sea, **110** 3D
Celtic Sea, **94** 1B
Central African Republic **97** 4E-F
Central America 84-85
Ceram, Indonesia **111** 4D
Cerro de Pasco, Peru **89** 7B
Ch'ŏngjin, N. Korea **104** 3E
Ch'ŏngju, S. Korea **104** 5D
Ch'unch'ŏn, S. Korea **104** 5D
Chachapoyas, Peru **88** 6B
Chad **96** 3E
Chad, Lake, **96** 3E
Chaleur Bay, NB **48** 2C
Chalon, France **95** 3H
Chalons, France **95** 2H
Chambery, France **95** 4H
Chandler, PQ **47** 3H
Chang Jiang (Yangtze) River, China 102-103 4H
Changchun, China **103** 2M
Changsha, China **103** 5J
Channel Islands, U.K. **92** 2B
Channel-Port aux Basques, Nfld. **50** 3B
Chapais, PQ **46** 3C
Chapleau, Ont. **43** 4E
Charente River, France **94** 4E
Chari River, **99** 1-2H
Charleville, Australia **113** 4H
Charleville-Mézières, France **95** 2H
Charlottetown, PEI **49** 2D
Chartres, France **95** 2F
Chase, B.C. **35** 3F
Chatham Island, New Zealand **113** 7P
Chatham, NB **48** 2C
Chatham, Ont. **44** 3B
Cheju-do, S. Korea **104** 7D
Chelyabinsk, U.S.S.R. **100** 4G
Chengdu, China **102** 4G
Cher River, France **94** 3F
Cherbourg, France **94** 2E
Chernovtsy, U.S.S.R. **100** 5C
Chester, NS **48** 3C
Chesterfield Inlet, NWT **33** 5H
Chéticamp, NS **49** 2E
Chetwynd, B.C. **35** 2E
Chiang Mai, Thailand **110** 2A
Chibougamau, PQ **46** 3C
Chiclayo, Peru **88** 6B
Chicoutimi, PQ **46** 3E
Chignecto Bay, NB/NS **48** 3C
Chihuahua, Mexico **84** 2C
Chilcotin River, B.C. **35** 3E
Chile **87** 10B
Chilko Lake, B.C. **35** 3D
Chilliwack, B.C. **35** 3E
Chimbote, Peru **89** 7B
Chimkent, U.S.S.R. **100** 5G
China, People's Republic of 102-103
Chincha Alta, Peru **89** 8B
Chinchaga River, Alta. **36** 3B
Chinju, S. Korea **104** 6D
Chipman, NB **48** 2C
Chisasibi, PQ **52** 3B
Chita, U.S.S.R. **101** 4M
Chittagong, Bangladesh **107** 5O
Chongqing, China **102** 5H
Chŏnju, S. Korea **104** 6D
Christchurch, New Zealand **113** 7N
Chu River, U.S.S.R. **100** 5H
Chubut River, Argentina **87** 13D
Churchill Falls, Nfld. **53** 3E
Churchill River, Man. **40** 2C
Churchill River, Nfld. **53** 3F
Churchill, Man. **40** 1D
Ciudad Bolivar, Venezuela **85** 6M
Ciudad Juárez, Mexico **84** 1C
Clair, NB **48** 2A
Claire, Lake, Alta. **36** 2E
Clarenville, Nfld. **51** 2E
Clark's Harbour, NS **48** 2C
Clarke's Head, Nfld. **51** 2D
Clearwater River, Sask. **38** 3B
Clermont-Ferrand, France **95** 4G
Cloncurry, Australia **112** 3G
Cluj-Napoca, Romania **93** 2G
Clyde River, NS **48** 4C
Coaticook, PQ **46** 5E
Cobalt, Ont. **43** 4F
Cobourg, Ont. **45** 3D
Cochranr, Ont. **43** 3E
Cold Lake, Alta. **36** 4F
Cold Lake, Alta. **36** 4F
Coleman, Alta. **37** 7D
Collingwood, Ont. **44** 2C
Colombia **86** 4C

Colombo, Sri Lanka **107** L8
Colón, Panama **85** J6
Colorado River, Argentina **87** 12D
Columbia River, B.C. **35** 3F
Comodoro Rivadavia, Argentina **87** 14D
Comoros Islands **97** 6H
Comox, B.C. **35** 3D
Conakry, Guinea **96** 4B
Conception Bay, Nfld. **51** 3E
Congo **96** 5E
Constanța, Romania **93** 3H
Constantine, Algeria **96** 1D
Cook Islands (New Zealand) **117** 4E
Cook Strait, New Zealand **113** 6N
Cook, Mt., New Zealand **113** 7N
Copenhagen, Denmark **90** 2E
Coppermine River, NWT **32** 4F
Coppermine, NWT **32** 4F
Coral Harbour, NWT **33** 5J
Coral Sea Islands Territory **116** 4D
Coral Sea, **113** 2J-K
Córdoba, Argentina **87** 11D
Cordoba, Spain **92** 4A
Cork, Ireland **90** 2C
Cornerbrook, Nfld. **50** 2C
Cornwall, Ont. **45** 2F
Corsica (France) **95** 5K
Corte, Corsica **95** 6N
Costa Rica **85** 6G
Cote d'Ivoire (Ivory Coast) **96** 4C
Coulonge River, PQ **46** 4B
Courtenay, B.C. **35** 3D
Cowansville, PQ **46** 5D
Cox's Cove, Nfld. **50** 2B
Craiova, Romania **93** 3G
Cranbrook, B.C. **35** 3G
Cree Lake, Sask. **38** 3C
Cree River, Sask. **38** 2D
Creighton, Sask. **38** 4F
Creston, B.C. **35** 3F
Crete (Greece) **93** 4G
Crete, Sea of, **93** 4G
Cross Lake, Man. **40** 3C
Cuba **85** 3H
Cuiabá, Brazil **86** 8F
Culiacán, Mexico **84** 3C
Cumana, Venezuela **85** 5L
Cumberland Sound, NWT **33** 4L
Curacao, Netherlands Antilles **85** 5L
Curitiba, Brazil **87** 10H
Cuzco (department), Peru **89** 8C
Cuzco, Peru **89** 8D
Cyprus **108** 1C
Czechoslovakia, **93** 2F

D

Da Nang, Vietnam **110** 2B
Da Yunhe Canal, China **103** 3K
Dacca, Bangladesh **107** 5O
Dakar, Senegal **96** 3B
Dalhousie, NB **48** 1B
Daloa, Cote d'Ivoire **96** 4C
Daly River, Australia **112** 1E
Damascus (Dimashq) Syria **106** 3C
Dandong, China **103** 2L
Daniel's Harbour, Nfld. **50** 1C
Danube River, Europe **93** 2E
Dar es Salaam, Tanzania **97** 5G
Darjeeling, India **107** 4N
Dark Cove, Nfld. **51** 2D
Darling River, Australia **113** 5G
Dartmouth, NS **49** 3D
Darwin, Australia **112** 1E
Daugavpils, U.S.S.R. **91** 2F
Dauphin Lake, Man. **41** 5B
Dauphin, Man. **41** 5A
Davao, Philippines **111** 3D
David, Panama **85** 6H
Davis Inlet, Nfld. **53** 3F
Davis Strait, NWT **33** 4N
Dawson Creek, B.C. **35** 2E
Dawson, YT **32** 5D
Dead Sea, **108** 2D
Debert, NS **49** 3D
Debrecen, Hungary **93** 2G
Deep River, Ont. **45** 1E
Deer Lake, Nfld. **50** 2C
Degema, Nigeria **98** 5D
Delhi, India **107** 4L
Delhi, Ont. **44** 3C
Deloraine, Man. **41** 6A
Denizli, Turkey **108** 1B
Denmark, 90
Denpasar, Indonesia **110** 4C
Derby, Australia **112** 2C
Deschambault Lake, Sask. **38** 4E

138

Hawalli, Kuwait **109** 3F
Hawke's Bay, Nfld. **50** 1C
Hawkesbury, Ont. **45** 2F
Hay River, NWT **32** 5F
Hay River, Alta. **36** 2C
Hayes River, Man. **40** 2E
Hearst, Ont. **43** 3E
Hebei (province), China **103** 3K
Hebrides Islands, U.K. **90** 2C
Hebron, Nfld. **53** 2F
Hecate Strait, B.C. **34** 2C
Hefa, Israel **108** 2D
Heifei, China **103** 4K
Heilong Jiang (Amur) River, Asia **103** 1M
Heilongjiang (province), China **103** 1M
Helsinki, Finland **91** 1F
Henan (province), China **103** 4J
Hengyang, China **103** 5J
Herat, Afghanistan **106** 3H
Herlen River, China **103** 1J
Herring Cove, NS **49** 3D
High Level, Alta. **36** 2C
High Prairie, Alta. **36** 4C
High River, Alta. **37** 6E
Highrock Lake, Man. **40** 3A
Himeji, Japan **105** 6F
Ḥimṣ, Syria **108** 2D
Hines Creek, Alta. **36** 3C
Hinton, Alta. **37** 5C
Hiroshima, Japan **104** 6F
Hitachi, Japan **105** 5H
Ho Chi Minh City (Saigon), Vietnam **110** 2B
Hobart, Australia **113** 7H
Hofn, Iceland **90** 1B
Hohhot, China **103** 2J
Hokkaidō, Japan **105** 2J
Holguin, Cuba **85** 3J
Holman, NWT **32** 3F
Holyrood, Nfld. **51** 3E
Honduras **85** 4G
Hong Kong (U.K.) **103** 6J
Hongshui River, China **103** 6J
Honshū, Japan, 105
Hope, B.C. **35** 3E
Hopedale, Nfld. **53** 3F
Hornepayne, Ont. **43** 3D
Huacho, Peru **89** 7B
Huallaga River, Peru **88** 6-7B
Huambo, Angola **96** 6E
Huancavelica (department), Peru **89** 8C
Huancavelica, Peru **89** 8C
Huancayo, Peru **89** 8C
Huang (Yellow) River, China **102** 2H
Huánuco (department), Peru **89** 7B
Huánuco, Peru **89** 7B
Huaraz, Peru **89** 7B
Hubei (province), China **103** 4J
Hudson Bay, Sask. **39** 5E
Hudson Bay, NWT **52** 2A
Hudson Strait, NWT **33** 5K
Hudson, PQ **44** 5C
Hue, Vietnam **110** 2B
Hull, PQ **46** 5C
Humboldt, Sask. **39** 5D
Hunan (province), China **103** 5J
Hungary **93** 2F
Hüngnam, N. Korea **104** 4D
Huntsville, Ont. **44** 2D
Huron, Lake, Ont. **44** 2B
Hyderabad, India **107** 6L
Hyderabad, Pakistan **107** 4J

I

Ibadan, Nigeria **98** 4B
Ica (department), Peru **89** 8C
Ica, Peru **89** 8C
Iceland **90** 1B
Idah, Nigeria **98** 4D
Ife, Nigeria **98** 4C
Igloolik, NWT **33** 4J
Ignace, Ont. **42** 3C
Ijebu Obe, Nigeria **98** 4B
Ikeja, Nigeria **98** 4B
Ikerre, Nigeria **98** 4C
Ikot Ekpene, Nigeria **98** 5D
Ila, Nigeria **98** 3C
Ilaro, Nigeria **98** 4B
Ile d'Anticósti, PQ **47** 3J
Iles Wallis (France) **116** 4E
Iles de la Madeleine, PQ **49** 2E
Ilesha, Nigeria **98** 3B
Iloilo, Philippines **110** 2D
Ilorin, Nigeria **98** 4B
Inambari River, Peru **89** 8D
Inch'on, S. Korea **104** 5D
India **107** 5L

Indian Ocean, **106** 7G
Indigirka River, U.S.S.R. **101** 3P
Indonesia 110-111 4C
Indore, India **107** 5L
Indus River, Pakistan **107** 4J
Ingersoll, Ont. **44** 3C
Innisfail, Australia **113** 2H
Innsbruck, Austria **90** 3E
Inukjuak, PQ **52** 2B
Inuvik, NWT **32** 4D
Inverness, U.K. **90** 2C
Ionian Sea, **93** 4F
Iqaluit, NWT **33** 5L
Iquitos, Peru **88** 5C
Iráklion, Greece **93** 4H
Iran, 109
Iraq, 108-109
Irawaddy River, Asia **110** 1A
Irbid, Jordan **108** 2D
Irbil, Iraq **108** 1E
Ireland, Republic of **90** 2C
Irian Jaya, Indonesia **111** 4E
Irish Sea, **90** 2C
Irkutsk, U.S.S.R. **101** 4L
Iroquois Falls, Ont. **43** 3E
Irtysh River, U.S.S.R. **100** 4H
Isachsen, NWT **33** 2G
Iseyin, Nigeria **98** 4B
Ishikari River, Japan **105** 2J
Ishim River, U.S.S.R. **100** 4G
Islamabad, Pakistan **107** 3K
Isle Madame, NS **49** 3E
Isle aux Morts, Nfld. **50** 3B
Israel 108
İstanbul (Constantinople), Turkey **108** 1B
Italy **93** 3E
Ivanovo, U.S.S.R. **100** 4E
Iverness, NS **49** 2E
Ivujivik, PQ **52** 1B
Iwo, Nigeria **98** 4C
Izhevsk, U.S.S.R. **100** 4F
İzmir, Turkey **108** 1B

J

Jabalpur, India **107** 5L
Jackson's Arm, Nfld. **50** 2C
Jaipur, India **107** 4L
Jakarta, Indonesia **110** 4B
Jalingo, Nigeria **99** 3F
Jamaica **85** 4J
James Bay, NWT **43** 2E
Jamshedpur, India **107** 5N
Japan, 104-105
Japan, Sea of, 104-105
Java, Indonesia **110** 4B
Jayapura, Indonesia **111** 4F
Jebba, Nigeria **98** 3C
Jega, Nigeria **98** 1C
Jerusalem, Israel **108** 2D
Jiangsu (province), China **103** 4L
Jiangxi (province), China **103** 5J
Jiddah, Saudi Arabia **108** 4D
Jilin (province), China **103** 2M
Jilin, China **103** 2M
Jimeta, Nigeria **99** 3G
Jinan, China **103** 3K
Jinzhou, China **103** 2L
Jodpur, India **107** 4K
Johannesburg, South Africa **97** 7F
Joliette, PQ **46** 4D
Jonquière, PQ **46** 3E
Jordan **108** 2D
Jos, Nigeria **99** 3E
Joseph Bonaparte Gulf, Australia **112** 1D
Juba, Sudan **97** 4G
Junín (department), Peru **89** 7C
Juniper, NB **48** 2B
Jurua River, Brazil **86** 6C
Juruena River, Brazil **86** 7F

K

K-2, Mt., **102** 3B
Kabalo, Zaire **97** 5F
Kabul, Afghanistan **107** 3J
Kaduna River, Nigeria **98** 3C-E
Kaduna, Nigeria **98** 2D
Kaesong, N. Korea **104** 4D
Kagoshima, Japan **104** 8E
Kalahari Desert **97** 7F
Kalámai, Greece **93** 4G
Kalemie, Zaire **97** 5F
Kalgoorlie, Australia **112** 5C
Kalinin, U.S.S.R. **100** 4D
Kaliningrad, U.S.S.R. **100** 4C
Kaliningrad, U.S.S.R. **91** 2F
Kalmar, Sweden **91** 2E

Kaluga, U.S.S.R. **91** 2G
Kamloops, B.C. **35** 3E
Kampala, Uganda **97** 4G
Kampuchea **110** 2B
Kamsack, Sask. **39** 6F
Kanaaupscow River, PQ **52** 3C
Kanairiktok River, Nfld. **53** 3F
Kananga, Zaire **97** 5F
Kanazawa, Japan **105** 5G
Kanchenjunga, Mt., India **107** 4N
Kandahar, Afghanistan **106** 3J
Kandalaksha, U.S.S.R. **91** 1G
Kandy, Sri Lanka **107** 8M
Kangaroo Island, Australia **112** 6F
Kangiksujuaq, PQ **52** 1D
Kangiksuk, PQ **52** 1D
Kangiqsualujjuag, PQ **53** 2E
Kangirtugaapik, NWT **33** 3L
Kano, Nigeria **99** 2E
Kanpur, India **107** 4M
Kaohsiung, Taiwan **110** 1D
Kapiskau River, Ont. **43** 2D
Kapuas River, Borneo **110** 4B
Kapuskasing River, Ont. **43** 3E
Kapuskasing, Ont. **43** 3E
Kara Sea, **100** 2G
Karachi, Pakistan **107** 5J
Karaganda, U.S.S.R. **100** 5H
Karbalā, Iraq **108** 2E
Karlskrona, Sweden **91** 2E
Katsina Ala River, Nigeria **99** 4E
Katsina, Nigeria **98** 1D
Kashechewan, Ont. **43** 2E
Kashi, China **103** 3B
Kassala, Sudan **97** 3G
Katherine, Australia **112** 1E
Katmandu, Nepal **107** 4N
Kaujuitoq, NWT **33** 3H
Kaunas, U.S.S.R. **91** 2F
Kaura Namoda, Nigeria **98** 1D
Kawasaki, Japan **105** 6H
Kayseri, Turkey **108** 1D
Kazakh S.S.R., U.S.S.R. **100** 5G
Kazan', U.S.S.R. **91** 2H
Kazan, U.S.S.R. **100** 4E
Kebi River, **99** 3H
Kechika River, B.C. **35** 1D
Kedgwick, NB **48** 2B
Keewatin, Ont. **42** 3B
Keffi, Nigeria **98** 3D
Kelowna, B.C. **35** 3F
Kelsey, Man. **40** 2C
Kemerovo, U.S.S.R. **100** 4J
Kemi, Finland **91** 1F
Kemptville, Ont. **45** 2F
Kenogami River, Ont. **42** 3D
Kenora, Ont. **42** 3B
Kensington, PEI **49** 2D
Kentville, NS **48** 3C
Kenya **97** 4-5G
Kerman, Iran **109** 2H
Kermānshāh, Iran **109** 2F
Khabarovsk, U.S.S.R. **101** 5Q
Khanka, Lake, U.S.S.R. **104** 1F
Kharkov, U.S.S.R. **100** 4D
Khartoum, Sudan **97** 3G
Kherson, U.S.S.R. **100** 5D
Kiel, F.R.G. **90** 2E
Kigali, Rwanda **97** 5G
Kigoma, Tanzania **97** 5F
Kilchu, N. Korea **104** 3E
Kilimanjaro, Mt., Tanzania **97** 5G
Killiniq, PQ **53** 1E
Kimberley, B.C. **35** 3F
Kimberley, South Africa **97** 7F
Kincardine, Ont. **44** 2C
Kindersley, Sask. **39** 6B
King Island, Australia **113** 6G
Kingston, NS **48** 3C
Kingston, Ont. **45** 2E
Kingston, Jamaica **85** 4J
Kinoosao, Sask. **38** 3B
Kinshasa, Zaire **96** 5E
Kirgiz S.S.R., U.S.S.R. **100** 5H
Kiribati Islands 116-117 4E
Kirikkale, Turkey **108** 1C
Kirkland Lake, Ont. **43** 3E
Kirkūk, Iraq **108** 1E
Kirov, U.S.S.R. **100** 4F
Kirov, U.S.S.R. **91** 2H
Kiruna, Sweden **91** 1F
Kisangani, Zaire **97** 4F
Kishinev, U.S.S.R. **100** 5C
Kishinev, U.S.S.R. **91** 3F
Kismaayo, Somalia **97** 5H
Kississing Lake, Man. **40** 3A

Kitakami River, Japan **105** 4J
Kitakyūshū, Japan **104** 7E
Kitchener-Waterloo, Ont. **44** 3C
Kitimat, B.C. **34** 2C
Kiyev, U.S.S.R. **100** 4C
Kizil Irmak River, Turkey **108** 1C
Klaipėda, U.S.S.R. **91** 2F
Kōbe, Japan **105** 6G
Kōchi, Japan **105** 7F
Kōfu, Japan **105** 6H
Kogaluc River, PQ **52** 2B
Koksoak River, PQ **52** 2D
Kolyma River, U.S.S.R. **101** 3Q
Komadugu Gana River, Nigeria **99** 2F
Komsomol'sk, U.S.S.R. **101** 4O
Kontagora, Nigeria **98** 2C
Konya, Turkey **108** 1C
Koocanusa, Lake, B.C. **35** 3G
Kootenay Lake, B.C. **35** 3F
Korea Bay, **104** 4C
Korea Strait, 104
Korea, Democratic People's Republic
of (North Korea) 104
Korea, Republic of (South Korea) 104
Kosciusko, Mt., Australia **113** 6H
Kosice, Czechoslovakia **93** 2G
Kota Baharu, Malaysia **110** 3B
Kotuy River, U.S.S.R. **101** 2L
Kraków, Poland **91** 2F
Krasnodar, U.S.S.R. **100** 5D
Krasnoyarsk, U.S.S.R. **101** 4K
Krishna River, India **107** L6
Kristiansand, Norway **90** 2D
Krung Thep (Bangkok), Thailand **110** 2B
Kuala Lumpur, Malaysia **110** 3B
Kuching, Malaysia **110** 3C
Kukawa, Nigeria **99** 1C
Kumamoto, Japan **104** 7E
Kumo, Nigeria **99** 2F
Kunming, China **102** 5G
Kunsan, S. Korea **104** 6D
Kupang, Indonesia **110** 4D
Kuopio, Finland **91** 1F
Kure, Japan **105** 6F
Kuril Islands, U.S.S.R. **101** 5Q
Kursk, U.S.S.R. **100** 4D
Kurume, Japan **104** 7E
Kushiro, Japan **105** 2K
Kuujjuaq, PQ **52** 2D
Kuujjuarapik, PQ **52** 3B
Kuwait **106** 4E
Kuwait, Kuwait **106** 4E
Kuybyshev, U.S.S.R. **100** 4F
Kwangju, S. Korea **104** 6D
Kyōto, Japan **105** 6G
Kyūshū, Japan **104** 7E

L

L'vov, U.S.S.R. **100** 5C
LG2, Reservoir, PQ **52** 3B
LG3, Reservoir, PQ **52** 3C
La Baie, PQ **47** 3E
La Coruña, Spain **92** 3A
La Libertad (department), Peru **88** 6B
La Loche, Sask. **38** 3B
La Malbaie, PQ **47** 4E
La Oroya, Peru **89** 7C
La Paz, Bolivia **86** 8D
La Plata, Argentina **87** 12F
La Pocatière, PQ **47** 4E
La Rochelle, France **94** 3E
La Ronge, Sask. **38** 4D
La Sarre, PQ **46** 3A
La Scie, Nfld. **51** 2D
La Tuque, PQ **46** 4D
La'youn, Morocco **96** 2B
Labe, Guinea **96** 3B, 0
Labrador City, Nfld. **52** 3E
Lac La Ronge, Sask. **38** 4D
Lac Seul, Ont. **42** 3B
Lac des Mille Lacs, Ont. **42** 3C
Lac du Bonnet, Man. **41** 5C
Lac la Biche, Alta. **36** 4F
Lac la Biche, Alta. **36** 4E
Lac-Ile-à-la-Crosse, Sask. **38** 4C
Lac-Mégantic, PQ **47** 5E
Laccadive Islands (India) **107** 8K
Lachland River, Australia **113** 5G
Lachute, PQ **46** 5C
Lacolle, PQ **46** 5D
Ladoga, Lake, U.S.S.R. **100** 3D
Lae, Papua-New Guinea **111** 4F
Lafia, Nigeria **99** 3E
Lafiagi, Nigeria **98** 3C
Lagos, Nigeria **98** 4B
Lahore, Pakistan **107** 3K
Lake Louise, Alta. **37** 6C

Tabriz, Iran **109** 1F
Tabūk, Saudi Arabia **108** 3D
Tacna (department), Peru **89** 9D
Tacna, Peru **89** 9D
Tadoule Lake, Man. **40** 1B
Tadzhik S.S.R., U.S.S.R. **100** 6H
Taegu, S. Korea **104** 6D
Taejŏn, S. Korea **104** 5D
Tagus River, Spain **92** 4A
Tahsis, B.C. **35** 3D
Taipei, Taiwan **103** 6L
Taiwan **110** 1D
Taiyuan, China **103** 3J
Tajrīsh, Iran **109** 1G
Takamatsu, Japan **105** 6F
Takaoka, Japan **105** 5G
Takla Lake, B.C. **35** 2D
Talara, Peru **88** 6A
Tallinn, U.S.S.R. **100** 4C
Tamale, Ghana **96** 4C
Tambo River, Peru **89** 9D
Tambov, U.S.S.R. **100** 4E
Tampere, Finland **91** 1F
Tampico, Mexico **84** 3E
Tamworth, Australia **113** 5J
Tanganyika, Lake **97** 5F
Tanger, Morocco **96** 1C
Tangshan, China **103** 3K
Tanzania **97** 5G
Tapajos River, Brazil **86** 6F
Tapti River, India **107** 5L
Ţarābulus (Tripoli), Lebanon **108** 2D
Ţarābulus (Tripoli), Libya **96** 1E
Tarbes, France **94** 5F
Tarn River, France **95** 4G
Tarsus, Turkey **108** 1C
Tartu, U.S.S.R. **91** 2F
Tashkent, U.S.S.R. **100** 5G
Tasman Sea **113** 6K-L
Tasmania (state), Australia **113** 7H
Tatamagouche, NS **49** 3D
Taz River, U.S.S.R. **100** 3J
Tbilisi, U.S.S.R. **100** 5E
Tegucigalpa, Honduras **84** 5G
Tehran, Iran **109** 1G
Tel Aviv-Yafo, Israel **108** 2C
Telukbetung, Indonesia **110** 4B
Temagami, Lake, Ont. **43** 4E
Temagami, Ont. **43** 4F
Témiscaming, PQ **46** 4A
Tennant Creek, Australia **112** 2E
Teresina, Brazil **86** 6J
Terrace Bay, NS **49** 3D
Terrace Bay, Ont. **42** 3D
Terrace, B.C. **34** 2C
Terrenceville, Nfld. **51** 3D
Teslin Lake, B.C. **34** 1B
Teslin, YT **32** 5D
Tête-à-la-Baleine, PQ **53** 4G
Thailand **110** 2B
Thailand, Gulf of **110** 2B
Thames River, Ont. **44** 3C
The Pas, Man. **41** 4A
Thelon River, NWT **32** 5G
Thessalon, Ont. **44** 1B
Thessaloníki, Greece **93** 3G
Thetford-Mines, PQ **46** 4E
Thimbu, Bhutan **107** 4N
Thompson River, Australia **112** 4G
Thompson, Man. **40** 3C
Thunder Bay, Ont. **42** 3C
Tianjin Shi (province), China **103** 3K
Tianjin, China **103** 3K
Tibet (Xizang) (province), China **102** 4D
Tierra del Fuego **87** 15D
Tignish, PEI **49** 2C
Tigre River, Peru **88** 5C
Tigris River, Asia **108** 1E
Tijuana, Mexico **84** 1A
Tillsonburg, Ont. **44** 3C
Timbuktu (Tombouctou), Mali **96** 3C
Timmins, Ont. **43** 3E
Timor Sea **110** 5D
Timor, Indonesia **110-111** 4D
Tirana, Albania **93** 3F
Tirgu Mures, Romania **93** 2G
Tisa River, Europe **93** 2G
Tisdale, Sask. **39** 5D
Titicaca, Lake, Peru **89** 8D
Titicaca, Lake, S. America **86** 8D
Toamasina, Madagascar **97** 6H
Tobermory, Ont. **44** 2C
Tobique River, NB **48** 2B
Tobol River, U.S.S.R. **100** 4G
Tocantins River, Brazil **86** 6H
Togo **96** 4D
Tokelau Islands **116** 4E

Tokushima, Japan **105** 6F
Tōkyō, Japan **105** 6H
Toliary, Madagascar **97** 7H
Tombouctou (Timbuktu), Mali **96** 3C
Tomsk, U.S.S.R. **100** 4J
Tonga **116** 4E
Toowoomba, Australia **113** 4J
Torino, Italy **92** 3D
Toronto, Ont. **44** 3D
Torrens, Lake, Australia **112** 5F
Torreon, Mexico **84** 2D
Toulon, France **95** 5H
Toulouse, France **95** 5F
Tours, France **94** 3F
Townsville, Australia **113** 2H
Toyama, Japan **105** 5G
Tracadie, NB **48** 2C
Trail, B.C. **35** 3F
Trenton, Ont. **45** 2E
Trepassey, Nfld. **51** 3E
Trieste, Italy **90** 3E
Trincomalee, Sri Lanka **107** 8M
Trinidad and Tobago **85** 5M
Trinity Bay, Nfld. **51** 3E
Trois-Pistoles, PQ **47** 3F
Trois-Rivières, PQ **46** 4D
Tromsø, Norway **90** 1E
Trondheim, Norway **90** 1E
Trout Lake, Ont. **42** 3B
Troyes, France **95** 2H
Trujillo, Peru **88** 7B
Truro, NS **49** 3D
Trust Territory of the Pacific Islands **116** 3D
Tselinograd, U.S.S.R. **100** 4H
Tuktoyaktuk, NWT **32** 4D
Tula, U.S.S.R. **100** 4D
Tuman River, China--N. Korea **104** 2E
Tumbes (department), Peru **88** 5A
Tumbes, Peru **88** 5A
Tumbler Ridge, B.C. **35** 2E
Tunis, Tunisia **96** 1E
Tunisia, **96** 1D
Turkana, Lake, Kenya **97** 4G
Turkey **108** 1B-E
Turkmen S.S.R., U.S.S.R. **100** 6F
Turks and Caicos Islands (U.K.) **85** 3K
Turku, Finland **91** 1F
Tuvalu Islands **116** 4D
Tweed, Ont. **45** 2E
Twillingate, Nfld. **51** 2D
Tyrrhenian Sea **93** 3E
Tyumen, U.S.S.R. **100** 4G

U

Ubon Ratchathani, Thailand **110** 2B
Ucayali (department), Peru **89** 7C
Ucayali River, Peru **89** 6-7C
Ucluelet, B.C. **35** 3D
Ufa, U.S.S.R. **100** 4F
Uganda **97** 4G
Ujang Padang, Indonesia **110** 4C
Ukrainian S.S.R. U.S.S.R. **100** 5C
Ul'yanovsk, U.S.S.R. **100** 4E
Ulaanbaatar, Mongolia **102** 1G
Ulan Ude, U.S.S.R. **101** 4L
Ulsan, S. Korea **104** 6E
Unggi, N. Korea **104** 2E
Union of Soviet Socialist Republics **100-101**
United Arab Emirates **109** 4G
United Kingdom **90**
United States of America **117** 2G
Unity, Sask. **39** 5B
Ural River, U.S.S.R. **100** 5F
Uranium City, Sask. **38** 2B
Urfa, Turkey **108** 1D
Uruguay **87** 11F
Uruguay River, S. America **87** 10F
Urumqi, China **102** 2D
Uticuma Lake, Alta. **36** 4D
Utik Lake, Man. **40** 3C
Utsonomiya, Japan **105** 5H
Uzbek S.S.R., U.S.S.R. **100** 5G

V

Vaasa, Finland **91** 1F
Val-d'Or, PQ **46** 3B
Valdiva, Chile **87** 12B
Valence, France **95** 4H
Valencia, Spain **92** 4B
Valletta, Malta **93** 4E
Valley East, Ont. **44** 1C
Valparaiso, Chile **87** 11C
Vancouver Island, B.C. **35** 3D
Vancouver, B.C. **35** 3E
Vanern, Lake, Sweden **90** 2E
Vanuatu **116** 4D

Varanasi, India **107** 4M
Varna, Bulgaria **93** 3H
Vatneyri, Iceland **90** 1A
Vattern, Lake, Sweden **91** 2E
Vegreville, Alta. **37** 5E
Venezuela **85** 6L
Venice, Italy **93** 2E
Ventspils, U.S.S.R. **91** 2F
Veracruz, Mexico **84** 4E
Vernon, B.C. **35** 3F
Victoria (state), Australia **113** 6G
Victoria Island, NWT **32** 3F
Victoria Lake, Nfld. **50** 2C
Victoria River, Australia **112** 2E
Victoria, Lake, Tanzania **97** 5G
Victoria, B.C. **35** 3E
Victoriaville, PQ **46** 4E
Vidal, Peru **88** 5C
Vienna, Austria **93** 2F
Vienne River, France **94** 3F
Vientiane, Laos **110** 2B
Vietnam **110** 2B
Vigo, Spain **92** 3A
Vilaine River, France **94** 3E
Villa Hermosa, Mexico **84** 4F
Vilnius, U.S.S.R. **100** 4C
Virden, Man. **41** 6A
Virgin Islands (U.K.) **85** 4M
Viscount Melville Sound, NWT **32** 3G
Vitebsk, U.S.S.R. **100** 4C
Vitim River, U.S.S.R. **101** 4N
Vladivostok, U.S.S.R. **101** 5O
Volga River, U.S.S.R. **100** 5E
Volgograd, U.S.S.R. **100** 5E
Vologda, U.S.S.R. **100** 4E
Vorkuta, U.S.S.R. **100** 3G
Voronezh, U.S.S.R. **100** 4D
Vyborg, U.S.S.R. **91** 1F
Vychegda River, U.S.S.R. **91** 1H-J

W

Wabasca River, Alta. **36** 3D
Wabowden, Man. **40** 3B
Wabush, Nfld. **53** 3F
Wadena, Sask. **39** 6E
Wadi Halfa, Sudan **97** 2G
Wagga Wagga, Australia **113** 6H
Wainwright, Alta. **37** 5F
Wakau, Sask. **39** 5D
Wakayama, Japan **105** 6G
Wakkau, Sask. **39** 5D
Walkerton, Ont. **44** 2C
Wallaceburg, Ont. **44** 3B
Walvis Bay (South Africa) **96** 7E
Wanapitei Lake, Ont. **44** 1C
Warri, Nigeria **98** 5C
Warrnambool, Australia **112** 6G
Warsaw, Poland **91** 2F
Washington, U.S.A. **117** 2H
Waterford, Ireland **90** 2C
Waterhen Lake, Man. **41** 4B
Watrous, Sask. **39** 6D
Watson Lake, YT **32** 5E
Wawa, Nigeria **98** 3C
Wawa, Ont. **43** 3D
Weagamow Lake, Ont. **42** 2C
Weipa, Australia **112** 1G
Wekusko, Man. **40** 3B
Welland, Ont. **44** 3D
Wellington, New Zealand **113** 7N
Wemindji, PQ **52** 3B
Wenzhou, China **103** 5K
Wesleyville, Nfld. **51** 2E
West Indies **85** 3L
Western Australia (state), Australia **112** 4C
Wetaskiwin, Alta. **37** 5E
Weyburn, Sask. **39** 7E
Whistler, B.C. **35** 3E
White Bay, Nfld. **50** 2C
White Nile River **97** 3G
White River, Ont. **42** 3D
White Sea **91** 1G
Whitebourne, Nfld. **51** 3E
Whitecourt, Alta. **37** 4D
Whitehorse, YT **32** 5D
Whitney, Ont. **45** 2D
Whyalla, Australia **112** 5F
Wiarton, Ont. **44** 2C
William River, Sask. **38** 2C
Williams Lake, B.C. **35** 2E
Williston Lake, B.C. **35** 1D
Windsor, Namibia **96** 7E
Windsor, NS **49** 3C
Windsor, Nfld. **51** 2D
Windsor, Ont. **44** 3B
Windsor, PQ **46** 5E
Wingham, Ont. **44** 3C
Winisk River, Ont. **42** 2D

Winisk, Ont. **42** 2D
Winnipeg River, Man. **41** 5C
Winnipeg, Lake, Man. **41** 4B
Winnipeg, Man. **41** 6C
Winnipegosis, Lake, Man. **41** 4B
Wisla River, Poland **91** 2F
Wolfville, NS **48** 3C
Wollaston Lake, Sask. **38** 2E
Wollongong, Australia **113** 5J
Wŏnju, S. Korea **104** 5D
Wŏnsan, N. Korea **104** 4D
Woodstock, NB **48** 2B
Woodstock, Ont. **44** 3C
Wroclaw, Poland **91** 2E
Wuhan, China **103** 4J
Wukari, Nigeria **99** 4E
Wunnummin Lake, Ont. **42** 2C
Wuxi, China **103** 4L
Wyndham, Australia **112** 2D

X

Xi'an, China **102** 4H
Xiamen, China **103** 6K
Xiang River, China **103** 5J
Xingjiang (province), China **102** 2C
Xingu River, Brazil **86** 6G
Xining, China **102** 3G
Xizang (Tibet) (province) China **102** 4D
Xuzhou, China **103** 4K

Y

Yakutsk, U.S.S.R. **101** 3N
Yalong River, China **102** 4G
Yalu River, China **104** 3C
Yamagata, Japan **105** 4H
Yana River, U.S.S.R. **101** 3O
Yaoundé, Cameroon **96** 4E
Yarlung Zangbo **102** 5E
Yarmouth, NS **48** 4B
Yaroslavl', U.S.S.R. **100** 4D
Yazd, Iran **109** 2G
Yedseram River, Nigeria **99** 2G
Yellow Sea, **103** 4L
Yellowknife, NWT **32** 5F
Yelwa, Nigeria **98** 2C
Yemen, **108** 5E
Yemen, People's Democratic Republic of **109** 5F
Yenagoa, Nigeria **98** 5D
Yenisey River, U.S.S.R. **101** 4K
Yerevan, U.S.S.R. **100** 5E
Yinchuan, China **102** 3G
Yining, China **102** 2C
Yogyakarta, Indonesia **110** 4C
Yokohama, Japan **105** 6H
Yokosuka, Japan **105** 6H
Yola, Nigeria **99** 3G
York Factory, Man. **40** 2E
York, U.K. **90** 2C
Yorkton, Sask. **39** 6E
Yuan Hong River, China **102** 6G
Yucatan Peninsula, Mexico **84** 3G
Yugoslavia **93** 3F
Yukon River, YT **32** 5D
Yumen, China **102** 3F
Yunnan (province), China **102** 6G
Yuzhno-Sakalinsk, U.S.S.R. **101** 5P

Z

Zacatecas, Mexico **84** 3D
Zagreb, Yugoslavia **91** 3E
Zāhedān, Iran **109** 3J
Zaire **97** 4-6F
Zaire River, Zaire **97** 4F
Zambeze River, **97** 6F-G
Zambia **97** 6F
Zamboanga, Philippines **110** 3D
Zanzibar, Tanzania **97** 5G
Zaporozh'ye, U.S.S.R. **100** 5D
Zaragoza, Spain **92** 3B
Zaria, Nigeria **98** 2D
Zemlya Frantsa Josifa (Franz Joseph Land), U.S.S.R. **100** 1E
Zhangjiakou, China **103** 2K
Zhanjiang, China **103** 6J
Zhdanov, U.S.S.R. **100** 5D
Zhejiang (province), China **103** 5K
Zhengzhou, China **103** 4J
Zimbabwe **97** 6F
Zinder, Niger **96** 3D
Zlatoust, U.S.S.R. **100** 4F
Zürich, Switzerland **92** 2D

CREDITS

Every reasonable attempt has been made to identify and credit sources. Any errors or omissions will be corrected in future editions, providing the publisher has received written notification. Credits are listed in clockwise order from the bottom of each spread, unless otherwise indicated.

p.4: top left, top right—Kent Smith. **p.5:** centre top—Suzanne Gauthier. **pp.8-9:** J. Jacquemain/Miller Comstock Inc.; R. Vroom/Miller Comstock Inc.; E. Otto/Miller Comstock Inc. **pp.20-21:** Image Finders/ The Stockmarket Inc.; Four By Five; B.C. Ministry of Agriculture and Food, Information Services Branch; Ted Russell/The Image Bank; Darren Sweet; Darren Sweet; Grant Heilman/Miller Comstock Inc.; Ontario Ministry of Agriculture and Food. **pp.22-23:** Abitibi—Price Inc. (all photos). **pp.26-27:** Department of Natural Resources; Noranda Inc. **pp.28-29:** Imperial Oil Limited; Imperial Oil Limited; Imperial Oil Limited; Imperial Oil Limited; Denis Thibodeau/Marystown Shipyard Ltd. **pp.30-31:** Via Rail; J. Jacquemain/Miller Comstock Inc.; W. Griebeling/Miller Comstock Inc.; Department of Transportation and Communications; CN Rail; Darren Sweet; Department of Transportation and Communications. **pp.32-53:** LANDSAT Satellite Imagery courtesy of the Canada Centre for Remote Sensing, Energy, Mines, and Resources Canada. **pp.120-121:** top row, left to right—Earth Satellite Corporation; George Hunter/Miller Comstock Inc.; D./J. Heaton/Miller Comstock Inc.; Earth Satellite Corporation. centre row, left to right—© The Stock House/Ma Po Shum; Earth Satellite Corporation; Korea National Tourism Corporation; Consulate General of the Republic of Korea. bottom row, left to right—Earth Satellite Corporation; K. Straiton/Miller Comstock Inc.; Four By Five; Earth Satellite Corporation. design—Sharon Foster.

The author thanks cartographers Jane Davie, Chris Grounds and Hedy Later for their assistance in producing this volume.

Design of Cover, Front & Back Matter: Sharon Foster
Editor: Deborah Lonergan

1 2 3 4 5 6 7 8 9 EB 7 6 5 4 3 2 1 0 9

Colour separation and film by Rainbow Graphic Arts Co., Ltd.
Printed and bound in Hong Kong by Everbest Printing Co., Ltd.